"Fascinating!"
—Desmond Morris

"The interrelation of men and menus has filled hundreds of texts. But none of them have digested so many facts so well."
—*Time* Magazine

"Gourmets will find *Consuming Passions* chock full of ingenious observations. Connoisseurs of culture will appreciate its serious anthropological analysis. Those who just plain like to eat can indulge in a smorgasbord of anecdote . . . for the everyday eater it is a solid meal!"
—*The Washington Post*

"A highly successful, up-to-date synthesis of what we know about food and diet—the science, the art, the symbolism and ritual. No other book covers the same territory."
—John Pfeiffer

"An altogether absorbing study . . . provocative and informative . . . richly illuminating."
—*Library Journal*

PETER FARB, who died shortly after the completion of this book, was the author of numerous works written from the perspective that the curiosities of human behavior have rational explanations. Among them are *Man's Rise to Civilization* and, most recently, *Humankind;* both were selections of the Book-of-the-Month Club. He wrote this book with the cooperation of GEORGE ARMELAGOS, professor of anthropology at the University of Massachusetts, Amherst.

Consuming Passions
The Anthropology of Eating

Peter Farb & George Armelagos

WASHINGTON SQUARE PRESS
PUBLISHED BY POCKET BOOKS NEW YORK

Cover photo: Helen Dill Collection, Denver Art Museum,
Denver, Colorado

A Washington Square Press Publication of
POCKET BOOKS, a Simon & Schuster division of
GULF & WESTERN CORPORATION
1230 Avenue of the Americas, New York, N.Y. 10020

Published by arrangement with Houghton Mifflin Company
Library of Congress Catalog Card Number: 80-12075

ISBN: 0-671-43420-9

First Washington Square Press printing April, 1983

10 9 8 7 6 5 4 3 2 1

FOR ORIOLE, MARK, AND THOMAS
FOR EDINA

A NOTE TO THE READER

The Reference Notes that begin on page 271 provide sources, substantiate points in the text that might appear contentious, and suggest readings that expand upon various topics discussed in this book. They also give some amplification and documentation that would be cumbersome in the narrative itself.

Contents

PROLOGUE   *1*

    Understanding Society and Culture Through
    Eating

I   EATING AND THE HUMAN ORGANISM   *17*

    1. The Biological Baseline   *19*
    2. The Emerging Human Pattern   *47*
    3. Eating as Cultural Adaptation   *67*
    4. The Life Passage   *87*

II   EATING AND THE WAYS OF
    HUMANKIND   *113*

    5. Meal as Metaphor   *115*
    6. Eat Not of Their Flesh   *133*
    7. Foods for the Gods   *152*
    8. The Feast and the Gift   *176*

III   THE PATTERNS OF EATING   *195*

    9. Taste and Distaste   *197*
    10. The Wisdom of Cuisine   *227*

EPILOGUE   *250*

    Hunger in the Social and Human Body

Acknowledgments   *269*
Reference Notes   *271*
Bibliography   *305*
Index   *329*

Prologue

Understanding Society and Culture Through Eating

ALL ANIMALS FEED but humans alone eat. A dog wolfs down every meal in the same way, but humans behave in a variety of ways while eating. In North American and European societies, for example, business negotiations are conducted over cocktails and lunch; seductions may begin with champagne and oysters; wedding and birthday parties center around an elaborately decorated cake; and gifts of food are part of the exchange at Christmastime. In simpler societies, eating is associated with initiation and burial rites, the roles of the sexes, economic transactions, hospitality, and dealings with the supernatural—virtually the entire spectrum of human activity.

Food faddists in recent decades have declared, "You

are what you eat." Before them so did Edmund Kean, the nineteenth-century Shakespearean actor, who ate mutton before going onstage in the part of a lover, beef when he was to play a murderer, and pork for the role of a tyrant. The classic formulation of this statement was set down a century and a half ago by Jean Anthelme Brillat–Savarin in his treatise on eating, *The Physiology of Taste:* "Tell me what thou eatest, and I will tell thee what thou art." But the attribution of character, behavior, and achievement to particular items in the diet did not originate with Brillat–Savarin. In *Julius Caesar,* Cassius says to Brutus: "Upon what meat doth this our Caesar feed,/ That he is grown so great?" And the idea was around long before Shakespeare. It goes back thousands of years—to a statement in the *Bhagavad Gita,* the sacred Hindu text, that particular foods are appropriate for those of a particular temperament, and even to the ancient Greeks, who codified the idea into their medical teachings, eventually passing it on to much of the world by way of Arab learning. The linking of food with human behavior has even been applied to stereotypes about entire nations: The French subtlety of thought and manners is said to be related to the subtlety of their cuisine, the reserve of the British to their unimaginative diet, German stolidness to the quantities of heavy food they consume, and the unreliability of Italians to the large amounts of wine they drink.

An anthropologist who knows what the members of a society eat already knows a lot about them. Learning how the food is obtained and who prepares it adds considerably to the anthropologist's store of information about the way that society functions. And once the anthropologist finds out where, when, and with whom the food is eaten, just about everything else can be inferred about the relations among the society's members. This is possible because human behavior has evolved in great part as an interplay between eating behavior and cultural institutions—and because behavior, in turn, influences anatomy, physiology, and the evolution of the human organism itself. Eating, in short, is inseparable from the behavior and the biology of the human species and from the adaptation that humans have made to the conditions of their existence on the planet. Cultural traits, social institutions, national histories, and individual attitudes cannot be entirely understood without an understanding also of how these have meshed with our varied and peculiar modes of eating. That is the thesis to be set forth by this book.

In all societies, both simple and complex, eating is the primary way of initiating and maintaining human relationships. In fact, the English word "companion" is derived from French and Latin words that mean "one who eats bread with another." The Bantu of southern Africa regard exchanging food as the formation of what amounts to a temporary covenant between individuals—"a clanship of porridge," as they call it. For most Chinese, social transactions are almost inseparable from eating transactions. The giving and sharing of food is the prototypic relationship in Chinese society, as if the word were literally made flesh. Only a Chinese living alone and in abject poverty would sit down to a solitary meal. It is usual to eat with one's family or kin; when these are unavailable, people eat in teashops or at work rather than by themselves. No important business transaction and no marriage arrangement is ever concluded without the sharing of food. The quality of the meal and its setting convey a more subtle social message than anything that is consciously verbalized; attitudes that would be impolite if stated directly are communicated through the food channel.

Food and drink have such intense emotional significance that they are often linked with events that have nothing to do with nutrition. The perpetrators of the Boston Tea Party were angry not over tea but over taxation; the breadline and apple-sellers of the Great Depression became symbols of what was wrong with the economy. Guests at a dinner party usually leave a little food on the plate to let their hosts know they have been fed to repletion. A child who misbehaves is sent to bed without dinner, while obedience is rewarded with candy or ice cream. The simple fact of sitting down to eat together may convey important statements about a society. The civil-rights movement in the southern United States during the 1950s began as a dispute about the right of blacks not simply to eat at lunch counters but to sit down there with whites; blacks insisted on that right because in North American society people customarily sit down to eat only as equals.

Eating is intimately connected with sex roles, since the responsibility for each phase of obtaining and preparing a particular kind of food is almost always allotted according to sex. Members of one sex, generally the males, may be served first, and particular foods may be regarded as appropriate to each sex. Husbands and wives in some parts of Melanesia and Polynesia are not supposed to see each other eat; in Arabia, Japan, and parts of eastern Europe, women do not eat until the men in the family have finished their meals. In some societies, on the other hand, eating with the family is so traditional that workers are given long midday breaks so that they can go home for lunch. After World War II, hungry Greeks preferred to carry home the hot soup given them by the Red Cross and eat it there with their families rather than in the warm Red Cross canteens. At marriage celebrations in northern Europe during the Middle Ages, it was considered an important moment when the couple ate together—which is apparently the origin of the custom that prevails today in North America and in parts of Europe of watching the new bride and groom share the first slice of wedding cake.

Each society's culture is transmitted to children through eating with the family, a setting in which individual personalities develop, kinship obligations emerge, and the customs of the group are reinforced. Children learn at mealtimes to express a formal reverence for food through the custom of saying grace, as in what Christians know as the Lord's Prayer ("Give us this day our daily bread"), and they become acquainted with the regulations governing what their society considers edible. For many African children, this amounts to learning that a meal is not a meal unless it includes porridge. Europeans are brought up to feel much the same way about bread, and many North Americans genuinely believe that dinner is not really dinner without meat.

Finally, what is eaten establishes one's social, religious, and ethnic memberships. The coarse black bread that is the standard fare of a European peasant is a function of social rank, and so is the meal of roast dog that was served to the Aztec noble. Who can mistake the status of a German who drinks Trockenberenauslese, a wine made from grapes so rare that finding enough to produce a single bottle is a day's work even for a skilled picker? The surest way of discovering a family's ethnic origins is to look into its kitchen. Long after dress, manners, and speech have become indistinguishable from those of the majority, the old food habits continue as the last vestiges of the previous culture. Taboos against certain foods mark one as an adherent of a particular religion: Moslems and Jews reject pork, Hindus beef, and some Protestant denominations alcohol. Food customs as a badge of rank are particularly evident in India, where rules for each caste define both whom a person is permitted to marry and also with whom that person is permitted to eat; the interweaving of these prohibitions tends to keep young people in the same caste as their parents.

With so much cultural importance attached to eating, it is no wonder that food to a large extent is what holds a society together. For example, the rice that is fundamental to the existence of the Malays of Southeast Asia is believed to possess an essential life force; so the ceremonials that mark every stage of life—from birth through coming of age, marriage, and death—involve a symbolic meal of rice. For a Malay, rice is synonymous with food, and its presence is what distinguishes a meal. The Malays' first food of the day, at what North Americans and Europeans think of as the breakfast meal, usually consists of a sort of cake and coffee. Malays regard this as a snack rather than as a meal, simply because no rice is eaten. People in modern societies as well have notions about what is appropriate food for each meal. A typical North American breakfast consists of fruit, cereal, and a milk product—but strawberry shortcake, which includes all three, is considered inappropriate.

Maize interpenetrates the entire culture of the Pueblo Indians of the southwestern United States: the family, religion, hospitality, friendship, and the concept of sharing. It is inseparable from ritual; chants praise the eating of maize, the field amounts almost to an altar and cultivating the plant to an act of worship. Every Pueblo Indian who can walk takes part in the Corn Dance. The anthropologist Dorothy Lee has summarized the central place of maize in Pueblo culture: "When I take away corn from such people, I take away not only nutrition, not just a loved food. I take away an entire life and the meaning of life." Possibly the reason why numerous American Indian groups have surrounded maize with myths, legends, and religious ceremonies is that they have never found the plant growing wild. Seeming to exist by some miracle entirely for human benefit, and being of unknown origin, maize may have been deemed a gift of the supernatural.

For the Bemba of Zambia, daily life revolves around food and beer. The village echoes all day with shouts from hut to hut about what is to be eaten at the next meal, what was eaten at the previous meal, and what is in prospect for the future. The Bemba refer both to the various habitats within their environment and to the passing seasons in terms of eating, describing a certain place as "where only pumpkin leaves are eaten" or referring to a time of year as "the time when we eat mushrooms." The polite greeting to a returned traveler is not an inquiry about the things seen or the people met, but rather the question: "Have you eaten well?" Wealth among the Bemba is measured by the amount of food available to offer hospitality to others. A man has not been fully described without some mention of how much he has in his granary, how many relatives he feeds, and how much beer he contributed to the last feast.

The many associations between eating and human behavior can be seen most clearly in simple and isolated societies, such as that of the Trobriand Islands off the eastern tip of New Guinea. Trobrianders do not consider eating a biological necessity for sustaining life, nor do they consciously recognize certain foods as having a higher nutritive value than others. They eat not simply because they have an appetite but because eating is a social necessity. To give food is a virtuous act, and the man who distributes large amounts of it is by definition a good man. The formal distribution of food is so important to all Trobriand festivals and ceremonies that some anthropologists describe it as a "cult of food." Distributions figure not only at feasts, but at competitions between rival groups, and at an annual festival. They are particularly lavish at funerals, marriages, and certain rituals when food is offered not only to the human guests, but also to the spirits as an encouragement for them to participate.

Even when formal distributions are not involved, food is used as a medium for most economic exchanges. A Trobriander who wants to engage the services of a specialist, such as a canoe-maker, first sends a gift of food, which is followed up with a succession of others after the artisan has agreed to the project. Food is also a measure of a person's sense of worth and pride. Hunger, or even a lack of superabundance, is not considered an occasion for the exercise of charity but rather as an extreme cause of shame. To say to a man, *"Gala kam"* ("Thou hast no food"), is to insult him. People will endure real hunger rather than expose themselves to such derogatory comments by asking for food. Above all else, foodstuffs are a prime medium for the enhancement of prestige. Yams are accumulated because they are easily stored, but also because they can be displayed as valued possessions. The storehouse is built with openings between the beams wide enough so that everyone can admire the quantity and quality of the yams, which are so arranged that the best specimens are visible—much as grocers in European-derived societies display their produce in a store window. Before filling the storehouse, magic is performed to decrease the appetite of the owners and thus insure that the supplies will last as long as possible. The Trobrianders believe that this magic also prolongs supplies by encouraging the eating of breadfruit from the village groves and wild fruits from the bush. Such magic is nutritionally and ecologically advantageous; it forces the Trobrianders to exploit their environment more fully, to consume a wide range of foods, and thereby to obtain a greater variety of vitamins and minerals.

Given the social importance of food, it might seem strange to discover that the Trobrianders eat alone, retiring to their own hearths with their portions, turning their backs on one another and eating rapidly for fear of being observed. Whereas premarital sexual relations are an accepted feature of Trobriand social life, couples are prohibited from eating together before marriage. People in Western societies sometimes object when an unmarried couple share a bed; the Trobrianders object just as strongly when they share a meal. Food taboos further divide the Trobrianders along the lines of rank. Those of the highest rank obtain food from, and have it prepared by, people of similar rank because their diet is different from that of commoners. A man of the highest rank would never knowingly eat, for example, a bush pig or a stingray—and were he to learn that he had done so unwittingly, he would vomit up the meal.

The attitudes toward eating that prevail in the Trobriand Islands can be found in more complex societies as well. At one time in North America and Europe, both tuberculosis and rickets, for example, were attributed to a lack of proper food, and thus were a source of shame for the afflicted and their families. Just as the Trobrianders pay an artisan with gifts of food, painters and sculptors during the Middle Ages and the Renaissance were often paid in food and wine. Trobrianders gain status through their display of yams, but we also achieve status through the consumption of certain rare or expensive foods: caviar, wild game, and the truffles that must be rooted out by trained dogs and hogs. And although we do not use food directly as a medium of exchange, we discharge obligations that cannot appropriately be repaid with money by inviting people to a lavish meal. Trobrianders use food to reward and punish, but Europeans and North Americans long punished prisoners by feeding them only bread and water. For all that we denigrate the magical beliefs connected with food in simpler societies, it should be remembered that some of us throw salt over a shoulder to ward off bad luck, or eat fish in the belief that it is a superior brain food, or order oysters with the hope of increasing sexual potency. All the major religions continue to attach symbolic meanings to food and drink (even though the Roman Catholic prohibition against eating meat on Friday has been lifted): the bread and wine of the Christian communion service, the taboo observed by Jews against mixing meat and dairy products at the same meal, and the reverence for the sacred cow in Hindu India. In the political sphere, injustice is dramatized by fasting, as practiced by Gandhi and Martin Luther King, Jr., among many others. And we continue, like the Trobrianders, to observe the rites of passage—birth, coming of age, marriage, and death—with food and drink.

A people's niche in the environment is determined, as surely as it is for any other animal species, by that people's eating behavior. That is because eating inevitably brings humans into broader contact with their total environment—not only their natural surroundings, but also their social, economic, and political relations with neighbors—than any other essential behavior. Some theorists have looked upon adaptation to the environment as involving unconscious "strategies" for increasing the gains from a successful adaptation and decreasing the losses from an unsuccessful one. Gain might, for example, result from a decreased need for food energy or from producing it more efficiently. On the other hand, loss might result from the poor nutrition that lessens the amount of human muscle available to the society for extracting energy from the environment. A strategy that is adaptive supports the number of individuals appropriate both to a particular environment and to the complexity of their culture.

The esthetic emphasis placed on food by the Japanese might appear maladaptive because human energy is expended on niceties rather than on the primary need of stoking the body with energy. Actually, though, their method of food preparation is a beneficial adaptation to the environmental conditions that have long prevailed in Japan. Lacking the abundant food and the readily available fuel of North America and Europe, the Japanese have adapted their food and its preparation to scarce resources. The scanty amounts of food, particularly meat and fish, that do become available are sliced into small pieces, which are then served in small portions and spiced in different ways to give them variety. This practice conserves fuel, since thin slices can be cooked in a short time at high heat, thereby using less fuel than would be required by prolonged cooking over a low flame; and, of course, those fish and meat dishes that are served raw need no fuel at all. Preparing many foods in a single vessel, as is done in the Japanese version of the wok—a thin-walled vessel which transmits heat to food with virtually no delay—also saves fuel. Finally, the Japanese have expanded the range of their food resources by using the same foods in varied and contrasting ways, offering dishes that are sweet or sour, hot or cold, crisp or slippery in texture—all presented in ways so pleasing to the eye as to add an esthetic dimension that further overcomes monotony.

Japanese cuisine is clearly adaptive. (The elegant French-derived word "cuisine" refers to nothing more than the sum total of nutritional resources, the technology of their preparation, and the taste preferences entailed.) Is it possible also that the many apparently capricious and irrational customs found in societies around the world are similarly adaptive? People starve to death in India, leaving unbutchered the sacred cows that roam the streets. New Guineans eat their pigs only on ceremonial occasions, but they eat one another. For all their seeming irrationality, it can be argued that such food customs are adaptive—and it will be so argued in this book.

Many eating practices that appear strange to us may actually be adaptive in that they enhance or preserve nutritional value. The consumption of bean sprouts—that is, the germinated seeds of legumes—in China and India might seem to be merely a quaint means of achieving variety. Soybeans in the raw state, though, are both toxic and indigestible, and they must be subjected to prolonged cooking, which makes certain amino acids, fats, and vitamins available to the digestive system and at the same time destroys the toxins in the beans. Although the fuel necessary for prolonged cooking is in short supply in China and India, the people there have been able to make soybeans a nutritious part of their diet by such processes as germination (to produce bean sprouts), fermentation (to make soy sauce), and breaking down the structure of complex proteins by using smaller amounts of fuel for steaming (which results in bean curd). Other national cuisines have also been affected by a lack of fuel or by an abundance of it. The quick frying of much Italian cooking is the result of a shortage of fuel there, whereas the slow stewing and roasting typical of French cuisine was made possible by an abundance of wood and the presence of hearths that were kept burning anyway to heat the house.

Peasants in Mexico prepare maize for making tortillas by soaking it in water in which they have previously dissolved particles of limestone, a practice which we certainly consider unusual. But studies have shown that this preparation multiplies the calcium content to at least twenty times that in the original maize while possibly increasing th ` availability of certain amino acids— important because the peasants inhabit an environment where animal foods are scarce. Some Quechua Indians of Peru dip potatoes into a clay solution as a way, they claim, `o prevent a sour stomach. Closer investigation has shown that this practice is scientifically valid: The clay they use is mostly kaolin, a substance prescribed by physicians for the protection of the mucous membranes of the digestive system. In places in Africa people eat fish wrapped in a banana leaf whose acidity dissolves the fish bones and thereby makes the calcium in them available; the French practice of cooking fish with sorrel has the same effect. Putrefied food is eaten in numerous societies—among them the Eskimo, several Indian groups of North and Central America, the Bemba of southern Africa, the Lepchas of Sikkim—and also by many Europeans (those, for example, with a taste for "high" venison or for such cheeses as Limburger, Roquefort, and Gorgonzola). In fact, people in some places go to such unusual lengths as burying food or keeping it wet to insure that rotting takes place. The Vedda of Sri Lanka (Ceylon) actually search out five different kinds of rotted wood, which they eat after garnishing them with honey, leaves, and fruit. The preference for rotted food may be partly a matter of taste, but rotting also enhances the nutritive value of certain foods, since the bacteria that cause putrefaction manufacture such vitamins as B_1.

In citing preferences that are also adaptive, let us not overlook the British custom of pouring milk into tea.

The protein in the milk reacts chemically with the tannin in tea to break it down and prevent its absorption; and the calcium in milk neutralizes its acidity. That milk is effective in counteracting the harmful effects of tannin is seen by the fact that the rate of cancer of the esophagus is very much lower in Britain, where milk is customarily added to tea, than in other tea-drinking countries (such as Japan) where it is not. In the eighteenth century, when tea was the national drink of Holland and it was not taken with milk, esophageal cancer was common; the disease became rare after the Dutch switched from tea to coffee.

How can the multiplicity of unusual food customs around the world be accounted for? The many attempts to do so can be placed into a few categories: the fortuitous, the mentalist, the ecological, the innate, and the cultural. The fortuitous can be quickly dismissed. Any explanation of human behavior based on the assumption that it "just happened" obviously explains nothing. It furthermore postulates a world in which human behavior is meaningless, accidental, capricious— things which the science of anthropology long ago showed to be untrue.

The mentalist view regards eating behavior as part of a cultural code that expresses the world view of each society. To the French structuralist Claude Lévi-Strauss, for example, food taboos become explicable once they have been interpreted in terms of mythology. He observes that the species of animals tabooed for food are those that in some way deviate from the norm in anatomy, behavior, or habitat—anomalies which render them "unclean" and therefore inedible. His categorization is inadequate for at least three reasons: It does not explain how the members of particular societies arrived at their world view in the first place; it offers no logical explanation for why animals that people regard as unusual must necessarily also be unclean and inedible; and it ignores more obvious explanations, such as that the prohibited animals are dangerous, scarce, or notably vulnerable to overhunting.

The ecological explanation, on the other hand, does attempt to account for the differences and similarities in eating behavior of various peoples by way of a detailed analysis of environments and the potential foods within them. This approach, though, is flawed in that it reduces the problem to the environment alone, whereas human behavior is demonstrably influenced by a considerable number of other variables.

The innate explanation, which has long been fashionable, can be found in the statement by Dr. Benjamin Spock that very young children possess an "instinctive knowledge" about their dietary needs. This belief seemed to be given scientific validity by an experiment more than half a century ago in which three very young children were allowed for six months to select from foods offered to them. Although the day-to-day variations in the nutritive value of what the children selected were substantial, the total of all the foods selected added up to a healthful diet. But these experiments were so naively conceived that they are scientifically inadmissible. The array of highly nutritious foods presented—meat, fish, eggs, milk, cereals, fruits, and vegetables—was such that the children could not possibly have selected an unwholesome diet. The experiments included none of the junk foods that make up a large part of what children eat: candy, soda pop, high-fat cookies, jams and jellies, and potato chips. Until a similar study is made that incorporates junk foods as well as nutritious ones, and in which a large number rather than just a few children take part, the claim that children instinctively select the foods they need cannot be sustained.

Perhaps the most common explanation for the variety of eating customs is enculturation—that through the learning experience members of the younger generation come to accept the traditional ways of their society. Proponents of enculturation theories would say that Chinese children eat with chopsticks instead of with forks, and consider milkshakes inedible, simply because they have been enculturated into Chinese rather than North American society. But things are by no means as simple as that. Enculturation can account for only a portion of the eating behavior found in different societies—and in fact that of the older generation is never duplicated exactly, or there would be no "generation gap."

Rather than attempting to pin down eating customs as fortuitous, mentalist, ecological, innate, or due to enculturation, this book will approach the subject from a broader perspective, taking account of the cultural system as a whole. Any such system is composed of three interlocked sectors: first, the techno-environmental (the way in which the cultural system is adapted to its habitat in extracting, transforming, and distributing food and other forms of energy); second, the social structure (the maintenance of orderly relations among individual members of the society who obtain the energy and also produce the next generation); and third, the ideology (the way the members of the society view the world, their techno-environmental adaptation, and their social structure).

Before the basic proposition of this book—that by knowing how people eat, anthropologists can know much about them and their society—can be explored in depth, the question to be answered is: How did humans arrive at their present attitudes, beliefs, and behaviors in connection with eating? The next four chapters will be concerned primarily with the biological aspects of eating and with the influence of these on behavior. The first two of these chapters will emphasize the evolutionary aspects of eating—the way in which the entire adaptation of the human body has been molded by the need to acquire, prepare, and consume food.

Part I

EATING AND
THE HUMAN
ORGANISM

1

The Biological Baseline

THE DIET of most mammals is limited to one category—either animal or plant food—and often to only a few items within that category. Cattle eat grass, chipmunks eat seeds, and hyenas eat mostly carrion. Monkeys and apes, the human's primate relatives, are usually given both animal and plant foods in zoos, but few of them eat much in the way of animal foods under natural conditions. Humans, on the other hand, are distinguished anatomically and physiologically by the wide range of foods they can utilize. Their teeth include the cutting incisors of a rodent, the grinding molars and premolars of a herbivore, and the pointed canines of a carnivore. The human digestive system includes an extremely long gut that can digest green food, gastric juices that convert complex starches to simple sugars, pepsin that metabolizes proteins, and a pancreatic bile that emulsifies fats. No other mammals, with the possible exception of the rats and mice that live in human settlements, possess the same ability to adapt themselves to a variety of conditions—and consequently the capacity to evolve an enormous range of behavior connected with eating.

Thanks to omnivorous eating, humans are not dependent on particular foods and are therefore better able to
find food despite plant blights, insect depredations,
droughts, and other calamities. This enormous adaptability allows humans to move readily into new environments containing different food sources. Why, then,
did not all mammals evolve as omnivores? One reason
is that although omnivores do well at obtaining a wide
range of foods, they may lose out to the specialized
mammals that have become adapted to a specific diet.
Omnivorous baboons, for example, cannot equal the
efficiency of warthogs in digging out roots. Another
reason is that being omnivorous demands a certain kind
of intelligence. The world is filled with plants and animals that have little nutritive value, are difficult to
obtain or to digest, or may actually be toxic; knowing
what is edible and what is not requires both intelligence
and memory. Whereas the specialized mammals have
food-recognition programmed into their genes, an omnivore must be able to evaluate whatever potential
foods the environment offers to make judgments about
the relative merits of one food over another, and about
the hazards of obtaining it. No wonder that only a few
other mammals besides humans and certain other primates have evolved as omnivores—among them the
garbage-feeding domestic rat whose fare includes lasa-
gna in Italy, crêpes in France, and moo goo gai pan in
China.

The human digestive system deals in essentially the
same way with every cuisine. No matter how elegant
the meal, whatever is eaten consists in the end of chemicals to be metabolized—that is, combined with oxygen,
thereby releasing the heat that provides energy. This
heat represents the calories about which so much confusion exists. A calorie (technically, a kilocalorie) is the
amount of heat required to raise the temperature of one
kilogram of water (about 2.2 pounds, a little more than
half a gallon) by one degree Celsius (about 1.8 degrees
Fahrenheit). Different kinds of food provide differing

numbers of calories: Fats, for example, have two and a quarter times more calories than equal amounts of proteins or carbohydrates. Calories are needed to sustain the body even while it is lying completely at rest—about 1400 each day for an average North American woman weighing 121 pounds. Merely sitting up requires about seventy additional calories per hour, slow walking about two hundred, bicycling on a level road nearly three hundred, chopping wood more than four hundred, swimming as many as six hundred—and sexual intercourse about one hundred and fifty per orgasm. (To get an approximation of the number of calories needed for moderate activity each day, multiply your body weight in pounds by sixteen; active people should multiply it by twenty and those whose work is strenuous by twenty-four.)

Calories are essential for stoking the body's furnace; they become unwanted only when an excess of them is not burned up and instead turns to fat. North Americans are in general overweight, and those excess calories in the form of stored fat total about 2,300,000,000 pounds for all the adults in the United States alone. Recent calculations show that if these adults were to eliminate the excessive calories they have stored as fat, the slimming-down process would produce, in terms of fossil-fuel energy, 160 trillion BTUs—enough to run about 900,000 automobiles for 12,000 miles a year. And if all of these same adults were to maintain their ideal weights, they would consume 97 trillion fewer BTUs each year, more than enough to supply electricity for a year to the residents of Boston, Chicago, Washington, and San Francisco combined.

For many North Americans, a dinner consisting of shrimp cocktail, T-bone steak, baked potato with sour cream, tossed salad with French dressing, hot rolls and butter, and apple pie à la mode, accompanied by wine and coffee, represents a special treat. To the digestive system, however, it is intrinsically just a collection of nutrients, forty-four kinds altogether, that go into the process of growth and the replacement of dead cells. Virtually all of the nutritional elements in this meal can be found on the shelves of a supermarket and a pharmacy—such as six and a half ounces of liquid protein, half an ounce of salt, about six ounces of sugar, somewhat less than three ounces of lard, thirty ounces of mineral water, and so on. These could be purchased at a considerably lower cost than would go into purchasing the foods on the menu. At 1979 prices, the cost of these equivalents in standard portions, as measured by nutritionists, was $4.25. (Technical data on the nutritional elements in this meal are in the Reference Notes on pages 271–304.) In other words, the cultural appetite for a tasty and varied meal, prepared in interesting ways, is irrelevant to the digestive process—so long as the preferred items continue to supply the calories and nutrients essential for sustenance.

What happens when the items in the dinner menu itself are eaten and digested? Contrary to the usual assumption, the digestive system is, in a sense, not inside the body, for all that it is sometimes referred to as "innards." It consists of a single convoluted tube, some twenty-eight feet long, with openings at each end—the mouth and the anus—which is enlarged at intervals for holding food and mixing it with glandular secretions. Foods in various stages of digestion are propelled along the length of this tube by muscular contractions. It is only after being mechanically and chemically reduced to particles simple enough to be absorbed that the nutrients enter the blood and the lymphatic system and are carried to the cells of the body. The digestive system is therefore an exterior part of the body in the same sense that the hole is exterior to the doughnut. Indeed, after being taken into the mouth, some food particles, such as the cellulose in bread and vegetables, travel the entire length of the digestive tract without ever entering the body itself.

In the mouth, the entranceway to the tube, food is chewed and broken into small pieces, which are mixed with the saliva that begins to break them down further. Just the sight of food will stimulate the glands to produce saliva—which is, of course, where the expression "mouth-watering" comes from. Whether or not food is actually accepted depends not only on whether it falls within the category of those foods considered to be edible by the society, but also to some extent upon sensory perceptions: appearance, aroma, taste, texture, and even sound. Color can be important, which is why a steak colored bright green would automatically be rejected. Food technologists add orange coloring to synthetic orange juice because marketing surveys have shown that people will not believe it tastes right unless it has the familiar color. Similarly, grape-flavored drinks are colored purple, cherry drinks red, and lemonade yellow (even though natural lemon juice is colorless). Texture and sound also have much to do with the acceptability of food: The expectations are that an apple or celery will crunch in the mouth, whereas milk whose texture is curdled will usually be rejected.

Often, in fact, the sensory properties of food play a greater role in the choice of food than does nutritional value. The senses react to an almost unlimited number of chemical compounds that have odor, flavor, or taste. Odors do not spur us to eat until they have been evaluated by the brain; for example, the odors of milk and of after-shave lotion are both usually acceptable, but milk is associated with nutrition and after-shave lotion is not. Certain foods have been prized since ancient times because of their flavors rather than because of their nutritional value. During the wanderings of the Israelites in the Sinai Desert, they were provided as though by a miracle with a food they called "manna." (Considerable dispute has taken place about what this manna might have been; most probably it was the secretions of certain scale insects that feed at night on the tamarisk thickets of the Sinai.) The Israelites complained to Moses that manna had no flavor compared to the leeks, onions, and garlic (foods that are valued chiefly because of their flavor) and the fish, cucumbers, and melons (which offer strong and distinctive odors in addition to their nutritional benefits) they had left behind in Egypt.

A further example of the influence of aroma is hot chicken soup, sometimes called "Jewish penicillin" because of its reputed powers in curing colds and fevers. Its efficacy in speeding the flow of mucus through nasal passages has now been demonstrated. Volunteers who drank hot chicken soup showed a thirty-three percent increase in the velocity of the mucus; those who drank plain hot water also showed an increase in velocity, but at a much lesser rate, while those who drank cold water showed a markedly decreased flow of mucus. Drinking any hot liquid, either plain water or chicken soup, obviously increases mucus velocity, but chicken soup seems to provide some additional benefits in clearing the nasal passages, probably because of its aroma. Presumably other soups with distinctive aromas would produce the same effect.

The tongue samples the taste, texture, and temperature of food and then signals the body either to accept or to reject it. The surface of the tongue is covered with about ten thousand taste buds, which are clusters of sensitive nerve endings. These decline in both number and sensitivity with increasing age—people by the age of seventy-five have lost two-thirds of the taste buds they had at thirty, thus accounting for the common complaint by the elderly that food nowadays does not have the flavor it did in their childhood. Ever since Aristotle sensations of taste have traditionally been divided into four categories—sweet, salty, bitter, and sour—but scientists have long debated whether only four basic taste sensations exist or whether the tongue detects a spectrum of almost countless tastes, each somewhat different from all the others. Nineteenth-century researchers believed that the perception of taste was similar to color vision, in that several tastes could be mixed to produce a new one, just as mixing blue and yellow produces green. Taste, though, has been shown to be quite different. When foods with different taste qualities are mixed, these qualities do not fuse to produce a new taste but rather suppress or enhance one another: A salty substance added to a sweet one enhances the latter, whereas acid suppresses sweetness.

It is now known that the taste of water—which people often describe as being sweet, sour, bitter, salty, flat, or even having no taste—often depends on what food has just been eaten. Most people, after eating an artichoke, for example, find that water tastes sweet. Although the artichoke has served as a food for humans for at least 2750 years, this phenomenon went unnoticed by scientists until about half a century ago, and it was not until recently that two substances in the artichoke that account for the transformation in the taste of water were isolated. These substances do not mix with the water; rather, they temporarily alter the taste buds of the tongue so that nonsweet substances appear to have been sweetened. For this reason the chemicals in the artichoke are now being investigated as possibly offering a substitute for sugar.

Taste and smell are quite different sensations; it is impossible, for example, to smell the sweetness of ice cream or the saltiness of fish. Cane sugar, maple sugar, and honey have the same sweet taste; they vary only in their aroma. Some people believe they detect a metallic taste in foods that have been canned or stored in metal pots; gastronomes accordingly recommend storing meat in wooden containers and stewed fruit in glass ones. North Americans have gotten so used to the metallic character of canned orange juice that according to marketing surveys they even prefer it to that of the freshly squeezed juice. What the metal adds, though, is not a taste but a smell, probably the effect of oxides. The more subtle flavors of foods are detected as aromas in the nasal cavity adjacent to the mouth. Sensory cells with this function are much more discerning than the tongue. The tongue can detect sweetness at a dilution of one part in 200, saltiness at one in 400, sourness at one in 130,000, and bitterness at one in 2,000,000—but odors can be detected at a dilution of one part in 1,000,000,000.

The detection of tastes has, throughout the evolution of mammals, undoubtedly been essential to survival. The evolutionary path from sea-dwelling creatures to modern humans has given us salty body fluids, the exact salinity of which must be maintained. The human desire for salt appears to be inborn, but it is also influenced by individual physiology. People who do not produce enough of certain adrenal glands excrete salt in unusual amounts; consequently, their craving for salt leads them to douse even grapefruit with it. The tongue's ability to detect bitterness must have had great survival value throughout human evolution, since natural toxins usually taste bitter. A "sweet tooth" is inborn in all mammals, humans included, and it too is adaptive because sugars are a source of energy. Sugar became maladaptive—for the teeth, for the cardiovascular system, and for the entire metabolism of potential diabetics—only after humans learned to grow sugar cane and beet sugar in quantities much larger than had ever occurred naturally. If the assumption is correct that early human food habits were similar to those of modern apes and monkeys, then a marked craving for sweet foods such as fruit is part of the human evolutionary heritage. This heritage is reinforced in each generation by the sweetness of mother's milk and by even a bottle-fed infant's preference for sweet solutions over water.

The humans' very remote ancestors—those that some four hundred million years ago left the sea and took up life on land—were presented with a problem in swallowing that does not exist under water, where the liquid helps ease the passage of food through the mouth toward the gut. For land mammals, therefore, the salivary glands came to be of great importance, and so did the tongue for manipulating saliva-moistened food. Human culture has also contributed such means of aiding the passage of food through the mouth as lubricating dry bread with butter, margarine, lard, oil, or gravy. The chewed food is swallowed when the tongue catapults it into the esophagus, where muscular contractions squeeze it downward into the stomach. There, the semi-liquid mass is mixed with gastric juices. Among these is hydrochloric acid, which kills bacteria in food and drink, softens fibrous foods, promotes the formation of the digestive enzyme pepsin—and is also one of the most corrosive acids known. At the concentration secreted by the stomach lining, it is deadly to living cells and powerful enough to dissolve zinc.

Why, then, does not the hydrochloric acid cause the stomach to digest itself? Sometimes, of course, it does, as when emotional upsets, caffeine, or cigarette smoke markedly increase the amount of acid in the stomach, and ulcers are the result. For most people, though, a complex physical–chemical barrier that is not yet fully understood prevents the acid from corroding the stomach wall. During the digestion of a meal, which stimulates the secretion of hydrochloric acid, many tiny hemorrhages do occur in the lining of the stomach; these are usually superficial, and heal quickly. Alcohol and aspirin are common substances that can penetrate this barrier. A single aspirin tablet causes the loss of only about a thimbleful of blood, but in combination with alcohol it can lead to extensive bleeding.

After anywhere from half an hour to five hours in the stomach, the kneaded mass of the meal is flushed by muscular contractions into the small intestine, which is about twenty feet long in adults, and from which the bulk of the food is absorbed by the body. The small intestine is the place where many of the complex starches in the potato, roll, and dessert are reduced to the simplest sugars, which can be absorbed into the blood within about half an hour. The enzymes in the small intestine divide the proteins from the shrimp, steak, butter, sour cream, and ice cream into the amino acids that are found in all living things. The amino acids and the simple sugars, together with vitamins, are absorbed rapidly by the huge number of fingerlike cells that line the small intestine and extend into the liquid mixture of nutrients and digestive juices; the total surface area of these absorbing cells is about two-thirds that of a basketball court.

By this time, all that is left of the dinner this chapter started with are minerals, fluids, and the fats (triglycerides) in the steak, butter, salad dressing, and dessert. Fat takes some hours longer to digest than protein or carbohydrates; the more fat in a meal, the more slowly the stomach empties and the longer a person has the feeling of satiety. Alcohol takes longer to affect the person who eats fatty hors d'oeuvres such as cheese before drinking than the person who eats non-fatty ones such as carrot and celery sticks. That cheese eaten before drinking serves to "coat the stomach" (in other words, to protect it against the mechanical irritation of alcohol) is not the only reason for this. In addition, alcohol takes longer to reach the intestines, where the major part of it is absorbed into the body, when the accompanying fats cause the stomach and upper intestine to slow down the process of absorption. The minerals and fluids from a meal generally do not enter the body until they reach the large intestine, anywhere from twelve to seventy-two hours after being eaten. The large intestine also receives the undigested remnants of the meal, which represent about five percent of the total intake. Contractions in the colon push this soggy mass toward the rectum, absorbing water from it along the way.

An understanding of the process of digestion does not, however, explain why humans every few hours halt their work, put aside their obligations, and seek out food. Until several decades ago, questions about this would hardly have seemed necessary. Since hunger was regarded as merely unpleasant churnings and spasms ("hunger pangs") of a stomach that had been empty for too long, filling it presumably stopped the pangs and the hunger as well. The same notion persists to this day, even though a moment's thought will show it to be an incomplete explanation of why people eat when they do. An empty stomach does not lead inevitably to eating. A sick person, for example, may not experience any desire to eat even when the body is in need of food. Scientists and dieters alike have observed that tobacco, caffeine, and alcohol can suppress the pangs of an empty stomach, as can a number of drugs. Various emotional states as well as vigorous exercise can reduce or eliminate the pangs of appetite. On the other hand, a person whose stomach has been surgically removed may still experience feelings of hunger and satiety.

The motivation to begin eating now appears less dependent on hunger than on such psychological influences as the arrival of the usual mealtime or the sight and smell of food. Few humans in modern societies go without food long enough to know what real hunger is like; and research indicates that humans cannot gauge accurately the difference between slight and moderate hunger, so as then to make the appropriate adjustments in the amount of food they consume. Experimental animals have been shown to respond promptly and accurately to the need for calories, but humans possess no innate mechanism for distinguishing between meals with high calories and those with low. Instead, they rely on cultural knowledge and on trial and error. In one recent experiment, humans who were given meals in which the caloric content was disguised in gruel could not distinguish between one providing 3000 calories and another providing only 400.

People eat a lot or a little for reasons that obviously do not have much to do with their awareness of the food's energy value, but those reasons are subject to at least four internal controls that regulate the body's intake of calories and thus keep the weight of most adults nearly constant. First, the brain acts as a monitor of the store of body fat and the rate at which sugar in the blood is being consumed, collecting this information in a small organ at its base, the hypothalamus. Second, the body monitors the process of eating: The mere filling of the stomach and gut produces a signal to stop eating, even before sufficient time has passed for the nutrients to be absorbed into the bloodstream. Third, like all warm-blooded animals, humans possess internal regulators that adjust the body temperature within certain narrow limits in relation to the environment. Because eating increases body temperature, the familiar loss of appetite in hot weather is biologically adaptive, and so is the desire to eat more when air temperatures are low. Finally, from very early childhood through life, the learning of those food preferences and avoidances that become part of the personality has its effect on what and how much is eaten.

Scientific interest in the regulation of eating has shifted in recent decades from the stomach to the brain, which is nowadays considered to be in effect the first part of the digestive system. This function seems to be centered in the hypothalamus and in the associated pituitary gland. One part of the hypothalamus is a "stop-eating" center; when a laboratory rat is electrically stimulated there, it will not eat even though it has been deprived of food for a long time. Another part is a "start-eating" center; stimulation here will cause a rat that has just finished feeding to begin again. By operating alternately, the two parts of the hypothalamus initiate periods of feeding followed by periods of fasting, in that way maintaining approximately the same body weight day after day. A rat from which one of the two centers is surgically removed will either die of starvation in the midst of food or literally eat itself to death.

Such experiments show that animals do maintain their weight as a response to settings on their internal scale—and the same thing seems to be true for humans as well. Human patients with damage to the hypothalamus may display similar symptoms. Normally, though, humans exercise a much greater extent of conscious control over eating and drinking than do laboratory rats. When the hypothalamus signals hunger, a human may respond in any number of ways that are not possible to the rat exploring a laboratory cage for food. A rat cannot go to the refrigerator, or shop at a supermarket, or panhandle for a coin to buy a cup of coffee, or draw a picture of something delectable to eat—or restrain itself out of a resolve to lose weight. The internal regulators in the brain that tell humans to eat every few hours can be overridden by cultural attitudes, as a result of which people may be in the habit of eating anywhere from one to six meals a day, or none at all because they are fasting. Feelings of revulsion about certain foods may also cause people to starve themselves rather than eat a food their culture has labeled inedible—as happened during World War II, when United States pilots in the Pacific went hungry because of cultural inhibitions against strange sea creatures, lizards, toads, and insects, even though they had been taught that these could safely be eaten.

The reason humans eat or do not eat is explicable neither in terms of a full or empty stomach nor as a result of any mechanism operating in isolation—such as the level of sugar in the blood, the emptiness or fullness of fat cells, or a need for caloric energy. Moreover, even if a combination of mechanisms does send humans in search of food, no single part of the brain dictates that they will eat the food once it has been found, since it might turn out to have been labeled as inedible by the particular society. In the final analysis, whether or not humans eat depends upon the interactions among numerous physiological and environmental variables.

Why humans eat is one thing, and another is what they eat. The chemical compounds obtained from food by the human body are classified as proteins, carbohydrates, fats, vitamins, and minerals. Proteins make up part of every living cell, and would in fact account for half of the weight of the entire body if all its fluid content were drawn off. Muscle, bone and cartilage, skin, membrane tissue, hair, and just about everything else are composed at least partly of protein. The protein content of food is resynthesized by the digestive process into new forms of protein that the body can use for its growth and maintenance. A North American male between eighteen and twenty-two years of age who consumes about two ounces of protein a day—the equivalent to that in three hamburger patties—is getting all he needs, including a slight surplus to draw upon in the event of injury or disease. The body can tolerate as much as five or six times that amount of protein a day—so long as sufficient water is drunk to help the kidneys dispose of their accumulated nitrogen—but no benefit from an excessive intake of protein has ever been demonstrated beyond its caloric energy.

Carbohydrates are occasionally scorned, especially by some proponents of miracle ways to lose weight, as providing only empty calories (that is, energy without much nutritional value). The accusation is justifiably made, however, only against refined carbohydrates such as honey (refined by bees) and table sugar (refined by humans from beets or cane), which are indeed lacking in such nutrients as are found in the raw carbohydrates provided by maize, wheat, and potatoes. A shortage of carbohydrates in the diet can bring about harmful biochemical changes. For example, glucose, which is one of the carbohydrate molecules, is being continually absorbed by the brain at a rate of some five hundred calories every twenty-four hours. To supply this glucose to the brain alone—quite aside from the needs of the rest of the body—a 125-pound woman requires about four and a half ounces of carbohydrates a day. Any reducing diet that reduces calories at the expense of the carbohydrates necessary for the brain to function must obviously be dangerous to health. If not enough carbohydrates are eaten at least every twelve hours—as they are not in some reducing diets—the liver must draw upon the protein stored in the muscles to supply glucose to the brain. If the liver cannot do this, the metabolic changes associated with starvation begin to appear. A rapid drop of ten percent in the amount of glucose available to the brain can cause mental confusion; a twenty-five percent drop leads to coma and cell damage; a drop even slightly greater can be fatal.

Although many athletes believe that they need large steaks at the training table to build up muscles, beef is really no better as a source of protein than pork, poultry, cheese, or even vegetables in balanced combinations. Instead of building up an excess of protein, athletes should concentrate on building up a reserve of stored glucose, which comes from carbohydrates, as fuel for prolonged physical exertion. This can be brought about by a temporary change in the usual patterns of eating. For several days before the particular event, the athlete consumes a diet consisting mainly of protein and fat, with a minimum of carbohydrates, and exercises to exhaustion the muscles that will be used. The day before the event, large portions of carbohydrates are added at each meal with the result that glucose will be preferentially stored in the muscles at a level almost double what it is normally, where it will be drawn upon for the needed energy.

The high esteem in which fats were once held is clear from many references in the Old Testament. In the book of Genesis, for example, Abel offers Yahweh "the firstling of his flock and of the fat thereof" (4:4); and Pharaoh promises Joseph that if he and his brothers settle in Egypt they "shall eat of the fat of the land" (45:18). Although nowadays fats have a poor reputation, they are important nutritionally for a number of reasons. They are essential for the absorption of fat-soluble vitamins from the digestive tract. Certain fatty acids (such as those in oil made from maize, peanuts, and soybeans) are necessary for the growth of very young children, and in smaller amounts are needed also by adults. Fats remain in the stomach longer than almost any other kind of food, and thus produce a feeling of satiety. A meal in a Chinese restaurant—which often consists mostly of fish, chicken, rice, bean curd, and vegetables—is low in fat, and this is the reason why people complain of being hungry again only a few hours afterward.

Evidence of the role played by vitamins—or at any rate by one of them, vitamin C (ascorbic acid)—was available as long ago as the time of Columbus. Some of his sailors who showed symptoms of what is now known to have been scurvy—pain in the joints, hemorrhages of the blood-vessel walls, and a loss of weight—were left behind on a Caribbean island, where they lived on fruit and recovered. Later they were picked up by a Portuguese ship, and so miraculous did their recovery seem that the Portuguese word for "cure"—Curaçao—was given to the island, a name it bears to this day. Despite the experiences of these and later seamen, the causes of scurvy were not established until the eighteenth century, when James Lind, a physician for the Royal Navy, carried out an experiment. When he divided seamen suffering from scurvy into six groups, and fed each group on a different diet, the only men to show rapid recovery were those who every day had been given the juice from oranges and lemons (which are, of course, rich in vitamin C). Although he published his results in 1753, it was not until 1795 that the Admiralty made a citrus ration compulsory, thereby freeing the fleet from scurvy by the time of the sea battle against the French at Trafalgar in 1805. The British at that time used the word "limes" for what are known as lemons today; the warehouse district around the London waterfront where the fruit was stored got the name of "Limehouse" as a consequence, and the British sailors were nicknamed "Limeys."

Vitamins consist of two large groups: those that are fat-soluble (A, D, E, and K) and those that are water-soluble (notably C and the nine B vitamins). Fat-soluble vitamins, as their name indicates, occur in fatty foods such as oils and meats, water-soluble vitamins mostly in fruits and vegetables. The latter tend to leach out into the water they are cooked in. This vitamin-laden "pot likker" was eaten by the black population of the southern United States—with the result that they were generally better nourished than whites at the same economic level, who regarded drinking it or even using it in soup as socially unacceptable. Of the four fat-soluble vitamins that are stored in the liver, where they form a valuable reserve, vitamin D is a natural constituent of only a few foods. Small amounts are found in eggs, cream, and butter, and somewhat larger amounts in fish. Otherwise vitamin D must be manufactured in the outer surfaces of the skin by the action of sunlight. Since vitamin D is necessary for depositing calcium and phosphorus in the bones, children who are largely deprived of sunlight—such as those who are brought up in the narrow, smog-darkened streets of northern slums— often suffer from the crippling disease known as rickets. Over the past several decades, pasteurized milk has been fortified with vitamin D as a means to prevent it.

No disease resulting from a deficiency of the fat-soluble vitamin E has ever been found, although experiments with rats indicate that it is necessary for reproduction. Vitamin A is usually associated with carrots, with other yellow vegetables such as sweet potatoes and squash, and with fruits such as peaches and cantaloupes, though what they contain is the hydrocarbon pigment carotene, which is converted into vitamin A by the liver. Some dark green vegetables (for example, spinach, turnip greens, asparagus, and broccoli) are also rich in carotene, the yellow of the pigment being masked by the green of chlorophyll. Animal livers are the richest source of vitamin A; the older the animal, the greater the concentration of the nutrient, making beef liver a better source than calf liver. A folk belief that eating quantities of carrots allows a person to see in the dark has no basis in fact, other than that one symptom of vitamin A deficiency is an inability to adapt quickly to changes in the intensity of light. Nevertheless, the belief is so ingrained that during World War II the Royal Air Force was able to keep the invention of radar secret by declaring the great accuracy of British fighter pilots at night to be the result of superior vision achieved by eating enormous quantities of carrots. Since the Germans subscribed to the same folk notion, they believed the story.

About fourteen minerals (among them calcium, phosphorus, iron, copper, iodine, and flourine) are found in the human body, and with one exception— iron—these are easily obtained from the normal diet. Particularly for a woman who is menstruating, pregnant, or nursing an infant, sufficient quantities of iron are extremely difficult to obtain except by eating large amounts of certain foods—notably liver, beef tongue, certain leafy vegetables, dried fruits, and nuts. Since even inorganic iron can be absorbed by the body, a soup or a stew simmered in a cast-iron pot will usually be enriched by the leaching of mineral traces from the pot into the food. The problem of obtaining sufficient iron is further compounded by the fact that only about ten percent of the amount eaten is absorbed by the body. A deficiency of iron can lead to a form of anemia that has been common at various times and places. The "green-sickness" mentioned by Shakespeare and other Elizabethans as a disease of women—as when Juliet is berated by her father for having fallen in love with Romeo: "Out, you greensickness carrion!"—was almost certainly anemia.

Several attempts have been made to determine the allowances of these nutrients that will satisfy the needs of all human beings. Such are the Recommended Dietary Allowances (RDA), which often appear in abbreviated form on the labels of prepared foods, and which have been established by the United States Food and

Nutrition Board and by the British National Committee on Nutritional Sciences. Such recommendations should not be looked upon as requirements; they are, in fact, deliberately calculated in excess of the needs of most people under current living conditions in the United States and Britain, as a way of insuring that the needs of all are met.

That everyone leaves a unique set of fingerprints is a fact readily accepted, yet little attention has been given to the uniqueness of the nutritional blueprint for every human body. Two individuals of the same age, sex, and physical proportions do not have precisely the same metabolism. One of them, in fact, might burn calories ten times faster than the other because of the varying rates at which the chemical reactions involved in metabolism take place. Extensive studies have shown that some healthy people secrete as much as two hundred times the amounts of pepsin and hydrochloric acid secreted by others equally healthy. Even more surprising is the discovery of some women in India who synthesize vitamin C—a feat of which the human body was thought to be incapable.

Another enigma has come to light in New Guinea in a nutritional study of about five hundred children. As many as seventy-four percent of them were subsisting on a diet so extremely deficient in both calories and protein that they could have been expected to exhibit clear signs of malnutrition—yet the only visible effect was that they grew more slowly than white children in North America and Britain. Not only did the children seem to have no ill effects from this diet; the health of young adults also was good, and adult females paid no penalty in decreased fertility. How are these findings to be explained? One possibility is that estimates of food requirements using North America and Europe as the standard may not necessarily apply to other populations of the world. Some of those who have investigated the problem believe further that New Guineans might have a special kind of nutritional adaptation. For example, one highland group consumed an extremely unbalanced diet: between eighty and ninety percent of their calories from a single food source, the sweet potato, a mere four percent from protein sources, and the remainder from leafy vegetables and beans. Metabolic studies of these people show a number of anomalies that have yet to be explained, but which suggest that they might possess unusual intestinal bacteria that fix nitrogen (an essential component of protein) in the same way as do bacteria in the roots of soybeans and alfalfa—thus becoming what one investigator has labeled "walking legumes," equipped to thrive on carbohydrates and a minimal amount of protein.

No wonder, then, that nutritionists have great difficulty in recommending an appropriate daily intake of various nutrients for people generally. The problem is compounded by the fact that not everyone eats every part of every kind of food. Those, for example, who peel off the skin of a white potato and then boil it or make French-fries have thrown away about twenty percent of the nutrients it contains. Each year an average North American family of four throws out more than a hundred pounds of potato peelings—losing thereby the equivalent of the iron from five hundred eggs, the protein from sixty steaks, and the vitamin C from nearly two hundred glasses of orange juice.

These are not the only problems in the way of standardizing nutritional requirements. Another difficulty is that variations in the chemical form in which a nutrient enters the digestive tract largely determine whether it is absorbed and utilized by the body. Only about ten percent of the form of iron found in red meat is absorbed—and it may be less if the meat has been eaten along with substances that inhibit its absorption, such as the oxalic acid in spinach. (Spinach also binds calcium and prevents its absorption by the body. Well-intentioned parents who provide children with spinach and milk—each in itself a nutritious food—at the same meal are actually preventing the body's utilization of the calcium in the milk.) A second complication has to do with the bacteria that are permanent inhabitants of the large intestine, where they live on organic molecules from food and contribute to the digestive process by manufacturing vitamins, particularly K and some of the B vitamins, which their human hosts absorb. Ill health or an unbalanced diet would tend to inhibit this activity, and in that event some additional nutrients would be needed.

A third major complication is that the absence of just one nutrient may prevent the utilization of others. The human body cannot synthesize protein without amino acids; most of these can be synthesized by the body, but anywhere from eight to ten of them, depending upon a person's age, can be obtained only from the food that is eaten. If just one of these is absent from a meal, then none of the others can be utilized fully by the body. And to the extent that a single one is insufficient, then all become equally insufficient. Animal products—meat, fish, poultry, eggs, milk, cheese—supply all of the essential amino acids in the necessary proportions, but plants usually lack at least one of them. Maize, for example, lacks lysine and tryptophan; beans and peas are good sources of lysine but lack methionine; leafy green vegetables contain the tryptophan that is absent from maize but lack other essential amino acids. Every culture—through a long selective process—has surmounted the deficiency of plant foods in amino acids by developing dishes that combine and balance them. Mexicans eat beans, rice, and leafy vegetables with a maize tortilla; Jamaicans eat rice, wheat, or maize combined with peas; many American Indians ate succotash, a combination of maize and lima beans.

Although a proper balance of proteins, carbohydrates, fats, vitamins, and minerals is obtained most readily by eating both animal and plant foods, in some societies the diet seems to consist of either meat or plant food almost exclusively. Certain Eskimo groups, for example, were long thought to subsist solely on meat. When hunting had been good, an adult might eat as much as twelve pounds of it a day. One would think that Eskimos pay a nutritional penalty, but studies reveal that most of those living on a traditional diet suffer from no major nutritional diseases. Several things account for their ability to achieve a balanced diet even though they inhabit an environment where few plants grow. One is that in fact they do eat some plant foods. Many of the more southerly Eskimos gather a variety of wild plants for food, and even the northern Eskimos manage to obtain them in small amounts—mainly roots, berries, and the buds from willow thickets on the tundra, supplemented by the fermented stomach contents of planteating mammals such as the caribou they hunt. These stomach contents are in fact regarded as a delicacy and, although meager in quantity as compared to the large amounts of meat that Eskimos consume, they are rich in carbohydrates and in the many vitamins synthesized by bacteria during the process of fermentation.

Another reason Eskimos are well nourished is that they consume nearly all parts of the animals they kill, including the internal organs, which furnish virtually the entire range of vitamins and minerals they need. One comparative study of an Eskimo diet showed ten times more of vitamins A and D, and also more iron and other minerals, than in an average North American diet. A deficiency of vitamin C might be expected to be particularly common among Eskimos, since they lack the vegetables and citrus fruits that are primary sources of this vitamin, yet cases of scurvy are almost never found among them. This is because meat contains small amounts of vitamin C, and these are not lost in cooking, since Eskimos either eat their meat raw or roast it only slightly. Vitamin C also occurs in willow leaves, and some berries that grow on the tundra are exceptionally rich in it; these are preserved for the winter in seal oil, which happens also to be an excellent source of vitamin A. In summary, the traditional adaptation of the Eskimos to the far north requires no arcane knowledge of nutrition to keep them well nourished during most of the year. Only in recent decades, as the Eskimos' way of life has changed and they have begun to consume increasingly large amounts of processed foods bought at trading posts, have nutritional diseases become common.

At the opposite extreme from the meat-eating Eskimos are those peoples who consume plants almost exclusively. Some are vegetarians by necessity, because they have no money to buy meat, or because neither wild nor domesticated animals are abundant where they live; others may abstain from meat as a result of ethical or religious sanctions. Most vegetarians by choice do eat some animal products in the form of milk, butter, cheese, and eggs, which even in small amounts contribute important nutrients to what is basically a plant diet. Some people described as vegetarians, though, do not really fit the category. The Amhara of Ethiopia observe approximately 150 fast days each year during which they eat no flesh from either birds or mammals and no milk products; and especially pious people observe 220 such fast days. They are allowed fish at these times, though, and during the remaining days of the year the Amhara eat enough animal foods to give them a balanced diet.

Some of those who are vegetarians by choice point to the successful adaptation made over a few thousand years by adherents of Buddhism, which preaches vegetarianism because of a moral repugnance toward the killing of animals. Although it is true that a devout Buddhist will not knowingly deprive any creature of life, it is not true that Buddhists in general consume no animal products whatever. Many eat butter and drink milk, and in some countries that are largely Buddhist— among them Tibet, Sri Lanka, Burma, and Thailand— even the priests eat meat. In India, those belonging to the lower castes eat meat whenever they can obtain it, and those belonging to the higher castes often eat eggs, cheese, and butter (while some of the more liberated urban dwellers even eat meat itself). In China, both Buddhist and Taoist influences have discouraged the eating of meat, yet complete vegetarianism has not generally been practiced except by the clergy and a small number of particularly devout people.

Many people in the world are, of course, vegetarians by necessity rather than choice. The typical peasant of Gambia in West Africa consumes various cereals (most commonly rice, but also millet, sorghum, and maize) as well as nuts, beans, green leaves, and fruits. This is not to say that the peasants prefer such a diet; they readily eat meat, dried fish, and eggs on whatever rare occasion any of these can be obtained. As a result of having been forced to subsist on a low-protein, high-carbohydrate diet, many Gambian peasants suffer cirrhosis of the liver, pellagra, beriberi, kwashiorkor, and other deficiency diseases, all of which become particularly evident during the "hungry season"—those months each year after the food from the previous harvest has been used up and before new fields have begun to produce. At such times, energy must be obtained by drawing on the body's store of fat; consequently, adults lose weight and the growth of children comes nearly to a halt. Things would be even worse for the peasants if they were not able to obtain small amounts of protein from insects, rodents, and other small animals that North Americans and Europeans would regard with repugnance as a source of food.

Although little meat is eaten in certain societies simply because it is so rarely available, no society has ever been discovered that is exclusively vegetarian. The reason apparently is that such a society would not be able to produce offspring generation after generation, and it would eventually die out. One reason for this is the obvious fact that diet affects the nutritional quality of a mother's breast milk. Any woman who adhered strictly to a vegetarian diet, one not including even eggs or milk, would lack vitamin B_{12}, which is obtained almost exclusively from meat and animal products and which is essential to avoid anemia. Nevertheless, it is possible to achieve a healthy diet from plant foods alone, so long as they are combined in accordance with current nutritional knowledge and are occasionally bolstered by nutritional supplements. This was demonstrated by a study in Israel of some eighty strictly vegetarian households, who were satisfactorily nourished by consuming a wide variety of plants that complemented one another in providing essential amino acids and vitamins. Dishes made from sesame seeds and soybeans provided calcium, iron, and thiamine; wheat germ and bran were excellent sources of iron and B vitamins; vitamin A was obtained from carrots and leafy vegetables, vitamin C from green peppers and guava.

Before anyone concludes from this study that a strictly vegetarian diet provides adequate nutrition for all people, several facts must be emphasized. First, these Israelis belonged to the urban middle class and therefore both could afford a varied plant diet and were able to purchase it in convenient city markets. Furthermore, as members of the Israeli Vegetarian Association, they made a practice of being well informed about nutrition and the need for vitamin supplements. The same cannot be said of Gambian peasants or of any other peoples who are vegetarians by necessity. Nor were the knowledge of nutrition, the long-distance transportation necessary to import a variety of plant foods, or today's vitamin supplements to be had during the more than 99.99 percent of evolution in which human adaptations to eating took place.

Such adaptations made over long periods of time can often explain differences among human groups in regard to physique, body dimensions, and the size of the face and skull. Anthropologists used to attribute such differences solely to the genetic makeup of populations, but many physical characteristics are now known to be influenced greatly by diet. Two groups of the Hutu people of Ruanda, for example, subsist on markedly different diets and also exhibit marked differences in their size and physical proportions, even though they are genetically similar.

If a superior nutrition can indeed promote growth, will not an improved diet eventually produce a human species of such gargantuan size that it is destined for extinction, as happened to the Irish elk and the giant dinosaurs? A study of Harvard students published in 1932 did seem to give support to this notion. On the whole these male students were distinctly larger than their fathers had been at the same age; and similar increases in size appeared to have been occurring from one generation to another. A more recent study, though, found that no further increase in stature had occurred among Harvard students. For the United States population as a whole, data from the National Center for Health Statistics show average gains in height for both males and females totaling about four inches over the past hundred years—but, as was true for the Harvard students in recent decades, the trend toward increased size has virtually ceased.

Such increases in stature are a phenomenon that has been observed in many parts of the world during the past few centuries, particularly in modernizing nations. The increase is strikingly evident during a visit to a museum or a historic home; clearly, most humans living nowadays in Europe or North America would have trouble fitting into those small beds or suits of armor. Between 1880 and 1960, the average height of French army conscripts increased by nearly two inches. An increase was also observed among Japanese immigrants into Hawaii and the two subsequent generations of Japanese–Hawaiians born there. The average stature of first-generation males increased by more than four inches over their immigrant male parents; in the second generation, though, no further increase took place. For females the pattern was different: The increase in stature was much slower, but it took place for both generations born in Hawaii, eventually totaling nearly three inches.

No explanation based on genetics can account for all of the observed facts, and neither do most environmental explanations, except where a change in diet is taken into account.The diet of the two generations born in Hawaii included much more protein and calcium than had been commonly eaten in Japan. Why, though, did a difference in patterns of growth occur between males and females? Culture undoubtedly played an important part. Whereas the Japanese immigrants were concerned that their sons should adopt the new Hawaiian ways, including the superior diet, the daughters were frequently kept at home, where they had only the traditional foods available. Furthermore, the preferential treatment given Japanese males meant that they were served first and that the females of the household ate only the leftovers. Being better fed, the males could reach their genetic potential of growth much more rapidly than the females, who required two generations to achieve the same thing. But once an improvement in diet had brought their stature to the genetic potential, further increases for either sex ceased.

Although the phenomenon of increased growth is apparently both genetic and environmental, changes in the latter, especially in regard to nutrition, have obviously been more influential. This may explain why, despite the worldwide increase in the stature of adults, the size of infants at birth has not changed appreciably over the past several centuries. Once the outer limit for growth set by genetics has been reached by an individual who is well nourished, further increase in growth is halted. Increases in stature such as occurred from generation to generation in Hawaii and elsewhere can be explained as beneficial adaptations to an abundance of food: The added size, in well-fed individuals, allows a diet high in calories to be metabolized more easily. Once the genetic limitation on size has been reached, however, an excess of calories results not in more growth but in added fat, leading to circulatory disorders and various diseases associated with obesity.

These changes in stature are an illustration of how eating, culture, and biology cannot be separated from one another—and that indeed, as elemental facts of existence for the human species, they are in constant interaction. Every animal species is unique in the kinds of food it takes from the environment and the ways in which they are metabolized. But human metabolic needs are like those of no other animal, in being continually influenced by culture. The human adaptation thus produced did not develop suddenly or by some accident of history; rather, it emerged by degrees along the unique evolutionary path taken by the ancestors of modern humans.

2

The Emerging Human Pattern

HUMANS—from the tips of their fingernails to their facial proportions—have been shaped by the ways they acquire and utilize food. The exact details of how humans gradually developed into omnivorous animals with a wide range of cultural associations between eating and social behavior, symbols, status, and sexual relations can never be known for certain. A surprising number of facts about the origins of the human diet can, though, be inferred from observing our living primate relatives among the apes and monkeys, from fossils, and from surviving hunter–gatherer societies. A number of biological and behavioral features that are the foundation for the way humans eat were inherited from the primates, whose living species display them in rudimentary form: adaptability in foraging, the occasional sharing of food, and clear preferences for certain foods and ways of obtaining them. The physical structures inherited by humans from primate ancestors include mobility of the digits, a reduction in the size of the snout and the teeth, and stereoscopic vision.

Most apes and monkeys are adapted to a diet of plant foods, and some—such as the colobus and howler monkeys, and the gorilla—even have specialized digestive tracts whose lengthened intestines can cope with the leaves that are indigestible for almost all other mammals. Many other primates are more omnivorous, and some feed on a wide variety of roots, seeds, fruits, flower buds, nuts, and such animal foods as insects, bird eggs, reptiles, even other primates. In zoos, almost all primates easily adapt to a diet of chow and offal, along with the peanuts and ice cream offered by visitors. Despite the basic orientation of apes and monkeys toward plant food, the need for vitamin B_{12} means that they must eat some food of animal origin to survive—as they all do, either intentionally or unwittingly, in the form of insects that are consumed along with the plants they feed on.

The direction to be taken by human feeding behavior was foreshadowed when, perhaps seventy million years ago, ancestral primates became adapted to an arboreal environment. There they were able to exploit a nutritional wealth of fruits, nuts, and seeds—as well as insects—that had not previously been tapped to any great extent by mammals. As a way of locating this new food source, the primates evolved refinements in vision: The stereoscopic placement of the eyes and the ability to discriminate colors were advantageous because at a distance it is of course easier to see a banana than to smell it. Other adaptations were equally necessary for success at exploiting the new niche in the trees. For example, the hand developed as an organ of manipulation, which meant that the mouth no longer had to be used for investigating and seizing what the eyes had detected, but was liberated to develop the rich vocal communication of the non-human primates and eventually the symbolic language of humans.

The human ability to make tools would have been impossible had not the primate ancestors evolved fingers of great dexterity, bearing nails instead of claws. Unlike squirrels and other arboreal mammals that climb by digging their claws into the bark, primates climb by grasping, an efficient way of moving about in search of new food sources that did not interfere with the manipulative ability of sensitive fingertips. A lessened emphasis on smell, the preeminent sense in almost all other mammals, had important consequences for human evolution. Sight became paramount; the mammalian snout was nearly eliminated, thereby bringing the eyes forward to a position that not only made stereoscopic vision possible but also afforded a better view of the ground while walking upright. The disappearance of the snout further allowed the lips a new mobility, widening the possible range of facial expressions.

Language, upright posture, tool-making, a large brain—these and other hallmarks of the human species can be traced back in one way or another to the primate adaptation to food sources in the trees. Upright posture probably developed as much in response to the need to carry food as it did to the need to use the hands in making and using tools; and once humans were on their hind legs, the hands were freed to evolve into the marvelous organs of manipulation they now are. The very shape of the human head is a result of evolutionary changes associated with eating: The jaws and the teeth became smaller, as did the brow ridges of the skull, once buttresses for powerful chewing muscles were no longer essential; and an increasingly large brain gave humans a superior ability to process information, much of it originally having to do with the availability of food and the best ways to obtain it.

All of the categories of foods that humans find edible are also consumed by primates in the wild, except for the milk of domesticated mammals, certain spices, and cola and caffeine beverages. Like humans, but unlike most other mammals, primates are selective in that they show clear preferences not only for specific foods but also for specific parts of these. The gorillas of Central Africa, for example, at various times of the year will feed on a hundred or more species of plants that grow there; yet the bulk of their nourishment is derived from the few species they prefer to eat. Despite such preferences, nonhuman primates maintain their flexibility in choosing foods, which indicates that the evolutionary basis for food choice in humans was not completely ordained by the genes. The ancestors of certain baboons were forest-dwelling monkeys that moved onto the tree-dotted savanna—an ecological shift that was also made, at least five million years ago, by the ancestors of humans. Although ninety percent of the diet of the olive baboon is grass, it has also been known to eat flowers, vines, lizards, insects, immature birds, and small mammals—a flexibility indicating that nonhuman primates, like humans, have been able to take advantage of changing opportunities offered by the environment.

At least some animal food is consumed by virtually all primate species. In fact, certain monkeys and prosimians (the tarsiers, lemurs, lorises, and other relatively primitive species that still survive in Africa and Madagascar) apparently consume more worms, insects, frogs, lizards, and bird eggs than they do plant foods. The actual proportion of animal to plant food is less important than that primates have probably always been able to obtain and to digest animal foods. Apes and monkeys were not under any evolutionary pressure toward a more largely carnivorous diet, for the reason simply that the forests contained a diverse and nearly unlimited supply of plant foods. Even so, chimpanzees and baboons cooperatively seek out and pursue animal prey, such as other primates or young grazing mammals. During a recent twelve-year period, about 170 examples of hunting by chimpanzees were recorded by primatologists at Tanzania's Gombe National Park, and undoubtedly numerous other hunts took place unobserved.

Most primate species that were once considered herbivorous are now known to expand the proportion of animal foods in their diet to levels as high as ninety percent at times when insects are abundant and can be easily captured. This was dramatically seen in the behavior of several groups of baboons in Botswana several years ago, when an explosive increase in the numbers of insects on certain kinds of trees occurred. Baboons in the vicinity during this period immediately switched from their usual diet, consisting largely of plants, and devoted seventy-two percent of their foraging time to capturing insects.

The repugnance of modern North Americans and Europeans toward the eating of insects obscures the large proportion of protein they must have supplied for early humans, and still supply for some American Indians and groups in Africa and the Near East. Grasshoppers and other members of the locust family, for example, are an exceptionally nutritious food. Merely a handful provides the daily allowance of vitamin A, as well as protein, carbohydrate, and fat. In addition to locusts, early humans must also have consumed, as hunter–gatherers still do today, beetle grubs, caterpillars, bee larvae, termites, ants, cicadas, and aquatic insects. An analysis of the fried termites eaten in West Africa has shown that they contain about forty-five percent protein, a higher proportion even than in dried fish.

Given such nutritional benefits, the repugnance toward insects as food in modern societies is difficult to understand, as is the eagerness to eat other kinds of invertebrates: clams, mussels, oysters, snails, squid, and especially the lobsters, crabs, and shrimp that are more closely related to insects. The distinction between invertebrates that are eaten and those that are not seems to hinge on whether they live in water; living in the sea apparently removes a species from everyday associations. People in Florida, for example, eat crabs from the sea readily enough, yet they disdain land crabs, which are closely related and equally tasty. The avoidance by people in Western societies of grasshoppers and locusts is especially mystifying. Even though these were specifically recommended to the Israelites in the dietary laws of Leviticus, one of the books of Moses, modern-day Jews avoid them. And although John the Baptist, according to Matthew (3:4), lived in the wilderness of Judea on "locusts and wild honey," modern Christians avoid them also.

The human tendency to switch to animal foods whenever these become available is apparently a legacy from primate ancestors. But the preference for meat on the part of early humans could be indulged only to a limited degree in the absence of sophisticated tools and weapons, of domesticated animals, and of the long-distance transportation that today makes meat available in quantity to large numbers of humans. Nowadays, though, with meat readily available, the preference for it has become hazardous to health. Animal products are now consumed regularly in quantities that earlier in evolution were achieved only irregularly.

Anthropologists used to assume that in the evolution of human behavior, once erect posture left the hands free to use weapons and other tools, the early humans could become hunters of game in the open country into which they had moved from the forests. According to this hypothesis, cooperative hunting eventually led to the sharing of food within some kind of family structure. Since it is now known that apes and monkeys cooperate in the hunt and in sharing the kill afterwards, this behavior may actually have evolved millions of years before the advent of "ape–men." Hunting by humans, though, differs from that of apes and monkeys in two major ways. Humans communicate through speech, which makes possible strategies more complex than those of any kind of nonhuman primate. And whereas nonhuman primates could kill only small animals, humans developed weapons and complex systems of cooperation that enabled them to bring down prey much larger than themselves.

When human ancestors left the forest cradle of the primates to walk upright on the African plains, perhaps five million years ago, they apparently became increasingly carnivorous in contrast to the apes and monkeys. Humans retain the long gut of a herbivore and the sweet tooth of fruit-eating primate ancestors, but human teeth suggest those of a carnivore; and the fact that in virtually every human society animal foods are the most desired, even though they are usually the most difficult to obtain, is another sign of the carnivorous heritage of humans. But just as the basically plant diet of apes and monkeys became the more carnivorous diet of early humans, a return to an emphasis upon plants for food occurred with the invention of agriculture in various parts of the world some ten thousand years ago. Rice and wheat alone account for more than forty percent of the foods, whether plant or animal, eaten in the world today. Agriculture has meant, in fact, a great decrease in the variety of foods eaten. Whereas tens of thousands of plant species are known to be edible, only about six hundred of these are cultivated, and virtually no plants of importance for food have been added to the list of domesticated species for thousands of years.

Although humans share many features with the nonhuman primates, the differences between the behavior of the humans' closest relatives, the chimpanzees, and even the simplest hunting–gathering society are enormous—and most of these differences stem from contrasts in their quest for food. Humans carry food from place to place, either inside containers or suspended from poles, and once the food is back at the settlement, they regularly share it according to established rules and customs; they exchange recipes, and culinary techniques are passed from generation to generation. No chimpanzee or any other primate even approaches these practices. And whereas roughly seventy percent of an ape's time each day is devoted to finding food, hunters and gatherers need spend only a few hours a day.

For more than ninety-nine percent of its history, down to the beginnings of agriculture, the human species sustained itself by hunting and gathering. This cultural adaptation is based on two facts: First, some sort of plant food is always available, regardless of the season or the weather, thus becoming the mainstay of the diet; second, game animals provide certain essential nutrients, but they represent a smaller proportion of the food consumed because they are not always available or because hunting has been unsuccessful. From these two facts, several conditions of hunter–gatherer life necessarily follow: a willingness to cooperate in the quest for food, to share afterwards, and a submission to the rules that assign tasks according to sex—the hunting of large animals by males, the gathering of plants, insects, and other small animals by females. Perhaps 300,000 human beings around the world still follow the hunting–gathering way of life, some in the northern tundras, others in the deserts of Australia and southern Africa, in the rain forests of Africa, and in parts of South America and Southeast Asia. Vestiges of hunting–gathering ways may be seen in the behavior of modern humans. A roast is ritually butchered at the dinner table by the senior male in the household, wielding a weapon larger than a carving knife need be, and by the practice of leaving on the head of the pig, pheasant, or fish that is about to be eaten—occasionally with an edible object such as an apple in its mouth, as though it had been killed in the very act of feeding.

The overriding importance in human evolution of cooperative hunting and sharing is indicated by archeological excavations at several sites in East Africa. These, dating back to between two and three million years ago, have provided unambiguous evidence that large mammals were hunted successfully, butchered on the spot, and carried back in pieces to camps. Hunter–gatherers of course cannot preserve meat except by drying small strips of it in the sun (as jerky) or, as the Eskimo and other Arctic people do, by freezing it. The efficiency of the natural deep-freezer of northern climates was shown by the discovery in Siberia of mammoths that had died about fifty thousand years ago—and that were so well preserved in the ice that steaks were cut from them by the explorers who made the discovery.

The transportation of food back to the camp means that the early humans, unlike apes and monkeys, postponed food consumption—which made possible the success of the hunting–gathering adaptation, because transportation implies a camp that everyone agrees to return to, the division of labor in the tasks relating to food, and the sharing of the foods obtained. When several families come together in one camp, they engage in endless exchange of information typical of human activity: that nuts in a certain grove two miles to the east are ripe, or that a hunter has crossed the spoor of a large animal. They can become much more efficient in the quest for food through dividing tasks according to sex and age—the women to gather, the men to hunt, the young and the elderly to take care of things around the camp. The division of labor not only brings in much more food, but it also makes possible a greater variety, which means in turn a balanced diet for everyone. The exchange and sharing of food mean that the one who gives today can expect to receive tomorrow. And from that expectation stem reciprocal obligations, rules to enforce fair sharing, and marital ties between kin groups to make sharing permanent. The human family probably could not have arisen without those early and simple steps toward the sharing of food.

In this hypothetical reconstruction, hunting by males is not the central event. That it was so, and for so long, in the minds of anthropologists, came about largely because few archeological remains of plant-gathering have been unearthed. The wooden stick used by women for digging out roots and tubers would have decayed, whereas the man's stone hunting points and butchering tools would have been preserved. Likewise, the bones of food animals are more likely to be fossilized than are roots or berries. Two facts, though, indicate how important the female role of plant gatherer must have been: The patterns of wear on the fossil teeth of early humans show that plant food was consumed in quantity, and statistical studies of present-day hunter–gatherers reveal that on an average two-thirds of their food supply consists of plants. The drama of males hunting dangerous game long obscured for anthropologists the less dramatic, but much more important, aspect of the hunting–gathering adaptation: the fact that males and females agree to return to a common meeting place to share what they obtained in the quest for food.

Hunting–gathering societies have various rules about sharing meat. In the case of the San (sometimes referred to as Bushmen) of the Kalahari Desert of southern Africa, the owner of the arrow that made the kill gets the choicest parts; the next in line is the hunter who first sighted the game, followed by the one who threw the first spear, and so on until each man in the hunting party has received a share. If the kill is a large animal, each hunter then divides his portion with relatives, who in turn distribute what they have received to others. This means that when an animal the size of a giraffe has been killed, virtually everyone in several neighboring camps will have received some of the meat through a process that spreads outward like ripples through water. The consumption of huge amounts of meat whenever it becomes available survives today in the human species as the so-called "hunter's appetite": People still eat as though in anticipation of a shortage of meat even though none is imminent. Plant foods, which are shared by women with their children, their husbands, and very close relatives, usually do not go beyond the immediate household, simply because any family will be able to find plants for itself.

Among the Copper Eskimo of central Canada, each hunter goes into partnership with a large number of others for the reciprocal sharing of the ringed seals they kill. Each seal is divided into fourteen agreed-upon cuts, six of which (including the two front flippers, the two rear flippers, and the shoulders) consist of pairs, thus providing portions for a total of nineteen partners besides the hunter himself. When a successful hunter returns with a seal on his sled, the wives and children of his partners wait patiently while the animal is dismembered. Each then speaks the partner's name, whereupon the hunter's wife offers the stomach, the liver, the front left flipper, or whatever. The event has become institutionalized under the name *nippiqtuq,* meaning "he waits to get his share"—and each of the partners is called by a name corresponding to the portion of the seal to which he is entitled: "Stomach-Meat-Companion," "Neck-Companion," "Liver-Companion," and so on.

It might seem that the hunter who made the kill in the first place should have a claim to all or most of it. But the reputation of those who freely distribute meat is enhanced both for skill in hunting and for generosity as members of their society. The presence of even a few very successful hunters in a camp often draws families from other camps; these hunters are also able to attract the most desirable females; and they are listened to when important decisions must be made. The successful hunter who shares generously places an increasing number of people in his own band, and in neighboring bands as well, under obligation to him. He thereby adds to his own prestige, and he also gains the power of a creditor—one to whom others must reciprocate by sharing meat when they are successful in the hunt. The gathering of plant foods does not give women the same prestige, even though at certain times of the year they may have provided eighty percent of a band's food supply. Plants simply do not have the prestige that meat does, presumably because a man can always go out and pick some berries or nuts, whereas a woman cannot suddenly decide to go hunting.

Why should males be the hunters and females the gatherers? Males tend to be somewhat stronger and more aggressive than females, but that cannot be the entire answer because in any band of foragers at least some of the females are every bit as qualified physically as some of the males for hunting. The reason appears to be the need to travel light on the hunt because any burden would interfere with the hunter's ability to chase game over long distances; it would throw off the balance and coordination needed to hurl a spear or to shoot an arrow. In this females are handicapped because of the burdens they must carry—the fetus during pregnancy, and the nursing infant for at least two years (no other source of milk or other infant food being available to hunter–gatherers). Since the periods during the life span of an adult female when she is not either pregnant or nursing are relatively short and sporadic, a small band would be squandering its human resources if women were trained in the many skills needed for hunting. Much greater survival value attaches to training them from childhood in the far different skills needed for gathering—identifying an underground tuber by its stem or knowing when the fruit of a certain tree will be ripe.

Numerous new sharing relationships are created whenever two people in a hunting–gathering society marry, as new roles are assumed by each member of the two united families. The new husband becomes a son-in-law to the bride's parents and a brother-in-law to her brothers and sisters, and in such ways the network of kin from whom food can be received and to whom it will be distributed is enlarged, thereby reducing the risk of hunger for any one of them. Even the unrelated members of the society benefit from a marriage because it forges alliances between kin groups and between bands, further enlarging the network of sharers and reducing the likelihood that anyone will be in want. Early in human evolution, the subsistence bond between a male hunter and a female gatherer must have provided an important basis for stability in the band. Each partner to a marriage might have managed to dispense with the other for sex, for companionship, or for protection—but not for the exchange of plant and animal foods.

Since humans, bears, and pigs consume basically the same sort of omnivorous diet, the teeth of all three show many similarities even though they evolved along very different paths. In fact, the fossilized teeth of a pig unearthed in Nebraska were once mistaken by biologists for those of an early human—an indication of the obvious fact that the food an animal eats largely determines the number, kinds, and shapes of teeth it has. Omnivorous mammals, including humans and some other primates, depart little from the basic mammalian pattern of dentition; they lack such specializations as the enormous front teeth used by horses for cropping grass or the slashing canines used by tigers to kill their prey. Apes and monkeys have lost the long muzzle of the mammals, and with it a number of teeth, leaving all primates (the New World monkeys excepted) with only thirty-two teeth instead of the usual mammalian forty-four. Despite many similarities, the teeth of modern primates and of modern humans do show clear differences. As compared with the arched jaw of humans, the ape's jaw suggests three sides of a rectangle, with the sharp-edged incisors in front, the pointed canines at the corners, and the premolars and molars on the sides.

The four pairs of incisors evolved, as their name implies, for cutting. Primates use them for biting into fruits, nuts, and shoots, and for stripping bark from branches. The incisors enable primates, along with many other kinds of mammals, to bite off portions of food that would otherwise be too large to swallow. The sharply pointed canines are smaller in humans than in other primates. These might seem to be associated with a carnivorous way of life—indeed, their prominence in dogs, known scientifically as *Canis,* accounts for their name—but the fact that they are usually much larger in primate males than in females suggests that their function is not directly related to feeding. Males and females do, after all, eat the same foods and would therefore be expected to have similar teeth. Rather, primate males employ their canines for defense and for competitive displays to threaten a rival male. They do this by opening the mouth wide in what appears to be a yawn, drawing back the lips so that the canines are entirely uncovered; to appease another male, on the other hand, an ape or monkey covers the canines with the lips. Humans who display the teeth in a smile intended to appease are doing exactly the opposite. Even so, they usually take care not to display too many teeth, since the wide smile that reveals the canines indicates the scoundrel in melodrama, movies, and folk belief. Although some anthropologists have argued that smaller canines in humans stemmed from the increasing use of tools for piercing, the canines had already decreased in size, as compared to those of nonhuman primates, at least two million years ago. At the same time, the entire jaw was becoming less massive, making it possible for the skull to become enlarged and thus accommodate a larger brain.

In the course of evolution, as the flat premolars on the sides of the mouth decreased in number from the eight pairs found in most mammals to the four pairs in apes and monkeys, they became more efficient. The back teeth or molars, meanwhile, evolved in such a way as to combine the functions of grasping, grinding, and cutting. This kind of economy has been an ongoing trend in primate evolution as fewer, smaller, and more efficient teeth perform more work. The human's thirty-two teeth are thus more generalized than those of other primates, and considerably more so than the forty-four teeth of most other mammals. The trend toward fewer teeth apparently is continuing; witness the increasingly common absence of the molars farthest to the rear, the "wisdom teeth." Individuals who do have them may suffer from impacted third molars, which frequently have to be extracted by a dentist.

Parents in modern societies often send their children to orthodontists to give them what is now considered a "correct" bite—that is, with the upper incisors slightly overhanging the lower ones to produce the shearing action of a pair of scissors. Considerable evidence, though, indicates that in the characteristic bite of hunter–gatherers, both today and in the past, the upper and lower incisors meet edge to edge, like a pair of pincers. When hunter–gatherers eat a tough haunch of meat, they use the "stuff-and-cut" technique: Part of the haunch is stuffed into the mouth, firmly clamped by the incisors, and then either torn away by a vigorous tug of the hands or sliced off near the lips with a knife. Thus for hunter–gatherers, the incisors are used less as cutting tools than as clamps. If the front teeth are used in this manner several times a day, beginning in childhood, they soon develop in the edge-to-edge position of pincers.

The scissorlike bite of modern humans can be attributed not to genetic or dietary changes but to the practice of cutting food into bite-sized morsels before putting it into the mouth, thereby largely bypassing the incisors. This began in Europe several centuries ago, and much earlier in China, as a result of the introduction of the fork and of chopsticks. Bronze chopsticks have been unearthed from royal tombs dating as far back as 3500 years ago, but they did not come into general use until at least a thousand years later, when the custom became widespread of preparing food in small pieces that could be manipulated with chopsticks and did not require any further cutting at the table. The use of the fork did not really become common until about two hundred years ago, although it had spread through the royal courts of Europe as early as the sixteenth century. At first used to transport food to the plate or to the mouth, the fork was increasingly used to hold down the food on the plate while it is cut into small pieces with a knife—"butchering at the table," as the Chinese derisively call it. In the use of both chopsticks and forks, the result was the same: a reduced involvement of the incisors in eating and a subsequent loss of the edge-to-edge bite of hunter–gatherers.

A second preoccupation in modern societies with teeth and diet concerns caries or "cavities." Although dental decay is often thought of as a disease of civilization, brought on when humans switched to effete or mushy foods, it has in fact been found in many species of mammals—among them rats, pigs, and monkeys—as well as in fossils of early humans. The *Homo erectus* fossils from Java (formerly known as "Java Man" or "Pithecanthropus erectus"), dating from well over half a million years ago, show signs of caries. Although caries are obviously not caused solely by the modern adaptation, they do tend to increase as the diet changes to soft foods and a large intake of sugar. Aristotle touched on the major cause of caries when he asked in his *Problems:* "Why do figs, which are soft and sweet, damage the teeth?" The prevalence of caries among Greeks at this time was no doubt due to their heavy consumption of honey and dried fruit (roughly half of a dried apricot or fig consists of sucrose, one of the simple sugars). Honey and dried fruit were also eaten in large quantities during the Roman occupation of Britain, where toothlessness then became common. Skulls dating from the subsequent Anglo-Saxon period, when the Roman diet was replaced by one that used large amounts of tough meat and abrasive grains, show that caries practically disappeared during that time. The trend was reversed once again in the twelfth century, as sugar became increasingly available from the new trade routes to the Mediterranean that were opened up by the Crusaders. By the fifteenth century, Venetian ships were bringing a hundred thousand pounds of sugar to England each year. Shakespeare's *The Winter's Tale*, written a century later, gives a shopping list for twenty-four people at a country feast; it includes three pounds of sugar, as well as raisins and other fruits with a high sugar content.

Probably no cultural influence on the evolution of teeth has been more important than cooking. Charles Lamb, in his "Dissertation on Roast Pig," accounted for the origin of cooking in this way: A farmhouse accidentally burns down, and the pigs kept there by its owners are roasted in the flames. A boy poking through the ruins accidentally burns his fingers on the carcass of a pig, cools them in his mouth—and immediately discovers the delicious taste of roast meat. The only probable thing in Lamb's account is that the discovery must have been accidental; the rest of the story is incompatible with what is known about human behavior.

Human beings are extremely finicky about what they eat; the first foods roasted by accident would probably have been disdained, since the taste for roast food is culturally acquired. Why ruin a good haunch of bloody meat or kill the taste of a tuber by putting it into a fire? A human preference for cooked foods must have developed gradually over a very long period of time as the advantages came to be recognized: Cooking destroys the toxins, bacteria, and parasites in food, and it makes the protein in meat and fish easier to digest. Whereas the human digestive system cannot cope with the cellulose and raw starch that make up the bulk of most plant foods, the cellulose walls of plant cells are broken down by heat and the starch is changed chemically into more easily digested sugars. Cooking amounts, therefore, to a sort of external predigestion.

Two basic kinds of cooking are known, one of which must have developed early, the other more recently in human evolution. The process of roasting or applying heat from a fire directly to food is very ancient. The archeological remains of "Peking Man" (*Homo erectus*) at the Choukoutien caves in China, dating from some half a million years ago, indicate that meat was roasted there. Traces of hearths that were apparently used for roasting have also been found in the caves of southern France and of Hungary, and date from approximately the same time. Before the arrival of Europeans, roasting was the only kind of cooking known to the Australian Aborigines, the Tasmanians, the Tierra del Fuegians who live at the southern tip of South America, and some other hunting–gathering peoples.

Cooking that does not apply heat directly to the food, but transmits it through another medium, is most probably a more recent invention. When the medium is water, the process is boiling; when it is oil, the process is frying. Whereas roasting could have been discovered by accident, hot water is a rare natural phenomenon, not easily produced by humans in the absence of containers that are to some degree waterproof and fireproof. It was therefore long believed that boiling and frying did not develop until after ceramics and metallurgy had been invented, in the Near East, between 6,000 and 9,000 years ago. Human invention did, though, devise ways of boiling food without manufactured pots—by making use of the shells of tortoises, turtles, and large mollusks as containers. A considerably more complex method was to dig a hole, line it with stones and clay to prevent seepage, fill it with water, and raise the temperature of the water to boiling by dropping in heated stones. While the food boils, more and more hot stones are put into the water to keep the temperature high. By these and other methods, peoples lacking ceramic or metal pots that could withstand fire were able to cook their food in a variety of ways. The Tikopians of the South Pacific, for example, baked food on hot stones in earthen ovens; they boiled it by sliding heated stones into wooden bowls filled with water; they wrapped fish in thick leaves and suspended it over a fire (much as seaweed is used at a New England clambake). Despite the limitations of their technology before they obtained manufactured pots from European traders, the Tikopians managed to exploit the possibilities of their environment with an imaginative cuisine.

The origins of cooking are more probably to be found in religion than in the fiction of Charles Lamb. In many societies fire is considered to be a spirit capable of suffusing food with supernatural powers that are thereby passed on to the humans who eat them. Many religious rituals call for animals to be sacrificed, burned, and then eaten—a practice that would have allowed the gradual development of a taste for roast meat. Hunter–gatherers and simple horticulturists must have learned early not only that certain plant foods are more easily prepared and digested if they have first been cooked, but that others, although poisonous when eaten raw, are so altered by the process as to become an edible food. Excavations at some of the earliest villages of the Near East show that wheat was roasted before being mixed with water to make gruel. American Indians even developed a special variety of maize whose kernels burst with heat—the forerunner of today's popcorn.

The traditional notion that hunter–gatherers must carry on a solitary, unremitting search for food, that they supposedly wake each morning not knowing whether or not they will find the day's supply, and that they usually die young from famine happens to be untrue. Hunter–gatherers, who are not solitary but live in small bands and observe many intricate social rules for the distribution of food, are far from impoverished. The San in the bleak Kalahari Desert forage for food for no more than a few hours a day on the average; moreover, the unmarried young people and those older than fifty do hardly any work at all. Medical examinations of the San have shown that their diet, both abundant and nutritious, has enabled them to escape many of the health problems associated with diets that are common in modern societies: obesity and "middle-age spread," dental caries, hypertension and coronary heart disease, and elevated levels of cholesterol. And far from being short-lived, many of the San live into their sixties and seventies. An important point made by studies of surviving hunter–gatherers is that their generally excellent nutrition extends to all members of the society and not just to a privileged few—simply because the prevalence of sharing insures that everyone eats the same way. In those rare hunter–gatherer societies where some individuals were notably more privileged, as were the chiefs of the Northwest Coast Indian tribes, the inequality did not usually extend to nutrition.

The beginnings, more than 10,000 years ago, of horticulture and pastoralism led to the emergence of privileged classes whose diet differed greatly from that of the laboring and peasant populations. A study of skeletons from Central America has documented the changes that took place under the Mayan civilization. Between about A.D. 300 and A.D. 900 at Tikal, Guatemala, the average stature of Mayan males shrank by more than three inches to a mere five feet one inch, a size not much exceeding that of some Pygmies in Africa today. But certain males who during the same period were given elaborate burials at Tikal (and are therefore presumed to have been members of the elite) had an average stature of five feet seven inches, and their life span as compared to that of the commoners was notably longer. Privileged classes with a preferential access to food are a characteristic of the newer cultural adaptations that have been with us to this day.

3

Eating as Cultural Adaptation

ALTHOUGH for most people in modern societies a meal is an interval spent apart from the work day, for others in many parts of the world, obtaining and preparing food is itself the day's work. On the island of Tikopia, for example, the people go inland to dig up taro roots or yams and to harvest breadfruit from the trees; some may take their canoes to the reefs to fish; and children cull the forest for wild foods that might have been overlooked by their elders. The daily routine is similar for much of the world's population, whether they forage or plant crops, and has been so until the past several thousand years for all human beings on the planet.

Some ten thousand years ago, as a result of the pressure of increased population, the hunting–gathering adaptation gave way in many places to the deliberate planting of seeds and roots. Horticulturists differ from hunter–gatherers in that they usually obtain very little meat by hunting, their clearing of land having destroyed the habitat needed by game animals, and are likely to be short of protein unless fishing is possible or unless they can produce a surplus of crops to trade for meat with pastoralists. Whereas hunter–gatherers break up into small groups to forage, horticulturists establish large and permanent settlements close to the gardens that are their source of food. For horticulturists, the land becomes a strategic resource, not simply—as it is for hunter–gatherers—a location from which edible things can be obtained. Once this change of attitude takes place, some system must be agreed upon for apportioning the land. The most common solution among horticulturists is for corporate kinship groups, such as lineages and clans, to act as the owners. (A lineage is a group of blood relatives spanning several generations who trace their ancestry to common forebears; members of a clan trace common descent to an ancestor who is usually mythic, and may even be a totemic animal or plant.) From the land holdings controlled by each kinship group, the elders allocate plots for cultivation by the members.

The kinship group is obliged by the larger political organization to which it belongs—such as a tribe—to protect its lands against encroachment by outsiders. Warfare to defend the group's claim to its land, or to expand and take over the lands of others, is thus endemic in horticultural societies. When a conflict over resources arises among hunter–gatherers, one family or the other simply moves to a different place—an easy matter since all of a family's possessions would fill no more than a couple of small suitcases. Horticulturists, on the other hand, are encumbered by their granaries, their tools, and their permanent dwellings, and must remain to defend them along with the arable land. Land must be defended not only against encroachment by human beings but also against the disfavor of supernatural powers. The leaders of the kinship group are thus responsible for conducting rituals to pacify various spirits during the critical phases while a crop is growing.

The horticulturists who have been successful in war are usually the ones who have allies to call upon, and the best way to cement alliances is through marriages with other kinship groups. Marriage alliances are essential also to the system of exchange found among horticulturists—a much broader one, of course, than among hunter–gatherers, whose distribution of plant food, and even sometimes of meat, is limited to kin and to members of the camp. Among horticulturists, whole communities exchange food, often in the form of a feast at which one kinship group is host to others. To prepare for such occasions, the chief of a lineage is expected to collect food donated by the members of his group and then to redistribute it at a time when the stored food is most needed. The host group expects that in the future, when its members are in need of food, those who have been the guests will reciprocate. Once both the rights and the obligation to organize such feasts have been assigned to certain individuals in the society—such as a chief, a lord, or a priest—then something has developed that does not exist among hunter–gatherers: the rise of complex political organization.

Although the life of the simple horticulturists might appeal to romantics, it is rarely an idyllic one. Warfare is almost unremitting; too many children are produced for the land to feed them adequately; the shortage of meat and the lack of variety in plant foods makes for an unbalanced diet. Horticulturists can do little to improve their lot because they are caught up in a circle of events. Constant warfare means that each generation must produce as many offspring as possible to serve as warriors, and so young women must be stolen from neighboring societies—leading to yet more warfare. Because enough arable land is rarely available to feed the additional mouths, the lands of others must be encroached upon—which means again more warfare, the need for yet more offspring, and further attempts to steal the land of neighbors.

Horticulturists cannot return to hunting and gathering because their populations have become too large and too dense, and because they have already killed off most of the game animals and the wild plants that might have provided food in place of cultivated crops. They cannot easily turn to herding because diseases usually take a high toll of domesticated animals in the tropical regions where most horticulturists live. So they expand wherever possible into the remaining sanctuaries of the hunter–gatherers, thereby speeding up their disappearance. But the arable lands occupied by hunter–gatherers are limited, and so the horticulturists have little choice but to intensify production—a futile attempt, both because they usually lack the technology to do so and because their population increases in pace with the increased harvests.

Pastoralism has flourished for thousands of years in parts of Africa, the Near East, and Central Asia. One particular kind, known technically as the "cattle complex," has long existed throughout an extensive swath of East Africa from southern Sudan into South Africa. Almost all of the people who belong to it claim that they value their cattle for cultural reasons—prestige, power, use in ceremonials, and emotional associations—rather than for food. To the Karimojong of northeastern Uganda, for example, cattle represent wealth, social status, and community influence. They are a man's legacy to his sons. They change hands to seal formal contracts of friendship, mutual assistance, and marriage. The most valued present a youth can receive is a healthy calf, to which for years after he will sing songs while he decorates it with garlands. Throughout life, the prime occupation of every man is to increase the size of his herd.

The failure of such people to utilize their cattle economically would appall a farmer in the Western world. Selective breeding is not practiced, although most of the animals are scrawny; the herds have too large a proportion of bulls, which are not even used for plowing; large herds are moved from one distant grazing area to another, in the process degrading the very environment on which the success of herding depends. The cows provide only small amounts of milk: between 300 and 400 pounds a year per animal, as compared to a United States average that ranges between 8000 and 12,000 pounds. In short, what outsiders think should be the primary value of the herds—that is, providing meat and milk without overgrazing the habitat—seem to have become secondary to an irrational love for cattle.

A closer look at the relation of East Africans to their cattle, though, reveals that it is based on imperatives of subsistence and survival rather than on irrational attachment. The region inhabited by the East African pastoralists is one in which rainfall is sparse and unpredictable; it is in general not productive for horticulturists, yet it can support the grazing animals that are herded from place to place in search of water and forage. When the rains do finally come and the cattle fatten on the renewed vegetation, the animals serve advantageously as storage larders on the hoof. Such advantages do not explain the ecological disregard shown by these people in allowing overly large herds to crop the savannas bare. But in fact the cattle complex is the only adaptation possible to the East African herders under the circumstances. Outsiders might think that cattle are kept merely to enhance a man's status, but for the Karimojong, along with other East Africans, the scrawny cattle are the major source of subsistence, though the herders do also cultivate gardens, gather wild fruits and berries, and occasionally hunt. The role of cattle in Karimojong life is the same as it is for modern farmers: to transform the energy stored in grasses, herbs, and shrubs into a form easily available for human consumption.

The notion that the Karimojong do not obtain much in the way of food from their cattle arises because they do not systematically butcher the animals. They nevertheless do obtain a steady supply of animal protein in the form of milk and blood. They milk lactating cows every day and they obtain more than a pint of blood every month from each animal. They do this by piercing its jugular vein and then collecting the blood in gourds; the animals recover quickly and the herders have obtained balanced protein and important vitamins and minerals. Contrary to what is occasionally supposed, some cattle are killed by pastoralists for meat, though a ceremonial or a ritual justification is generally offered. The Pakot of western Kenya, for example, ritually slaughter cattle on any of ten specified occasions, ranging from the conclusion of a peace treaty with another tribe to an adulterer's payment of a fine. In addition, each Pakot male is expected to serve as host at a feast of meat once a year, which means that in a single vicinity nearly fifty such feasts might be held annually. While ritual consumption is promoting community solidarity, it is also making meat available almost every week.

That cattle have represented wealth to herders everywhere may be seen in the derivation of the English word "pecuniary" from the Latin *pecunia,* meaning "wealth in cattle." East Africans may place a high value on cattle for the social status they afford their owners, but the herders are certainly aware also of the cattle's economic worth. In wet years when the gardens yield a surplus, the herders use the excess grain to purchase another cow; the animal is more valuable than stored grain because it reproduces additional wealth in calves, and also because it yields more food than a garden for the same input of human labor. This same cow may be invested later on in cementing an economically important alliance or in paying the bridewealth that obtains a female with the reproductive potential to bear laborers for the kinship group. Even though a portion of the herd is invested in this way, ownership of at least several cows is maintained to validate a man's social status. Such ownership is actually an investment. It brings rewards in the form of power and influence, much as owning a yacht or a large diamond does in Western societies. The East Africans' ostentatious cows, though, at least give milk and blood.

Since cattle thus provide not only food but also

wealth and power, an outsider might rightly wonder why East Africans are so profligate in the management of their herds. Why do they not selectively breed their scrawny cows to obtain animals that produce more milk and meat? Why do they not reduce the size of their herds, rather than allow them to overgraze the savannas, thereby depleting the very habitat on which cattle and humans alike depend for survival? The seemingly irrational disregard for the welfare of the herds and the land is explained in part by a turbulent history of East African tribes driving one another off grazing lands. Herders would be foolish to practice conservation when any improvements made in the land serve only to increase its appeal to potential invaders. They would be equally foolish to reduce the size of their herds, since at any time a large number of their cattle might be stolen or wiped out by an epidemic.

Nor does it make economic sense to butcher a cow so long as it provides at least some milk and blood. A man who slaughters one of his animals will keep less than a quarter of the meat for his own family; the rest must be shared with relatives, neighbors, and allies. It is therefore in each herder's interest to keep taking milk and blood, which need not be shared, until the animal eventually succumbs to disease or old age. A man might, of course, also avoid the rules of sharing by selling for meat the bulls not needed for reproduction, or the cows that are too old or infirm to give milk. Meat buyers, though, prefer to purchase large and well-fed animals, and they pay very little even for such specimens. A large ox that might yield four hundred pounds of meat would bring no more cash than the purchase price for less than three hundred pounds of cornmeal—a food nutritionally much less valuable than beef. Better, the East African herders reason, to keep the animal for prestige purposes and use it in the future to pay a bridewealth or to cement an alliance, while in the meantime obtaining milk and blood from it.

No wonder, then, that the eroding savannas are populated by large herds of lean cattle. Each man is acting in ways that have proved best over the centuries for his family and his kinship group. Given the ecological and social realities that prevail in East Africa, it is difficult to see how the cattle complex could be altered.

The modern cultural adaptation that emerged first in Britain, then in western Europe and North America, is now spreading rapidly around the globe—and even penetrating into the lands of remote pastoralists, horticulturists, and hunter–gatherers. Often regarded as synonymous with the Industrial Revolution—which began almost exactly two hundred years ago with James Watt's improved version of the steam engine—modernization entails much more than the replacement of human muscle by energy from machines. It has involved developments in the structure of the family, the division of labor, the growth of population, and the environment, as well as diet.

The fact is often ignored that the Industrial Revolution could not have taken place without the Agricultural Revolution that preceded it, and that was based on an increase in production due both to new crops from the Americas and to new methods of farming. Yields of food were increased substantially by such simple techniques as the rotation of crops—a sequence from year to year, for example, of barley, clover, wheat, and turnips, instead of leaving the field fallow when its fertility had been depleted. The selective breeding of cattle also greatly increased the yields of meat and milk. In such ways, what had been an inefficient system of agriculture was eventually replaced by large-scale mechanized farming that took on the character of modern industry. Oliver Goldsmith in his poem "The Deserted Village"—published in 1770, five years *before* Watt's improved steam engine first came into use—described how the mechanization of agriculture had already forced many farmers to abandon their small holdings and migrate to the cities. This considerable portion of the British population provided the labor for an industrialization that would otherwise have been impossible.

One phenomenon of modernization has been an increasingly rapid increase in population. In 1750 the total population of the world was probably about 750 million; by 1830 it had increased to a billion; by 1930 it was two billion, and by 1975 four billion. In other words, the human species needed millions of years to reach a population of a billion; but thereafter the second billion was added in only a hundred years, the third in thirty years, and the fourth in a mere fifteen years. This growth was long attributed to a drop in the death rate that stemmed from advances in medicine, but some demographers now question whether medicine had much of an effect. Tuberculosis, for example, was the largest single cause of death in Britain in the last century, yet in the fifty years previous to 1882—when the tubercle bacillus was first identified, by Robert Koch—deaths caused by it had already declined by about half. Pneumonia, influenza, infectious bronchitis, and other diseases also began significant declines early in the nineteenth century, years before immunization and potent new drugs could have had any effect.

If not medical advances, then what can explain the change in the response to infection by people living in modern societies? The answer seems to be the profound effect of improved nutrition on the body's response to microorganisms. The decline in the death rate that occurred in Europe and in North America during the last century is being witnessed today in developing nations, and has the same probable cause. Well-nourished people have a much lower rate of infection and, even if infected, are much more likely to recover as compared to poorly nourished people. Before the widespread use of the measles vaccine, practically every child in every country caught measles, but three hundred times more deaths occurred in the poorer countries than in the richer ones. The reason was not that the virus was somehow more potent in poor countries or that these lacked medical services, but that in poorly nourished countries the virus attacked children who, because of chronic malnutrition, were less able to resist it.

Along with an improved agriculture came the introduction into Europe of new crops from the Americas, notably white potatoes into northern Europe and maize into southern. In both Spain and Italy, where the cultivation of maize was widespread, populations soared— nearly doubling in Spain and increasing from eleven to eighteen million in Italy between the beginning and the end of the eighteenth century. The potato was not accepted so readily in Europe, even though it had been cultivated in the Andean highlands of Peru for about 2500 years. It was at first regarded with suspicion, in part because it was grown from a tuber rather than from seeds, as were all other edible plants in Europe up to that time. But by the beginning of the eighteenth century, the potato had become a common food for peasants, who found in it the perfect crop for small parcels of arable land. Just one acre planted to potatoes could feed a family of five or six, plus a cow or pig, for most of a year. The plant could grow in a wide variety of soils and it required no tools other than a spade and a hoe; it matured within three or four months, as compared to the well over half a year required for grain crops, and it had the advantage of a high nutritional value.

The most dramatic effect of the potato's introduction into Europe was seen in Ireland. By the middle of the eighteenth century, most of the Irish population was subsisting almost exclusively on potatoes, and the perennially recurring famines there appeared at last to be ended. Potatoes do not have aphrodisiac powers, as was once believed, but they did contribute to the sudden increase in the Irish population, making large families possible because they provided a maximum of sustenance with a minimum of labor. The population of Ireland grew from just above three million in 1754 to more than eight million in 1845. Then a blight struck, bringing the Great Hunger—a famine that was to last four years.

An increase in population as a result of new foods rather than of industrialization and medical advances also took place in China. The sweet potato, long grown by South American Indians, was early imported as a crop into China and was established by 1594, when it provided sustenance while the native grains were succumbing to drought. An eighteenth-century agricultural commentary extolled it as a versatile crop that could be boiled, ground, or fermented, could be fed to animals as well as to humans, and could grow in sandy, mountainous, and salty soils where grains did not survive. By that century, other New World crops were being widely grown: Maize was allowing people from the crowded Yangtze region to migrate inland and farm drier lands; the white potato made it possible to bring into production lands that were too impoverished even for growing maize; and peanuts could be grown in the previously useless soils along rivers and streams. The new crops allowed a Chinese population that had reached the limits of its previous resources to begin a new spurt in growth. The numbers expanded from about 150 million people in the early 1700s to about 450 million only a century and a half later. A worldwide growth in population over the past several centuries has been similar to what occurred in China, and can be assumed to have occurred for similar reasons. As soon as food resources could be moved from one continent to another because of the invention of long-distance transportation, a surge in population took place—one that had little to do with industrialization, shorter work hours, or advances in the practice of medicine.

People in modern societies usually assume that their own kind of mechanized agriculture is the most efficient known. But if the question is asked whether mechanized producers are really extracting from the soil a greater number of calories of food in proportion to the calories of energy they expend, the answer is No. In fact, they are very inefficient in this regard when compared to other adaptations—as is shown by a simple equation that makes it possible to analyze the efficiency of any system for providing food energy:

$$\frac{E}{m \times t \times r} = e$$

That is, a society's annual production of food energy, E (as expressed in thousands of calories or kilocalories), divided by the number of food producers (m) times the hours each works at food production during the year (t) times the calories expended per producer each hour in doing the work (r) equals e, that society's techno-environmental efficiency (in other words, the calories produced for each calorie of energy expended). Obviously, e must be greater than one because no society can survive for very long unless it produces more energy than it expends; actually, the value of e must be substantially higher than one to provide for such nonproducing activities as tool-making, ceremonials, and recreation, among other things, and also to support the young, the elderly, the sick, and other nonproducers in the society. The larger e becomes, therefore, the greater is the society's techno-environmental efficiency in producing food energy above the amount it expends.

In a hunting–gathering society, as exemplified by a camp of San, the equation might be applied as follows:

$$\frac{E \ (23{,}000{,}000 \ \text{kilocalories produced annually})}{\substack{m \ (20 \ \text{producers}) \times t \\ (805 \ \text{hours worked} \\ \text{per producer annually}) \\ \times \ r \ (150 \ \text{calories} \\ \text{expended per hour})}} = \begin{array}{l} e \ \text{(a techno-environmental} \\ \text{efficiency of 9.5)} \end{array}$$

In other words, a camp consisting of about twenty adult San who hunt or gather has a techno-environmental efficiency of between nine and ten times the amount of energy expended.

This low efficiency does not allow much of a margin of safety and is insufficient to provide food for full-time specialists such as woodcarvers or priests. But the San cannot increase their efficiency, because the average expenditure per producer of 150 calories an hour cannot be raised substantially; the human body simply cannot withstand long periods of being overheated or out of breath (which is why the average value for *r* of 150 remains the same in all of the adaptations to be discussed in this chapter). For each adult in the camp to work more than 805 hours a year (an average of a mere two hours or so a day) would not solve the problem because the San can neither transport nor store a surplus; and any increased effort would quickly deplete the food resources around the camp. They might try to enlarge the population of their camp to increase the number of producers, but the food supply in the Kalahari Desert is insufficient to support dense populations that lack the knowledge and tools to build irrigation dams. So long as the San follow their traditional ways, they obviously can do almost nothing to increase their techno-environmental efficiency.

Nor would it be possible for the San to switch to horticulture, given both the harsh environment and their limited technology for overcoming it. Even if they could, energy data from a horticultural village in Gambia, West Africa, shows how little would be gained. Instead of the twenty food-producers in the San camp, this village had 334, as well as a better climate for plant growth and a more complex technology. Yet the application of the equation to these peasants shows an efficiency only slightly above that of the San:

$$\frac{E\,(460{,}000{,}000)}{m\,(334) \times t\,(820) \times r\,(150)} = e \ (11.2)$$

The main advantage of horticulture over hunting–gathering is not its much greater efficiency but rather that people can live together in larger and more permanent settlements. The denser population of a sedentary village allows for protection against enemies, and gives greater opportunity for cultural interaction.

Detailed energy data do not exist for pastoral peoples, but their efficiency is believed to be no greater than for hunter–gatherers and horticulturists. It may indeed be less, since to allow domesticated animals to eat plant foods and then to eat the animal or its milk and blood takes the process of production through an extra step, with a loss of calories along the way. This assumption seems supported by the few studies that have been made. One tribe of southern Tunisia, which herds sheep and goats and also practices a little horticulture, has a techno-environmental efficiency of about six; for some Indians in the Andes of South America who are almost exclusively pastoralists, the figure is only a little more than two.

Figures on efficiency under other adaptations do not increase by much until the complex level of irrigation agriculture is reached. This adaptation can feed more people on less land than any other, including mechanized agriculture. Over the millennia, it has developed most notably in eastern Asia because of particular conditions prevailing there: many people to provide the labor for building and maintaining irrigation works, abundant water, and the incentive of a shortage of arable land. As the irrigation system develops and production is intensified, more and more people are fed from the same amount of land—though at the price of increasing the amount of labor per unit of land, which means that the land must be worked ever more intensively by more people. Given this cycle, no one can become richer by working harder, because the payments allocated to labor must be divided among a larger and larger force. And since such systems can develop only in the presence of an autocratic government, any economic growth that occurs is inevitably siphoned off by the bureaucratic elite that exists outside of the energy system.

A detailed study of labor inputs and food yields for an irrigation village in Yunnan Province, China, before the fall of the Nationalist government shows a greatly increased techno-environmental efficiency over hunting–gathering, horticulture, and pastoralism:

$$\frac{E\ (3,788,000,000)}{m\ (418) \times t\ (1129) \times r\ (150)} = e\ (53.5)$$

A higher efficiency, it should be noted, does not produce an increase in leisure, as is often supposed. Rather, each producer must work harder *(t)*—in fact, some thirty-five percent more labor is performed by each of these Chinese than by each of the San.

Of the nearly four billion kilocalories produced annually by this Chinese village, the villagers were estimated to need no more than a sixth. What happened, then, to the more than three billion kilocalories they produced each year over what they consumed? The surplus was used to feed the scores of millions in Chinese towns and cities who did not participate directly in food production, or it was sent to market and exchanged for manufactured goods, or it was taken away in the form of taxes levied by the local, provincial, and national governments, and in the form of rent payments to large landowners.

Modern societies are too complex to be analyzed by the equation employed here, but a few generalizations can be made. Once again, it is a mistake to suppose that modern societies allow people to work less hard for their daily bread. Out of the 1129 hours worked by one Chinese irrigation farmer in a year, only 122 were needed to grow enough food to sustain that farmer. A blue-collar worker in the United States, on the other hand, spends 180 hours earning enough money to purchase a year's supply of food. Notwithstanding Western notions of the Chinese peasants' incessant labor, it is plain that they actually need to work less by a third than North Americans or Europeans to keep themselves supplied with food. Moreover, although a mechanized farmer in the American Midwest need put in an annual total of only nine hours of work for each acre to achieve an astounding six thousand calories for each calorie of effort, that figure ignores the enormous amounts of human labor that go into manufacturing and transporting the trucks, tractors, combines, fuel, fertilizer, pesticides, fence wire, and everything else used by the farmer, not to mention transporting the food itself. For every person who actually works on a Midwestern farm, the labor of at least two others off the farm is needed to supply equipment and services directly to the farmer—aside from the very many more whose labors contribute indirectly to the final product. Altogether, a total of 2790 calories of energy must be expended to produce and deliver to a consumer in the United States just one can of corn providing a total of 270 calories. The production of meat entails an even greater deficit: An expenditure of 22,000 calories is needed to produce the somewhat less than four ounces of beefsteak that likewise provide 270 calories.

In short, present-day agriculture is much less efficient than traditional irrigation methods that have been used by Asians, among others, in this century and by Mayans, Mesopotamians, Egyptians, and Chinese in antiquity. The primary advantage of a mechanized agriculture is that it requires the participation of fewer farmers, but for that the price paid in machines, fossil fuels, and other expenditures of energy is enormous. A severe price is also paid in human labor. Once the expensive machines have been manufactured and deployed on the farms, they are economically efficient only if operated throughout the daylight hours, and indeed farmers in the United States often labor for sixteen hours a day. The boast of industrialized societies that they have decreased the workload is valid only in comparison with the exploitation of labor that existed in the early decades of the Industrial Revolution. If the prevailing forty-hour work week of North America and Europe were proposed to the San, whoever did so would be considered to be exploitive, inhuman, or plain mad.

Clearly, not every adaptation is beneficial. Maladaptation often occurs when old subsistence patterns must be adjusted to new conditions—a situation which, because of high-speed and long-distance transportation developed over the last few centuries, has affected even isolated peoples. Particularly vulnerable are the peasant cultures, still found on every continent except North America and Australia. Unlike many tribal groups around the world that are also subsistence horticulturists—for example, those in New Guinea—peasants always live within the framework of a complex society in which they are subordinate to external sources of political and economic power.

One such peasant group consists of somewhere between 10,000 and 15,000 Miskito Indians who live along the Caribbean coast of Nicaragua. Traditionally they raised bananas, manioc, and plantain, and hunted a few species of animals, primarily the green turtle. Their economy had begun to change by the middle of the seventeenth century, when a British trading company offered to barter mirrors and glass beads with the Miskito for their shells of hawksbill turtles—the familiar tortoise-shell used to make combs, bracelets, and various trinkets. That trade had little ecological impact on the diet of the Miskito because the hawksbill turtle was not an important source of food. The lands of the Miskito were repeatedly invaded by rubber, mining, banana, and lumber interests; but each of these enterprises eventually faltered, and the Miskito returned to their horticulture and hunting of green turtles.

The Miskito had been hunting turtles for many hundreds of years, at least, but from the seventeenth century onward they had become exposed to the foreign goods that could be obtained by trading with outsiders. So they were prepared to collaborate with two companies that in 1969 established factories in their lands for the processing of green turtles. The two products to be obtained were meat, to be served in restaurants as turtle steak, and calipee—the six to eight pounds of gelatinous material from under both the top and bottom shells used to manufacture turtle soup for the fancy-food markets of North America and Europe. It might be supposed that the predilections of a few distant gourmets would have no more than an inconsequential impact; but as a matter of fact, they have almost totally upset the traditional economy of the Miskito Indians. Unlike the hawksbill, whose shells the Miskito had previously sold, the green turtle had been a mainstay of their food supply—and the Indians are now selling it with a rapidity that makes the demise of the species in that area inevitable. Two years after the processing factories opened, just one Miskito village had increased its catch of green turtles nearly three times over—yet almost none of this catch provided food for the village.

The Miskito must go ever farther in their search for the disappearing turtles, which they spend so much time hunting that they scarcely have any left to plant their gardens. They work harder than they did before, and for an irrational motive: They are selling their food supply to obtain money, which they then use to buy food at the company stores, a set of transactions that leaves them nutritionally poorer than before they had money to spend. A successful turtleman earns no more than $4.20 a week beyond his expenses, and for most the earnings are a good deal less. A small turtle steak now costs the Miskito about a dollar, and provides a family with only one meal. About a dollar a week goes to supply each member of the family with two cups of watered-down coffee a day. Ten pounds of rice or flour cost about $1.50. No longer able to eat well, many of the turtlemen subsist almost exclusively on carbohydrates and coffee, which at least take away their hunger.

Traditionally among the Miskito, food had been directly tied to their kinship group. Meat from turtles and a few other prized animals was freely shared with other members of the group, who in turn shared their food on other occasions. The sharing evened out for each family the peaks and valleys of an irregular supply of turtles and thus made efficient use of available resources. Nowadays, turtle meat that would once have been shared with kin is sold. Since meat is in short supply, kin who are not very closely related are excluded from the protein distribution system altogether. As ties within the kinship group are weakened and every fisherman looks out for himself, the immediate family increasingly replaces the group as the economic unit.

The green turtle is an endangered species everywhere throughout its range; by the time this book appears, its decreasing numbers may mean that it can no longer be hunted by the Miskito. They have thus entered an ecological blind alley, in which they are dependent upon a food resource that will soon not exist. What then will they do? A return to horticulture would be extremely difficult, not only because previous ventures into lumbering, rubber, and banana plantations have degraded the environment, but also because the Miskito are now trapped inside a market economy. They cannot increase their production of cattle and pigs because little fodder is available and because no rail or highway transportation exists to reach a regular market. It might seem that they should turn to fishing their shores; however, they lack not only the capital that would be necessary to equip themselves for deep-sea fishing, but also anything approaching the knowledge about turtles they have accumulated over the centuries. Even more of an obstacle is that fishing demands cooperation and a sharing of resources, but the experiences of the Miskito with a market economy have made them unwilling to trust even their kin in joint ventures.

Barring massive intervention by the government of Nicaragua—an unlikely event at this writing—the Miskito lack any way of making a new adjustment. Long after they have disappeared as a viable culture, anthropologists of the future will no doubt describe them as a classic example of a subsistence system that failed to adapt to outside economic forces, and so was eventually destroyed.

4

The Life Passage

IN ALMOST EVERY SOCIETY, the milestones of passage from one stage to another in the biological and social development of the individual are celebrated with food and drink. The birth of a child becomes the occasion for a feast. Initiation rites and graduation ceremonies are celebrated to mark the launching of a new breadwinner. A marriage frequently entails the exchange of scarce or prestigious foods between the two families. And the dead pass to another world feasted by those who remain in this one.

The customs of virtually all societies recognize the pregnant woman's need for special foods. Even before they become pregnant, the Mbum Kpau women of Chad in equatorial Africa are exhorted to eat no chicken or goat so as to escape pain in childbirth or the birth of abnormal children; and after becoming pregnant, they avoid still other foods, such as the meat from antelopes with twisted horns, which might cause them to bear deformed offspring. Since failure to bear healthy children is a major tragedy for a Mbum Kpau woman, these prohibitions do not have to be enforced; the women themselves react with horror at any suggestion that they might eat a prohibited food. Such beliefs, found in all cultures, seem to be foolish; but they are nevertheless valid as a recognition that the eating habits of pregnant women affect the health of their children. In North America, a pregnant woman is warned that she must eat for two, and it is expected that her husband will cater to her cravings for pickles, ice cream, and chocolate.

A study of the pregnancy cravings of about two hundred and fifty women in Albany, New York, showed everyday beliefs about both cravings and aversions to be not as irrational as they sometimes appear. Most women reported strong aversions to alcohol and to coffee, both of which they knew might cause birth defects. Their strong cravings for ice cream, other dairy products, and sweets (including chocolate and fruit) were possibly due to the need for extra calories and for calcium during pregnancy. When a pregnant woman's diet is deficient in calcium, the fetus will draw upon the calcium stored in her teeth and bones—thus explaining the folk statement that each child costs a tooth. The increased demand for calcium during pregnancy and lactation is a special problem for women living in societies in which milk and milk products are not consumed. Cultural attitudes toward other foods and methods of preparation do, however, often provide substitutes. In China, many expectant mothers express a craving for sweet-and-sour spareribs, which is nutritionally adaptive because the vinegar used in the recipe leaches calcium from the rib bones into the meat, thereby making it available for digestion.

In the United States, pregnant women of African ancestry are often reported to experience a craving for clay—and the cause seems to be a combination of history, nutritional needs, and the culture of slaves in the southern states. In many of the African societies from which the slaves were taken, the biological need for calcium and other minerals by pregnant and lactating women is partially met by eating clays from nutrient-rich sources, such as that from termite mounds, which contain concentrations of minerals deposited by the insects. These clays are collected, baked, and then sold or bartered. A number of the villages of the Ewe people of Ghana, for example, have made this a thriving industry. At certain sites, which are held in particularly high regard for the quality of their edible clay, it is shaped into the form of eggs, to be marketed in the Ewe lands and elsewhere in West Africa. Samples of these clay eggs that have been analyzed for their mineral content—calcium, magnesium, potassium, copper, zinc, and iron—have been shown to compare favorably with the mineral supplements prescribed for pregnant women in modern societies. The United States Food and Nutrition Board has estimated that pregnancy demands about twenty percent more nutrients in addition to the Recommended Dietary Allowances; for lactation, the increased need is approximately fifty percent. The iron content of clay in the amounts typically eaten by a pregnant woman in Ghana ranges between sixteen and sixty-four percent of the RDA; for copper, it is between fifteen and thirty-three percent.

With the nutritional value of eating clay beyond doubt, and with clear anthropological evidence that it is a cultural trait in West Africa, the eating of clay by black Americans, particularly pregnant women, becomes more understandable. Most of the slaves brought to North America came from West Africa, and in their new environment they continued to eat clay for both nutritional and cultural reasons. As the cotton plantations moved inland from the Atlantic coast, relocated slaves often asked friends and relatives from the old plantations to send them bags of clay because they did not consider what they found in the new places good enough. Even today, clay is shipped to farmers' markets in Georgia, where it is sold by the shoebox, and visitors to new mothers in hospitals often bring gifts of clay. Among blacks who have migrated to northern ghettos, pregnant women sometimes ask relatives still in the South to mail them clay dug from a favorite pit. Others, unable to obtain clay, have settled on laundry starch as a substitute. Despite its superficial resemblance to clay, starch is almost entirely lacking in valuable minerals and is a harmful stomach irritant besides.

The food taboos observed by pregnant women in some societies are occasionally difficult to understand. To outsiders, it seems contrary to reason that males who greatly desire healthy infants, and who also often understand the need for an adequate diet during pregnancy, should deprive the women in their society of adequate nutrition. The truth is, though, that the taboos do more to bolster male dominance in reserving the most desirable foods for themselves than they adversely affect female nutrition. The taboos are not usually very effective. The tabooed foods may simply be unavailable; the chickens and goats prohibited to the Mbum Kpau women, for example, are butchered only on rare ceremonial occasions. On the other hand, pregnant women may have their choice of substitute foods that are just as nutritious as the prohibited ones. The Sanio–Hiowe of Papua, New Guinea, prohibit their women from eating four kinds of mammals, but six others that are equally nutritious are eaten exclusively by women, and there are nine more that may be eaten by either sex. Finally, some taboos may be ignored altogether when food is in short supply or when those foods regarded as proper for females are not available.

The infant's earliest emotional experiences are linked inextricably with eating, and its feelings about these experiences are almost always intense. The absence of love while food is being provided can lead to rage or desperate anxiety on the part of the infant. The primitive emotional connections formed within the first months of life, linking food with the mother, remain in the unconscious of the growing child and even of the adult, where they are being continually reinforced and modified by later experiences. By adulthood, the connections have become complex indeed. No adults ever really eat alone, for always with them are the earliest eating experiences associated with the mother.

The way in which mothers give food a meaning beyond nutrition can be seen in the Gurage, a horticultural people of southwestern Ethiopia. An hour after birth, the godmother ritually administers the first feeding by placing a small amount of butter in the infant's mouth. Several hours later the infant is given the breast—and from then on crying for any cause is interpreted as a desire for milk. After five days a feast is held for kin and friends to celebrate the infant's survival—a true milestone, given the high infant mortality that plagues the Gurage. The mother then goes into seclusion, devoting herself exclusively to the care of her infant and constantly suckling it, whether or not its discomforts stem from hunger. Two months later the mother shifts most of the responsibility for the care of the infant to a female relative or servant. Since the surrogate mothers do not usually give it much attention, the infant cries almost continuously because of hunger and lack of care. Although the mother offers the breast whenever she is present, both to satisfy hunger and as a pacifier, the infant remains unfed for hours while she is gone. As the infant approaches the age for weaning, when it is between two and four, the periods allotted for breast-feeding will have declined to only a few minutes at a time. At each feeding, the infant makes a frantic attempt to satisfy its hunger quickly. Weaning is eventually enforced when the mother applies a bitter substance to her nipples.

The inconsistent behavior of the Gurage mother establishes a pattern of alternating glut and want, which some psychologically oriented anthropologists believe contributes to the extreme anxiety about food displayed by the Gurage. The anxiety is greater among boys and men than among girls and women, because males never prepare their own meals but depend totally upon females to provide them for them. Furthermore, the Gurage place many values on food—such as for curing illness, for ritual activities, and as compensation for services—that have nothing to do with nutrition; indeed, every social and ritual event among the Gurage begins and ends with eating. So it is not surprising that psychological studies of the Gurage have isolated several personality characteristics that seem related to their anxieties over food: selfishness, the notion of a hostile environment, feelings of unworthiness, and the emotional detachment shown by parents toward their children.

Human milk fills all of the infant's nutritional needs, just as whale milk—which is laden with fats suitable for mammals that live in cold water—specifically fills the different needs of infant whales. Human milk also furnishes the infant with antibodies from its mother that protect its immunologic system, which is immature at birth, from infectious organisms and allergens. And for about six months after birth it provides a powerful growth stimulator—a substance that is five times more powerful than the other growth factors found in the blood. Despite the demonstrated benefits of breast feeding, the bottle has increasingly been substituted for the breast. In the United States, breast feeding declined from a nearly universal practice in 1900 to a mere eighteen percent in 1966; and in most countries of western Europe the situation is about the same. Studies made since 1966 indicate a slow return to breast feeding, at least among more highly educated women. A survey made in the vicinity of Boston showed that about seventy percent of women married to university students breast-fed their infants, and that about forty percent of upper-class women did so, as compared to only about thirteen percent of those belonging to lower socioeconomic classes.

In developing countries, though, mothers are rapidly switching from breast feeding to bottle feeding. In 1960, ninety-five percent of Chilean mothers breast-fed their infants beyond the first year; just a decade later, only six percent did so. A laborer in Chile will sometimes spend twenty percent of his total wages to buy milk for a single infant; in Kenya the annual cost of the formulas that are being bought as substitutes for breast milk amounts to about a fifth of the foreign aid that country receives. Families spend this disproportionate share of their earnings despite the observable fact that the mortality of bottle-fed infants—as a result of gastrointestinal infections, malnutrition, and other ailments—is considerably higher than for those who are breast-fed. In Chile, for example, the mortality rate at the age of three months for bottle-fed infants is two and a half times higher.

The shift to the bottle in developing countries is one of the most perplexing dietary changes seen in this century. Mothers there often lack not only the knowledge, but also even the pure water, needed to prepare a formula correctly and hygienically. From a nutritional standpoint, moreover, human milk is dissimilar from cow's milk, the basis of most formulas, in nearly all respects. The proteins in human milk, for example, are specifically matched to the metabolic requirements of newborn humans rather than of newborn calves. The fats in human milk are less saturated and are utilized more effectively than the saturated fats found in cow's milk. With mother's milk demonstrably superior, the spread of bottle feeding apparently has only status to recommend it. Mothers in many parts of the world often consider breast feeding to be a vulgar peasant custom, to be abandoned as soon as the bottle can be afforded.

A folk belief in numerous societies states that breast feeding prevents the conception of another child. The fellahin of Egypt, for example, believe that a woman cannot conceive while she is observing the two-year nursing period demanded by Islamic law for each child; a father who wants another child sooner than that must give his permission for the previous child to be weaned.

For the Chaga of East Africa, a taboo prohibits sexual intercourse between a mother and her husband until the infant is weaned; social disapproval of women who become pregnant less than three years after the birth of the last child is so strong that those who conceive earlier have been known to kill themselves or to commit infanticide.

Studies of many populations around the world have shown that mothers who nurse their infants for one or two years experience considerably longer intervals between pregnancies than those who do not nurse. Conception while nursing, even though contraception is not practiced, is dramatically lowered during the first six months, and is not usual during the next six months; after that, however, the correlation diminishes greatly. San mothers, for example, nurse their infants for the first two or three years of life, and often longer than that. During much of this time the mother's sexual life is active, yet conception does not occur; in fact, lactation suppresses ovulation in so many women for so much of the time that in one group of San who have been closely studied, the average interval between births is 3.7 years.

All the available evidence indicates that nursing limits fertility, but it does not explain how. For the San and for mothers in other societies in which the custom prevails of nursing frequently and on demand, day and night, the stimulation of the nipples apparently leads to the secretion of prolactin and other hormones which tend to suppress ovulation. Even in societies where nursing is not so frequent, lactation still suppresses ovulation. One explanation for this is the critical-weight hypothesis, according to which a critical storage of body fat may control the cessation or resumption of the menstrual cycle. Reproduction requires an enormous expenditure of energy by the mother, with the result that an undernourished female begins menstruation later and enters the menopause earlier than a well-nourished one. Nursing can delay the resumption of menstruation because it delays the buildup of energy reserves in the female's body, owing to the caloric demands made on it by nursing that amount to about a thousand calories a day. Accordingly, the diet must allow a mother to provide milk for one nursing infant and at the same time have the surplus of energy needed to bring another infant to term. Body fat thus acts as a signal to the mother's reproductive system as to whether or not her body is capable of supporting the demands of a new pregnancy. The temporary suspension of ovulation is obviously an ecological adaptation to a reduced supply of food, and is less wasteful than mass mortality in regulating excess population.

Weaning is a critical time for any child. The danger of disease and psychological stress are both intensified by the poor nutrition that may occur while the adjustment to another kind of feeding is made. Often the transition must be enforced. Among the Bemba, mothers squeeze the red juice from certain fruits onto their breasts; the juice looks like blood and frightens the child. Thonga mothers in southern Africa wean a child by covering their breasts with pepper; in Iran, children are told that a witch has eaten the mother's breasts, which by way of proof are shown smeared with a black substance. These measures, and others such as ritual offerings to ancestors, are a recognition of weaning as an important transition. A newly weaned child is exposed to a great risk of infection from foods that are tainted or that have been prepared with polluted water. Infections increase the need for certain nutrients, particularly protein, and at the same time they not only reduce the body's capacity to absorb nutrients, but also cause a loss of appetite. Children who are marginally nourished as they undergo the stress of weaning may thus cross the thin borderline into outright malnutrition by contracting even a slight infection. Malnutrition in turn further lessens the resistance to infection and adds to the stress, again increasing the need for the very food that is in short supply.

After the vulnerable years of weaning, the problem of malnutrition becomes less severe. One reason for this is that by the age of five children grow less rapidly and therefore need fewer of the nutrients that had previously been essential. Another reason is that they can now chew and digest a wider range of foods. This is the period in life at which children in all societies learn to forage on their own for tidbits of food. In modern societies they may do so by searching in the cupboard or by begging, but in simpler societies children go out looking for wild fruits and berries, insects, and bird eggs. Such gathered foods are nutritionally important, particularly for children in a horticultural society where the staple foods are often deficient in vitamins and minerals. The diet of such children who forage out of necessity during a famine may actually improve.

During a famine, differences in what is fed to male and female children become starkly evident. In Nigeria during the 1970 war over Biafra, the daughters in many families suffered from severe malnutrition while the sons were adequately fed. Indeed, in many cases the sons belonging to high-status families showed almost no signs of malnutrition. In many societies of the world, male children are better fed at all times. Among the Gurage of Ethiopia, mentioned several pages back, brothers are fed before their sisters; they receive better food and more of it. A boy who receives food as a special treat is expected to share it with other boys but not with girls, including his own sisters. On ceremonial and festive occasions, boys are almost always allowed to eat with the adults, girls almost never. The preference shown in the distribution of food, beginning in early childhood and continuing throughout adult life, is one means by which the Gurage implant notions of male dominance. For many East African pastoralists, disparities in diet between the sexes are linked to differences in their subsistence tasks. Whereas the diet of the men and boys who herd the livestock includes milk and blood, the women and girls who remain in the settlement eat only the crops they grow in their gardens. Subsistence tasks also lead to differences in the diets of male and female hunter–gatherers, the males often eating a portion of the animals they have killed before carrying meat back to camp to be shared.

Every parent has seen young children display marked preferences concerning foods. Those they favor generally are soft in texture; those they object to tend to be dry, highly spiced, or very hot or cold. They prefer thin puddings to thick ones, mashed potatoes to baked, white to whole-grain bread, and juicy hamburgers to chops. Their preference for foods that are soft and moist can be explained by their lack of an abundant supply of saliva to lubricate the food. The reason they prefer lukewarm foods to those that are very cold or very hot is not clear, but it may be the effect of extremes of temperature on receptors in the brain that tend to suppress the sense of taste. This is, of course, true for adults as well, but they have a lessened ability anyway to detect flavors and so this suppression is not as crucial. Most parents also say that their children are sensitive to flavors that go undetected by most adults—such as vegetables that have been scorched or milk that is just slightly curdled. Children have as a result been credited with a heightened awareness of flavors, but no experimental evidence supports this notion. In this case also, the explanation probably is that adults deviate from the norm and have become habituated over a long period of time to foods with strong or unusual flavors.

Although the predilections of young children are often difficult to explain scientifically, a number of observations can nevertheless be made. Aside from milk, which continues to be used as a food after weaning in some (but by no means all) societies, no single food can be associated with children everywhere. In each culture, children are gradually exposed to what adults eat and probably never consciously ask whether this is what they ought to be eating. In Mexico, peasant children are exposed from the day they are born to the odor of tortillas, beans, and the spicy sauce made from chili peppers and tomatoes. The children absorb the flavors of these foods in their mothers' milk, smell them on the breath of older siblings, and take them in with the first bite of solid food. They grow up immersed in these smells and tastes—so it is no wonder that as adults they consider a diet of tortillas, beans, chili peppers, and tomatoes to be the normal one, and would look with suspicion on any other.

The growing child also gradually becomes conscious of kinship and of social distinctions through customs connected with eating. Among certain Bantu tribes of Zimbabwe that are organized matrilineally, children are free to run into the hut of a maternal aunt and take food without asking, but in the house of a paternal aunt they must ask politely—whereas among the patrilineal tribes of the southern Bantu the situation is exactly the reverse. In fact, relations with kin, and social relations generally, are learned better through customs connected with eating than through direct explanation. Just as children in modern societies learn sharing through the exchange of toys with other children, in southern Bantu society they are trained through the sharing of food. The complex rules concerning hospitality—to whom it is offered and in what degree of lavishness—that are part of the system of clan obligations are established through the lessons of early childhood. Children early become aware of who eats with whom, and in what order, thereby defining the roles of the sexes and the age groups in Bantu society. They learn that they are prohibited from taking food from the pot in the presence of elders, and that when given food by an adult, even in a miserly amount, they are to take it in both hands as though acknowledging an act of largesse.

By the time a Bantu child is eight or ten years old, distinctions of age and sex have become very important. Male children are forbidden to eat any longer with their mothers and sisters around the family hearth; rather, they must eat with other males of about the same age. Even older boys and girls who work together in the fields at harvest time eat their meals separately. The younger boys, who act as goatherds in the settlement, are divided from those slightly older, who care for the cattle and are permitted to eat in the quarters of the unmarried men. These and still other groupings according to age and sex eat apart from one another, even though all the food comes ultimately from one family hearth. The mother who continues to cook the food—thus maintaining a kind of monopoly—now has it delivered by a young child to the boys' group or to the men's quarters.

The end of childhood is marked in many of the world's societies by some kind of initiation rite. Initiation ceremonies sometimes involve circumcision and the revelation of hitherto secret knowledge; almost always they entail a change in diet and the relaxation of previous taboos—as, for example, the drinking of coffee and wine at dinner by older children in modern societies. Among the southern Bantu, initiation ceremonies take place when a sufficient number of boys have reached the appropriate age or when the chief's own son has done so. The male child is now separated both symbolically and in fact from the mother's household. Initiation makes him aware of a network of obligations that bind him to other huts and to other families; he learns to measure prestige by the ability to offer hospitality and by the company in which one eats.

People in many simple societies, and some complex ones as well, view the onset of menstruation as a stage of life in the female that is a threat to males. Men who have been near a woman in menstruation often will not risk the dangers of hunting—a taboo that is still unconsciously observed in modern societies by those men who allow no women at their weekend hunting camp. Even plants are considered not immune from contamination by menstrual blood. According to Pliny the Elder in his *Natural History,* it "turns new wine sour; crops touched by it become barren, grafts die, seeds in gardens are dried up, the fruit of trees fall off." Menstruating women are supposed to have a particularly baneful effect on food when it is halfway between one state and another, as in the fermentation of cider, the refining of sugar, the baking of bread, or the churning of butter.

One explanation for the custom in numerous societies of segregating men and women at meals is that females might begin menstruating at any time, supposedly with dire consequences to the males at the table. The precautions might have originated as a result of observations concerning the behavior of women at the time of their periods. These changes are now known to be due to sharp fluctuations in the production of hormones, particularly of estrogen and progesterone, which can affect emotional states at these times. Studies show that women are more likely to commit acts of violence, attempt suicide, become involved in serious accidents, and seek admission to hospitals for imaginary ailments in their first few days of each period than at other times of the month.

The passing from a single to a wedded state is marked in most societies by feasting (whence the word "bridal," a compound of Middle English "bride" plus "ale"), by the sharing of food between the newly married couple, and by an exchange of choice foods between the two families. For the Trobriand Islanders, no marriage can be considered valid without an intricate series of exchanges of food, consisting of eight distinct steps, by the kin of the two partners—first an offering by the woman's family to signify its consent to the marriage, followed by countergifts on both sides, and finally a large gift from the groom's father to the bride's father. As part of the marriage ceremony on Tikopia, the unmarried friends of the couple gather to share a farewell meal with them. All eat from the same basket what is referred to as "food of parting from the unmarried state." Eating in common, dipping into the same food container, is a symbolic farewell, even though all the participants continue to be members of the same society and may even meet daily, because the pair now belongs to a different social category from those who are still unmarried.

The onset of adolescence begins a close association between food and sex that is a feature of all societies. According to the Judeo–Christian tradition, eating the Fruit of Knowledge in the Garden of Eden was followed by sexual shame; first came food, then sex. Breasts evolved among the mammals as structures for the feeding of offspring, and they have remained no more than that for all the primates except human beings, in whom they are permanently fatty and protuberant whether or not the female is pregnant or lactating. For other primate females the nipples have the same relative position as in the human female, although the fat is distributed much more evenly over the entire chest. The fatty tissue in the breast of a human female expands with age and with the number of children she has borne; it is liberally distributed throughout the tissue of the mammary gland itself, and tends to displace that tissue with advancing age. But the common belief that large breasts guarantee a copious supply of milk is false. Actually, the size of the areola is much more indicative of the size of the gland behind it than the prominence of the breast as a whole.

The eroticization of the breasts, a uniquely human phenomenon, possibly evolved as a sexual signaling device—though at a cost to the human infant, who finds the nipple more difficult to grasp as a consequence. The mouth, over the course of evolution, likewise became a major erogenous zone, thereby forming so powerful a link between the two essential human concerns, eating and sexual gratification, that the same descriptive terms can be applied to either one: hungry, starved, sated, and satisfied, among others.

More words from the lexicon of eating than from any

other human activity have been used to describe sexual relations and organs. A woman is referred to as spicy, a dish, a hot tomato, a honey pot, a bit of mutton, a piece of cake, somebody who in fact looks good enough to eat. To lose one's virginity is to lose a cherry. Breasts are apples, melons, grapefruits, or fried eggs; testicles are nuts; the penis is a hot dog, a banana, or meat, the female organ is a bun. When the Aborigines of central Australia ask the question, *"Utna ilkukabaka?,"* it may mean either "Have you eaten?" or "Have you had sexual intercourse?" The Aborigines characterize a young girl as either "unripe" or "ready cooked" (that is, nubile). *Ngaiala* means "hungry," either for food or for sexual intercourse. Similarly, on the island of Tikopia, eating and the sex act are often equated linguistically, as when during copulation the female's organ is said to "eat" that of the male. For the Sinhalese of Sri Lanka, cooking for a man implies sexual relations with him. A woman refers to her lover euphemistically as "the one I cook for," and the word *kanava* can refer either to eating or to sexual intercourse. The close connection between eating and sex is not hard to explain, if it is assumed that early in the evolution of the human species males and females were brought together primarily by the two basic necessities for survival: food and procreation. Now many people eat without being hungry and copulate without producing offspring.

People often reveal through their taboos, myths, and rituals the connections they make between food and sexuality. Among the Eastern Tukano Indians of Colombia, children below the age of puberty are forbidden to eat the meat from such important game animals as deer, peccary, tapir, and monkey. The Tukano believe that if a youth who could not yet reproduce ate this meat, he or she would be accumulating useless energy, thereby diminishing the total energy in the environment without being able to add a new life. For the Tukano, potential foods in the environment are identified as masculine or feminine—those of the forest being generally in the masculine category and those of the rivers and gardens being thought of as feminine. One anthropologist who has studied these people describes the relationship between the hunter and his prey as "erotic." The hunter feels sexual excitement during the hunt. After the kill, he examines the genitals of the animal, and if he has killed a female he expresses his regret to have shot "such a pretty beast." When the hunter returns with the dead animal, the entranceway to the shelter, which is the female domain, is thought of as resembling a uterus, and the act of bringing meat to the shelter is described by words that also mean "to inseminate." The woman who receives the meat now subjects it to culinary processes that are equated with gestation. The hearth itself is a uterine microcosm for transforming the bounty of the forest into a meal.

The association between the production of food and the production of offspring is so close in most horticultural societies that the two sometimes amount to a single event. The Fipa of Tanzania, who associate copulation and ritual masturbation with the growing of food, are just one example. The night before they begin cultivating the garden, the husband and wife have sexual intercourse. After orgasm, the man spends the rest of the night with his hands touching his own genitals and those of his wife. The next morning, without washing their odors from his hands, he sifts the seeds he is going to sow in his gardens and then sits naked with the tray of seeds between his legs. While his penis rests on the seeds, he rubs millet porridge mixed with a magical substance over it until he achieves an erection. In this way, he believes, he is insuring the future crop that will grow and become big like his distended organ.

Associations between food and sex were probably made by the earliest hunter–gatherers. Eating, like the mutual grooming of apes and monkeys, brought males and females into close proximity in a situation that did not call for defensive tactics. Eating can bind a pair together more effectively than sex, simply because people eat more often and predictably than they have sexual relations. This is a function that continues in modern societies. When a man and a woman have been separated for one reason or another, they will often celebrate their reunion with a special meal. The close association between eating and sex is biological as well as social. Sexual intercourse makes people hungry because a considerable number of calories are quickly expended in the process. There is also a close parallel in the way the nervous system deals with both hunger and sexual excitement. A particularly sensitive nerve structure, known as "Krause's end bulbs," is found in the sex organs (the clitoris and the tip of the penis) and in the mouth (the tongue and the lips). Some neurophysiologists see a correspondence between the sensory surfaces of the sex organs and the taste buds in the mouth, which may explain why sexual desire and a delicious aroma both cause the mouth to water.

Claims have long been made that all sorts of foods increase sexual potency beyond the most optimistic fantasies. No complete listing has been made of these, but the number may run into the thousands. A random sampling includes hippopotamus snout and hyena eyes (both recommended by Pliny), pine nuts (from a long list given by Ovid), dried marrow and liver (Horace), camel's hump (an Arabian specialty), curry and chutney (recommended by Asiatic Indians), shark's fin and bird's nest soup (endorsed by the Chinese), haggis (a Scottish specialty), chocolate and cocoa (forbidden to their women by the Aztec)—along with fish eggs, clams, oysters, sea slugs, lobsters, cuttlefish, eels, snails, snakes, dove brains, goose tongues, the genitals of swans, the eggs of various birds, calf brains, the musk glands of deer, and various parts of goats and rabbits. Also extolled in one society or another for their effect on sexual desire and potency are such common plants as apples, bananas, cherries, dates, figs, peaches, pomegranates, pistachios, artichokes, asparagus, celery, cucumbers, garlic, leeks, onions, peppers, both sweet and white potatoes, and tomatoes. Prunes were so highly regarded as aphrodisiacs in Elizabethan times that they were served free in brothels.

The reason claims are made for the efficacy of particular foods is sometimes obvious—as for the sexual organs of animals, plants that resemble human sexual organs in shape, and meat from animals that have a reputation for fecundity, such as rabbits and goats. But in other instances the origin of the belief is not clear. Some foods, such as chili peppers, curry, and other condiments, do stimulate the body, or at least the heartbeat and the gastric juices. The reputation of cinchona bark, the source of quinine, as an aphrodisiac may have come about because people suffering from malaria, whose symptoms had been relieved by quinine, would feel less weak and consequently be more potent sexually. Indeed, the reason for the apparent efficacy of a great number of foods eaten as aphrodisiacs may be simply that they add to physical or mental well-being. In this sense, almost any food has the properties of an aphrodisiac because the very act of eating causes an increase in the pulse rate and the blood pressure, raises body temperature, and sometimes even produces sweating—physiological changes that also occur in connection with an orgasm.

Foods from the sea had been recommended as aphrodisiacs long before modern knowledge of their nutritional benefits. In the ancient Mediterranean world, the Greco–Roman goddess of love, known as Aphrodite or Venus, was said to have emerged from sea foam where Uranus' genitals had fallen, thus linking venery with the sea. A seventeenth-century French physician observed that those who eat large quantities of fish and shellfish are ardent in love. "In fact," he confessed, "we ourselves feel most amorously inclined during Lent." Although fish is of nutritional value in building up long-term health and virility, evidence is lacking that it produces immediate sexual stimulation. Fish roe has been widely recommended nevertheless for the obvious reason that it is directly related to reproduction—especially caviar, which is also, as a rare and expensive food, a symbol of one's high regard for another. The sea slug has long been a favorite sexual stimulant among the Arabs and the Chinese because it swells and enlarges like a penis when touched. The oyster, which resembles the female genitalia in both appearance and texture, has been considered especially stimulating, though it likewise is not an aphrodisiac.

Two other reasons must be included in any explanation for the singling out of particular foods for use as aphrodisiacs. The first is rarity or novelty. The Age of Exploration suddenly flooded the markets of the world with exotic plants whose very strangeness suggested the existence of secret powers. Tomatoes brought back from South America were at first thought to be the forbidden fruit of Eden, and were known as "love apples." When potatoes first arrived in Europe—the sweet potato probably brought back by Columbus and the white potato somewhat later—they were immediately celebrated as potent sexual stimulants. In Shakespeare's *Merry Wives of Windsor,* Falstaff says to a woman he is about to embrace: "Let the sky rain [sweet] potatoes; . . . let there come a tempest of provocation, I will shelter me here." A book of recipes for the English housewife published in 1596 tells how to bake a tart with sweet potatoes "that is a courage to a man or woman" and a work dated 1650 tells the English reader that the white potato will "incite to Venus."

A second explanation has to do with the ancient Doctrine of Signatures, according to which the hidden virtue of a plant or animal is revealed through its external appearance. The shape, the texture, or even the color of an edible substance might thus indicate whether or not it had the properties of an aphrodisiac. Various bulbs and tubers—onions and potatoes, to list only two—that somewhat resemble testicles could be expected to improve sexual potency. Bananas, asparagus shoots, and carrots obviously resemble the male organ, as artichokes and dates resemble the female. The English word "vanilla" comes from the Latin one for the vagina because of a similarity in shape between the vanilla root and the vaginal canal. The oldest known example of the application of the Doctrine of Signatures to an aphrodisiac concerns the mandrake, a forked root uncannily resembling a man's thighs and penis, and occurs in the book of Genesis: Leah is said to have used a mandrake root to make Jacob lie with her, with the result that she conceived a son. Apparently mandrake does contain pharmacologically active compounds that steady the nerves and might have the side effect of improving a high-strung lover's sexual performance.

The preparation known as "Spanish fly" or cantharides—derived from the dried and pulverized remains of a beetle found in southern Europe—when eaten as an aphrodisiac produces acute irritation of the gastrointestinal system and dilation of the blood vessels, all of which stimulate the genitals. Violent erections of both the penis and clitoris occur, but only at the expense of damage to the kidney that could prove fatal. Yohimbene, another substance producing the same effect, is obtained from the bark of a tree that grows in South America and in West Africa. It irritates the bladder, the urethra, and the lower end of the spinal cord, thus stimulating erection.

Although beer and wine have been known since antiquity, the use of alcohol as an aphrodisiac did not become common until Arab chemists invented ways to distill it in the ninth century. In the twelfth century, the physician and scholar Moses Maimonides wrote: "Drinking honey water promotes erections, but even more effective in this regard than all medicines and foods is wine . . . it arouses the erections all the more when one enjoys the wine with desire." Chaucer's zestful Wife of Bath recommended strong liquor because, as she pointed out, a lecherous mouth has a lecherous tail. More recently Ogden Nash observed that for seductions "candy is dandy, but liquor is quicker." Notwithstanding such testimonials, alcohol is basically a sedative that progressively dampens the activity of the mind, and too much of it will produce a clumsy and incompetent lover. In small amounts, alcohol relieves mental stress and thus can serve as a psychological stimulant to both partners. Although champagne is a noted ingredient in seduction scenes, whatever effectiveness it may have is probably due to the flattery of being offered an expensive commodity—as well as possibly the titillation produced by the ejaculative pop as the bottle is opened.

The elderly, whose taste buds have withered and whose palates are jaded, need fewer calories and have a lessened biological incentive to eat. As a person ages, the proportion of the body that is lean tissue (muscle and bone) decreases, while the proportion that is fat increases. Because fat requires less energy than lean tissue, and because people usually become less active in their later years, the need for calories declines each decade after the age of twenty—which means that a person who does not eat considerably less at sixty than was eaten at twenty will gain weight. At the same time that the need for calories lessens, the requirements for basic nutrients remain about the same; more nutrients obviously have to be packed into less food, and there is less room in the diet for junk foods that are high in calories and low in nutrition. Although the ability to taste salt, which gives flavor to food, also diminishes with age, the receptivity to sweetness does not diminish, and this may tempt the elderly into the consumption of junk foods. By the age of sixty, the salivary glands have degenerated, and a decrease in the secretion of saliva is noticeable. Other enzymes can take over the role of saliva in the digestion of carbohydrates, but not as a lubricant for food—which leads the elderly to prefer soft, moist foods such as mashed potatoes and thin soups, which do not provide sufficient fiber.

As a result of these and other biological changes, the elderly tend to eat progressively less. A study of more than five hundred elderly people in California, begun in 1948 and ended in 1962 when 141 were still alive, showed this strikingly. With each decade of life beyond the age of fifty-five, a clear decrease in the consumption of food was observed, particularly marked in those older than seventy-five. Contrary to common belief, though, the relative proportion in the diet of proteins, carbohydrates, and fats continued even though the total intake decreased. Those individuals who in 1948 had a low intake of animal protein, for example, tended to maintain the same pattern in 1962. A question of great interest not answered by the study was whether the nutritional habits of those who lived to an advanced age contributed to their longevity. Perhaps heredity had enabled these elderly people to survive; perhaps, more precisely, hereditary tendencies played a part in their selecting the diets they did. Some specialists are convinced, at any rate, that a healthy old age is more likely in those who had healthy and long-lived grandparents— so long as nutritionally alert parents have prepared them for old age by instilling wise dietary habits in childhood.

Since people tend to eat what they learned to eat when young, poor nutrition is likely to follow people into old age. Beneficial food habits may, however, be difficult to maintain in old age if one is poor, as old people generally are: In 1974 half of those in the United States over sixty-five had yearly incomes of less than $1500. With less money available, they tend to substitute less expensive bread and cereal for fresh fruits and vegetables—one reason why many elderly persons suffer deficiencies of vitamins A and C. Furthermore, the longer an individual lives, the greater the likelihood of losing the teeth. Out of every hundred people in the United States older than seventy, sixty-six no longer have any of their own teeth—and of these, eighty percent either have not replaced them at all or have done so with ill-fitting dentures. Finally, an elderly person living alone often lacks the motivation to prepare varied meals. It is not unusual to find erratic eating patterns among the elderly: a day or two of nibbling, followed by a day of overeating, for example, with an intake of calories that fluctuates between 800 and 3700 a day.

The question of whether particular nutrients promote longevity is so hedged by unknowns that general statements on the subject are almost impossible to make. Humans nevertheless go on looking for something magical to eat or some elixir to drink to insure prolonged youth. In certain populations of the world, an exceptional number of people are said to live to advanced ages because they eat one food or another. The inhabitants of the rugged Caucasus Mountains of southern Russia, for example, are said to owe their longevity to the consumption of a cultured milk product similar to yogurt. Although no great numbers of centenarians have been confirmed, a remarkable number of these people do live into their eighties and nineties—for causes that seem much more related to their entire diet and way of life than to yogurt in itself. The genetic component of longevity does not appear to be particularly important for these people, given that the large numbers of elderly persons include Georgians, White Russians, Armenians, Turks, and Jews—all of whom differ markedly from one another in genetic makeup.

One factor common to the Caucasus Mountain peoples, whatever their ethnic group, is a varied and balanced diet consisting of milk products, cereals, nuts, and fresh vegetables and fruits. Meat is eaten only a few times a week, and the intake of calories is low in comparison to the typical United States diet. The food is usually eaten when it is very fresh, while vitamins and other nutrients are still retained. For breakfast, an individual might go into the garden and pick a salad of watercress, tomato, and cucumber, to be eaten with goat cheese and a cereal. The people of the Caucasus have traditionally emphasized hospitality and feasting, but they consider overeating to be in poor taste, and obesity is looked upon as an illness.

Scientific research has not settled whether and to what extent diet has contributed to longevity in the Caucasus. Other influences may be at work in conjunction with the small amounts of animal fat, the low number of calories, and the high content of vitamins. Exercise, for example, is built into these people's way of life, and they go on walking great distances over rugged terrain for nearly as long as they live. Retirement is unknown; everyone does at least some work even into the nineties. The aged are respected for their accumulated wisdom, and play an important part in village councils. The Fountain of Youth of the Caucasus may be composed of nothing more than a good diet, the expectation of living to a great age, and continuing to have an active part in social life.

Whatever the true explanation for exceptional longevity, death does come inevitably—and when it does, food still plays an important role. Death is an occasion when the routine of life is broken not simply for the deceased, but also for many other people. Kinship ties must now be reshaped, inheritances distributed, and new roles assumed by the survivors. Recognition by the community of this upheaval has its effect on the one activity common to everyone: the preparation and distribution of food. The disruption of community life is often symbolized by basic changes made in customs of eating—fasting, temporarily extinguishing the hearths, placing new taboos upon foods, and special offerings of food to the gods.

In many of the Polynesian and Melanesian islands, symbolic distinctions are made at a funeral between prepared and raw foods. The environment of these people provides many raw foods—such as coconuts, fruits, and edible roots—that can be easily obtained (except, of course, during times of drought or hurricane). Prepared foods, on the other hand, demand human intervention, and are symbolic of the social and domestic life that has been disrupted by death. On the island of Tikopia, the mourners are given prepared foods, such as puddings, which they associate with the continuity of life. At the burial itself, raw food from the dead man's garden is placed on the grave, symbolizing the product of his labors.

Although this first section has been primarily devoted to the biology of eating, it has been impossible even here to separate that biology altogether from such symbolic aspects as the distinction between raw and prepared foods, the consciousness of sexual metaphors, and ritual abstentions from eating at various stages of life. The humans' basic biological need to eat cannot be separated from symbols and metaphors of status, gift-giving, feasting, social and kin relations, and sacred ritual—all of which will be considered in detail in the next section of this book.

Part II

EATING AND THE WAYS OF HUMANKIND

5

Meal as Metaphor

BECAUSE OF VALUES that go far beyond filling the stomach, eating becomes associated, if only at an unconscious level, with deep-rooted sentiments and assumptions about oneself and the world one lives in. In the central African country of Chad, for example, four tribes who live in close proximity have different attitudes toward the beans, the rice, the millet, and the many other kinds of food that are grown in the area. Each group ridicules the others about what they consider edible. One object of raillery is the rotted meat which one tribe not only devours, but in fact holds in special regard as appropriate for rituals. The name explorers gave the Eskimo—who proudly refer to themselves as *Inuit,* "the true people"—is a variant of *eskimantsik,* a derisive word applied to them by neighboring Indians, meaning "eaters of raw meat." Similarly, North Americans are making metaphorical reference to the supposed eating habits of the French, the Germans, and the Italians in speaking of "Frogs," "Krauts," and "Macaronis."

Most notably in simpler societies, but in some complex ones as well, eating is closely linked to deep spiritual experiences, as well as to especially important social ties. In North America and Europe, weddings and birthdays are celebrated with a cake, formal good wishes are offered with a glass of wine, the Christian rite of communion is celebrated with the distribution of bread and wine, and the Jews observe Passover by eating unleavened bread and bitter herbs. Various states of spiritual exaltation are spoken of in terms of eating, as when Jesus declares, "Blessed are they which do hunger and thirst after righteousness: for they shall be filled." Often particular food plants are endowed with metaphorical qualities, as was the olive tree in the Mediterranean world of antiquity to indicate hope, peace, and plenty. A dove bringing an olive leaf to Noah presaged the subsiding of the flood waters; the olive branch was traditionally extended as a peace offering; and Jeremiah described (11:16) Israel in the days of its prosperity as "a green olive tree, fair, and of goodly fruit."

Once a particular food has been elevated to symbolic status, its nutritional use may become secondary. The pumpkin nourished both the American Indians and the settlers from Europe, and was part of the Thanksgiving feasts held by the Pilgrims of the Massachusetts Bay Colony. In more recent decades it has been largely symbolic, a decoration associated with Halloween and Thanksgiving, little used for food. Nearly three million pumpkins are sold in Massachusetts each autumn, but ninety percent of them rot away after being carved into jack-o'-lanterns or used to ornament front porches, window sills, and dining tables. Even today's holiday pumpkin pie is usually made from other orange squashes rather than from the one that has become symbolic of the season.

That food is often more circumstance than substance is clearly demonstrated by the "milk tie"—a belief, widespread from the Balkans eastward to Burma, which holds that unrelated children who have been nursed by the same woman maintain a life-long social connection with her and with one another. Among Arabs, a male child and a female child fed by the same wet nurse are regarded as blood relatives who are forbidden to marry exactly as though they were actual brother and sister. In India, a child who is given milk at the table of another family is bound to it by special obligations on both sides. The milk tie would be less charged with sentiment were it not for the uniqueness of milk itself as the single food all mothers offer to their young, a food manufactured by their own bodies for that purpose and for no other. Besides milk, only one other substance eaten by humans is produced specifically to provide food: the honey produced by worker bees. People in many societies have made the link between milk and honey as the only natural foods. Not only was the Promised Land described to Moses as "a land flowing with milk and honey," but the two are often coupled in myth and religious rite as sacrificial offerings or as the food of the gods.

The vocabulary of eating has long been used to categorize and describe a variety of experiences. In American English, a casual conversation is chewing the fat, an argument is a rhubarb, a complaint is a beef. Shoddy workmanship is cheesy and a defective automobile is a lemon; a misleading statement is a waffle; an over-emphatic actor is a ham; a person may tell a corny joke and lay an egg; the meat-and-potatoes man objects to pork-barrel corruption; a statement may be full of baloney; someone who jeers is giving the raspberry. The taste of food is likewise applied to personalities: A woman can be spicy, delectable, a dish; she may have a sweet or a sour disposition; a man may be described as peppery or bland, as an oily sort, one who knows how to butter you up, and a sugar daddy. And a particularly trying person might be asked, "What's eating you?"

The categories of each language reveal unconscious conceptual assumptions not only about eating, but also about the world in general. Peasants throughout Latin America, for example, assign all foods to a continuum ranging from "very hot" through "temperate" to "very cold," but which has nothing to do with the actual temperature of the food and little to do with its seasoning. Rather, categories from hot to cold express these peasants' belief in a system of antagonistic opposites that control the universe: life and death, sickness and health, night and day, war and peace, and so on. Eating an excess of food that is either hot or cold is believed to produce sickness, which can be cured only by restoring a balance between the two. The mixing of foods that are very hot and very cold at the same meal will have no ill effects, these peasants believe, because the contrasting foods blend in the stomach and thereby temper each other.

These same peasants believe that the hotness of a food comes from the sun, or from the energy the plant or animal contained while it was alive. Nocturnal animals are therefore necessarily cold, as is the potato because it grows underground, unlit by the sun. Coldness can also come from contact with water—and cooked soups are accordingly described as cold because they are made from water, even though they may be boiling hot. For some foods, such as the egg of a chicken, the categorization is complex: The egg as a whole is temperate, but the yolk is hot and the albumen cold (yellow being a hot color and white a cold one).

Latin Americans have extended the categories of hot and cold to the whole of the world they live in. Comets, stars, and the sun are hot, being made of fire; the moon, as a thing seen at night, is cold; clouds carry rain water and are therefore cold; the world itself is temperate because it encompasses both hot days and cold nights. Everyday behavior, too, is constantly influenced by these concepts. A peasant woman is careful not to go outside while she is cooking tortillas; the collision of cold air with the heat of her body will supposedly make her sick. If a hailstorm threatens the crop, palm leaves (obtained from the lowlands, and therefore hot) are burned to drive away the cold hail. A woman who cannot sleep at night eats raw lettuce, whose temperateness will dispel the warmth of her insomnia.

Such beliefs can ultimately be traced to the Hippocratic doctrine of the Four Humors, which not only flourished in the ancient world, but became entrenched as well in Europe during the Middle Ages. According to this doctrine, the human body is made up of four substances or "humors" to which the qualities of heat, cold, moisture, and dryness were intrinsic in various combinations: Blood was thought to be hot and moist, yellow bile or "choler" hot and dry, phlegm cold and moist, and black bile or "melancholy" cold and dry. An imbalance of the humors was believed to produce an illness that could be treated by restoring the equilibrium. Even William Harvey, the seventeenth-century discoverer of the circulation of the blood, was a firm believer in humoral medicine, at a time when the doctrine had already been abandoned in much of Europe. It persisted on the Iberian peninsula, to which it had been brought originally during the Moorish occupation, and from there was carried to the colonies of the New World, where it was accepted with almost no reservations by physician and priest alike. By the time educated Latin Americans had ceased to believe in the doctrine, it had filtered down to the peasants and become established as a strongly held conviction about the world in general.

Somewhat similar to the hot–cold dichotomy is the duality of *yin* and *yang* in Chinese culture, which has been traced back 2500 years and is still a dominant concept. Yin is the passive, feminine force that complements the active, masculine yang. The Chinese believe that the qualities of foods can be classified as either yin or yang, and that a balance between the two in the body will maintain the equilibrium necessary for good health. Yang foods are very spicy, take a long time to cook, include much fat, and tend to excite whoever eats them; they include most meats, alcoholic drinks, and dishes prepared by deep frying. Bland foods, such as grains and vegetables harvested from the passive earth, have traditionally been categorized as yin. Each sex achieves health and well-being by balancing the yin and yang foods appropriate to it. Men, in whom the yang element already predominates, are counseled not to consume too many yang foods, which will bring a loss of harmony, with attendant fevers, ague, digestive disorders, and the aggravation of venereal disease. In women, on the other hand, an imbalance toward yin can cause weakness and a loss of vital energy.

From a nutritional point of view, the yin–yang system has been beneficial, implausible as some of its precepts might appear to outsiders. Varying the diet leads to a balance in the amounts of animal protein, starchy staples, and vegetables, together with an adequate variety of minerals and trace elements. Those who are pregnant, who are feeling weak, or who have just given birth—who, in other words, have an imbalance toward yin—eat yang foods to restore equilibrium, and thereby obtain the proteins necessary for repair of the cells; those suffering from common digestive ailments (indicating an imbalance toward yang) eat the lighter and more easily digested yin foods (such as rice, potatoes, porridge, and certain vegetables). The system confers the further benefit that no foods are tabooed; rather, eating a wide range of foods is encouraged, thereby promoting good nutrition.

North Americans and Europeans tempted to belittle as quaint the hot–cold and yin–yang folk taxonomies should be aware that equivalent systems of belief pervade their own societies. We too unconsciously categorize certain foods as hot or cold, as in the expression "cool as a cucumber." Many people still think of the stomach in much the same way described in humoral medicine—as a physiological stove where food is cooked to supply energy to the rest of the body. With this notion of cooking comes the belief that body temperature rises above normal for at least an hour after eating, a belief which has produced a number of precautionary rules that are still observed: against bathing immediately after eating, drinking cold water with meals, or going into the cold night air right after eating. The saying "Feed a cold, starve a fever" similarly reflects humoral beliefs about the stomach. Since eating produces heat, heavy meals are thought to generate the means of driving out a cold; reducing food to a minimum, on the other hand, is supposed to lower the temperature of the stomach and thereby to counteract a fever.

North Americans and Europeans are also thinking in yin–yang metaphors when they classify certain foods as masculine (such as thick steaks) and others as feminine (salads and thin soups), or when they assign a hierarchy of values to a fancy dinner and to a meal composed of leftovers, which nutritionally differ very little. In North America, being served leftovers so lowers the status of the food which at its first serving might have been considered a prestigious meal that the food may even be regarded as waste. The borderline between the categories of leftover and waste is often a shifting one. Food not eaten at the original meal might be regarded as appropriate for a meal of less social importance—in which case it may reappear in disguise, as part of a casserole or a stew. It might also be considered as waste, suitable only for servants, charity cases, and pets—or discarded outright as garbage.

In much the same way that Malaysians use the presence of rice to define the difference between a meal and a snack, English working-class families differentiate the two according to whether or not the event is structured. A meal always entails certain combinations of food served in the appropriate sequence, while breakfast—which might consist of toast, cereal, a milk product, fish, and fruit, but served in any sequence—is almost always regarded as a snack. At what they call a meal, careful distinctions are made by working-class families between salty and sweet, moist and dry, and hot and cold foods. With food that is piping hot, the accompanying drinks must be cold. A dessert accompanied by hot tea or coffee, on the other hand, should be a cold, dry solid. The plates for warm courses are stacked above the oven so as not to cool the food, and a cold teapot is heated before hot water is poured in.

A working-class "main meal" properly consists of at least three courses, each with its own qualities of temperature, sweetness, and moisture. The main course is always hot and salty; it consists of a staple (potato), a centerpiece (a joint of meat, a fowl, or fish), trimmings (hot vegetables), and liquid dressing (a thick gravy). Working-class families would never think of eating anything sweet (such as an appetizer of fruit) or cold (such as a salad) before a hot, salty main course. The second course or "sweet" lacks the trimmings but otherwise also consists of a staple (a cereal product), a centerpiece (fruit), and a liquid dressing (cream)—ingredients that might be in the form of a fruit tart, a trifle, or a pudding. Up until the third course the foods have been hot and the beverages, such as plain water, cold; the final course of hot tea or coffee and cold biscuits reverses that situation. The demand in England for expensive biscuits has been increasing every year, while the demand for almost all other kinds of breads, cakes, and pastries has declined—because the biscuit holds a special place in the metaphors of a working-class meal, a signal that the final course has come to an end.

When people in modern societies organize various social events, they are using food and drink as metaphors for the character of a relationship. Cocktails without a meal are for acquaintances or for people of lower social status; meals preceded by drinks are for close friends and honored guests; those entertained at meals are almost always entertained also at cocktails, but the reverse is not true. A cold lunch is at the threshold of the intimacy that is symbolized by an invitation to a complete dinner (characterized by sitting down for a sequence of courses contrasted by hot and cold). Other such bridges are the buffet, the cookout, and the barbecue, which extend friendship to a greater extent than an invitation to morning coffee, but less so than an invitation to a sit-down dinner. Once such values have become attached to eating, then any invitation to share a meal or a snack conveys its own nuance of social information.

Such subtleties can be seen in the way Japanese entertain with dinner. Unlike North Americans and Europeans, who often entertain business associates at home, the Japanese much prefer a restaurant. Home to a Japanese is a very private place, reserved for the family, for close relatives, and for old friends. Should a Japanese family for some reason entertain at home, guests are taken to a room specifically designed for outsiders, where they are expected to remain for the duration of the visit. Dinner guests are never shown around the house as they are in North America and Europe. A traditional Japanese restaurant is usually chosen over one of the new-style, Western restaurants for several reasons: The guests will be served by attentive geishas instead of impersonal waiters, in a private dining room; host and guests alike will eat the same foods, as a metaphor of shared values, a communion through commonality. In a Western-style restaurant, on the other hand, each diner is given a menu from which to select whatever is preferred—a metaphorical expression of individuality.

Even more important is that traditional Japanese restaurants serve *saki*, a liquor made from fermented rice, throughout the meal rather than cocktails before dinner and wine during it, as the Western restaurants do. Saki was originally brewed as an offering to the gods; mortals would then gather to share it at the altar. Although saki is no longer regarded as a sacred beverage, its communal function is still deeply imbedded in an elaborate drinking etiquette. Everyone pours for someone else, as an indication that each is at the service of the others. Because saki cups are extremely small and need to be refilled frequently, every diner must remain attentive to the others throughout the meal. A cup to be refilled is invariably lifted from the table, as an acknowledgment that in the pouring of the saki service is being rendered.

The most extended effort to understand the symbolic character of eating is the one made in recent decades by Claude Lévi–Strauss of the Collège de France. His approach is summed up in his statement that human attitudes toward plants and animals have less to do with what is good to eat than with what is "good to think"— in other words, that the conventions of human society decree what is and is not food and what is appropriate to a particular social occasion, all revealed through a people's myths and folk sayings.

The foods available to a North American or European who shops at a supermarket, and to an Amazonian Indian who obtains food from the garden and forest, are of course almost entirely different. Nevertheless, according to Lévi–Strauss, the categories and sub-categories for both are remarkably alike, in that the foods will be raw, boiled, roasted, fried, steamed, or rotted. In fact, Lévi–Strauss sees each category of food as having its own level of social prestige, roasted foods being in general highly prestigious and identified with masculinity, whereas boiled or steamed foods are for everyday consumption by women and children. In both complex and simple societies, a roasted bird, for example, is suitable for a festive occasion, but the same bird is usually considered an everyday dish when it is merely boiled. Although the specific pattern is not exactly the same in every society, Lévi–Strauss believes that a contrast between roasting and boiling is universal. The Trumai, Yagua, and Jívaro Indians of South America and the Ingalik Eskimo of Alaska, among others, prepare roasted foods for men and boiled foods for women. The Maori of New Zealand considered it fitting for a noble to eat roasted foods but to avoid all contact with boiled foods, more appropriate to people of low birth.

Lévi–Strauss sees human beings as straddling a position between Nature and Culture. As biological organisms, they are obviously a part of Nature; but as sentient beings they are a part of Culture. Eating is important in such a view because, although food is a part of Nature, humans impose their own cultural categories upon it. Lévi–Strauss has developed this line of thought in what he calls the "culinary triangle." Since in every human society at least some food is prepared by cultural methods, a system must exist, he states, for deciding which foods to prepare in what ways. So he visualizes a triangle in which the three categories of the raw, the cooked, and the rotted (intentionally, as in Stilton, Roquefort, and Limburger cheeses) compose the three points. Cutting through this triangle are two continuums: Culture vs. Nature and prepared vs. unprepared. Roasted food is directly exposed to the natural force of fire and thus belongs both to Nature and to the unprepared category; boiled food, on the other hand, must be immersed in a liquid contained in a vessel made by humans, and thus belongs to the realm of Culture and of prepared food; rotted food, which is a transformation of Nature, although to a lesser extent than boiled, is also a prepared food.

Lévi–Strauss observes that roasted food has an affinity with raw because it is never uniformly cooked, being either done on the outside but uncooked on the inside or else roasted only on one side. The affinity of boiled food with rotted, he believes, is attested by such familiar words as the French *potpourri* and the Spanish *olla podrida,* both of which mean literally "rotted pot" and refer to various meats cooked together with vegetables. Smoking as a method of preparing food has an affinity with the cooked category. Thus a simplified culinary triangle would look like this:

RAW

roasted

COOKED ———————————— ROTTED

smoked   *boiled*

It can, as Lévi–Strauss points out, be expanded to incorporate other categories of food preparation. In some cuisines, roasting may include grilling as a subdivision—the difference being mainly in that the latter places the food closer to the fire. Similarly, some cuisines distinguish between boiling and steaming, in the latter of which water is more distant from the food. The triangle assumes the complex geometrical shape of a tetrahedron when the categories of fried (boiled in oil instead of in water) and braised (boiled in a base of water and fat) are added to it. Lévi–Strauss believes that a system eventually emerges that can be superimposed on other dualities in the society: men and women, sacred and profane, the village and the bush, family and society, high status and low. In short, Lévi–Strauss looks upon the ways people prepare food as a sort of language which at an unconscious level communicates the structure of society. He furthermore believes that such unconscious categorization is applicable to human beings everywhere.

This book is not the place for a detailed exposition of all of Lévi–Strauss' hypotheses, or even for a detailed critique of his position. (Some of these critiques, based on his far-fetched examples and his careless use of facts, are listed in the Reference Notes on pages 288–89.) An otherwise sympathetic critic, Edmund Leach, calls the culinary triangle a "fandangle," adding that "the whole operation suggests a game of acrostics in which the appropriate words have been slipped into the vacant slots of a prearranged verbal matrix." One study of the cooking vocabularies used in nine languages around the world uncovered no evidence for the linguistic associations that Lévi–Strauss claims for the culinary triangle, but rather showed that different languages make different distinctions about preparing food.

Typical of the way Lévi–Strauss is unreliable in his generalizations are his statements about how different kinds of cannibals can be expected to cook human meat: Cannibals who eat their relatives will invariably boil them because kin are associated with Culture, whereas cannibals who eat strangers will roast them because these belong to Nature. A sample of sixty cannibal societies does not at all support this generalization. About thirty-five percent of these cannibals roasted the meat, regardless of whether it came from kin (Culture) or from strangers (Nature). Out of twenty-six cannibal societies who ate only their relatives, and who therefore would be expected to boil them, according to Lévi–Strauss, only two actually did so. The cannibals not only unpredictably roasted or boiled relatives and strangers alike; they also baked them, smoked them, or ate them raw—a veritable smorgasbord of human flesh.

Such objections notwithstanding, the culinary triangle has been an important contribution in that it has encouraged scholars to examine more closely the linguistic categories connected with eating. The English language, for example, employs at least thirty-five words for ways of cooking. Some of these (such as coddle) are little used, some are compounds (pan-fry, oven-bake), and some are applied to specific dishes (such as to scallop potatoes, to plank meat, or to shirr eggs). And some, such as the verb roast—for a process that overlaps with both broil and bake because of a change in cooking methods in recent centuries—are ambiguous. Roasting used to be done on a spit over an open fire, until modern stoves made it possible to prepare meat with much the same result by baking it in the oven. The amount of time required for a cooking process accounts for other distinctions made by speakers of English: Stewing is boiling that goes on for a long time, par-boiling for a short time. A large or a small amount of the cooking medium makes the difference between deep-frying and French-frying (both of which use large amounts of fat) and sautéing (which uses a small amount). Still other distinctions are based on the use of a special utensil (such as a covered pot for braising), a special ingredient (barbecue sauce), or even a special purpose to be achieved by cooking (such as poaching to preserve the shape of the the food or stewing to soften it). Food served flambé requires the presence of alcohol; rissoles are cooked by prolonged frying, whereas searing in fat is brief; to toast is to brown by applying direct heat without fat, to parch is to brown by baking without fat in indirect heat.

In these ways most speakers of English unconsciously categorize the preparation of food. Other languages make similar distinctions, including some not made in English. For example, the Amharic language spoken in Ethiopia has distinct words for the boiling of solids and of liquids—unlike English, in which the boiling of eggs is not set apart from the boiling of soup. Speakers of French similarly distinguish between *rôtir* ("to roast") and *griller* ("to grill") according to the shape of the food: *rôtir* being applied to a leg of lamb, a potato, or any other rotund food item, and *griller* to a strip of meat, toast, or any other flat one.

A remarkable thing about cooking vocabularies is not that distinctions made in one language are lacking from another, but rather that speakers of each language choose from certain possibilities and then arrange these conceptually in ways that are culturally indicative. Even more remarkable is the very small number of categories used to describe the preparation of food, no matter what language is spoken. Anyone could easily suggest other categories—such as one set of terms for everyday cooking and another for ceremonial cooking, or one group of words for the morning meal and another for the evening meal—but no language makes these distinctions.

Meals are taken at more or less fixed times of the day; they are eaten in certain places, such as at the hearth or in a dining room set apart for that purpose; and they are prepared under the supervision of people designated in each society to perform that task, usually females but also sometimes the surrogates known as chefs. The sequence of meals is inseparable from the day's routine, and even events in the world beyond the family are often associated metaphorically with the domestic hearth, as when the Basuto of southern Africa refer to the evening star as *sefalaboho* ("dish-cleaner") or as *kopa-selalolo* ("ask for supper"). In simple societies, almost everything about eating is hedged in by metaphoric associations, magical practices, ceremonies, and taboos—and to a somewhat lesser extent the same thing is true in complex societies as well.

The important metaphorical associations a society has are usually with the staples. In the Near East and in Europe, the staple is bread. Called "the staff of life," it is referred to not only in the Lord's Prayer but in 263 other instances throughout the Old and New Testaments. Jesus established the intimate symbolic connection between bread and Christian ritual in saying of it, "This is my body." The bread Jesus ate at the Last Supper (actually the Jewish festival of Passover) would have been the *matzoh* or unleavened bread symbolizing the flight from Egypt when the Israelites had no time to take leavening with them. Bread is also given a sexual symbolism. The ancient Egyptians fashioned it in the shape of a phallus, an association that may have been suggested by the way the loaf swells as it rises and bakes. The oven in which it was baked is likewise a symbol of the female organ in many societies—including North America, where the slang expression "put bread in the oven" refers to sexual intercourse.

The hot-cross buns eaten by Christians during Lent had their origin in pagan antiquity. The Egyptians offered cakes marked with the horns of sacrificial oxen to the goddess of the moon, and the Phoenicians presented horn-imprinted cakes to Astarte, the goddess of fertility. The horns were later modified into the form of a cross to represent the four quarters of the moon, and the Romans are known to have eaten buns marked in this way at religious feasts. The Saxons also marked loaves with crosses to honor Eastre or Ostara, the

Teutonic goddess of the dawn, who was worshiped with a feast at the spring or vernal equinox. All these practices came together in the celebration by the early Christian Church, around the time of the vernal equinox, of the resurrection of Jesus. The festival acquired the name Easter for the Teutonic goddess, and the associated custom of making bread with a cross at this season was assimilated to it. The cross cut into the surface of the bun also has a practical purpose: It allows the loaf to expand without cracking as it rises.

Bread was of enormous symbolic importance to the ancient Egyptians, a people who were referred to by Herodotus and others as "The Bread Eaters" because they were said to have baked about fifty different kinds. Sacred animals, even cats and wasps, were offered bread to eat. Graves were stocked with huge amounts of bread as food for the deceased—although these were sometimes in the form of clay models, as both more durable and less likely to tempt pilferers. Throughout the whole ritual life of the Egyptians—the stocking of tombs, the cults, and their endless offerings to the gods—bread was a central symbol. During certain festivals in which pigs were to be sacrificed, the poor who could not afford living pigs made models of them out of bread dough and offered these instead.

In the modern world, probably no one gives more symbolic attention to bread than the Greek peasants. Christmas breads are decorated with a cross made of dough, and are embedded with the walnuts said to symbolize the fruits of the earth; sometimes the cross is made from eggs, which are regarded as symbols of fertility. At the new year, breads are baked with a coin inside to insure good fortune. Easter breads are baked in a variety of shapes, but most often they are round to symbolize eternity. On Easter Day itself, people give their godchildren presents of decorated breads indicative of sex roles: a horseshoe shape for the boys, who might someday become officers, and an ordinary loaf shape one for the girls, who will remain at home to be bakers of bread. A man going into the army is given a piece of bread to carry in his knapsack because it is thought to confer power. As protection against harm, workers carry to the fields a crust of bread that is kept separate from their lunch and is eaten only after safely returning home in the evening. Children are similarly protected while they sleep by a small piece of bread placed under their pillows.

Such richness of symbolism might seem irrelevant to people in industrial societies for whom bread is often cottony commercial loaves. The white loaf, though, is nothing new, for it has long symbolized well-being and prosperity. It was esteemed by the Romans as the bread of aristocracy. When Rome was besieged by invaders from the north, the people are said to have thrown white bread at them as though flaunting their wealth and their confidence that they would not be reduced to famine. In possibly all societies that consider bread a staple food, its color has been associated with rank: white bread for the wealthy and prestigious, black bread for the peasants. Vestiges remain today of times when bread symbolized fertility. The shoes tied to the back of the newly married couple's car are a relic of a custom in some parts of Europe: A piece of bread was put in the bride's shoe to assure that her marriage would be a fruitful one. The ancient Greeks spread barley around the temple of Demeter to encourage fertility; the barley later gave way to wheat, the wheat to rice, and the rice finally to the confetti that today is often thrown after a bride and groom.

A meal in North America or Europe involves certain assumptions having to do with the time of day, the seating arrangements, and the sequence of the courses. Most families also observe certain rules: Who sits where is based either on status or on habit; there is a restriction on moving about; conversations are expected to be free from disgusting topics; and usually there is a prohibition of other activities (such as speaking on the telephone). A meal also presupposes certain minimal requirements about the food itself. A serving of baked beans with coffee usually does not qualify in North America as a proper lunch or dinner, but the same beans cooked with chopped meat and chili peppers—in short, chili con carne—would qualify. That is because people in North America know intuitively that chili con carne is in accord with the formula $A + 2b$ for a meal—that is, one central ingredient A (in this case, beans) together with two unstressed ingredients b (meat and chili peppers). For the same reason people given eggs, bacon, and toast will feel that they have been served a meal, whereas those given eggs alone (that is, A without $2b$) will not.

Such intuitive assumptions about what a meal must consist of led to the invention of the dish known as Chicken Marengo. In 1800, when victory over the Austrians at the battle of Marengo, in Italy, seemed assured, Napoleon ordered his chef to prepare a festive dinner. The supply wagon had not caught up with the advancing army and so the master chef sent his men to scavenge for food. They managed to collect only a hen, three eggs, six crayfish, four tomatoes, a little garlic, and some oil—out of which the chef produced a dish consisting of chicken surrounded by eggs, fried with tomato sauce and garlic, and crayfish, with a sauce poured over it. Chicken Marengo qualified as an appropriate meal because it incorporated the fish, egg, and fowl courses traditionally regarded by the French as essential to a feast.

Eating is symbolically associated with the most deeply felt human experiences, and thus expresses things that are sometimes difficult to articulate in everyday language. Nowhere are the metaphors of eating stronger than in the taboos that societies around the world place upon certain foods.

6

Eat Not of Their Flesh

THE TWO most important Judeo–Christian–Moslem myths about the origins of the human species describe the consequences of eating. According to the book of Genesis, Yahweh created Adam on the sixth day, entrusted him with dominion over all the animals, and then created Eve as a helpmeet. In Eden the humans and animals lived in harmony until Adam and Eve broke a taboo against eating a certain fruit. (The fruit, by the way, was certainly not an apple, a species that did not grow in the ancient Holy Land, but was probably an apricot.) Adam and Eve were expelled from Eden, condemned to eat bread "in the sweat of thy face" (Genesis 3:19). The second myth is concerned with the origins of meat-eating in the human diet. To cleanse the earth of wickedness, Yahweh unleashed a catastrophic flood. Along with Noah and his family, a pair of each kind of animal was kept safe from the waters in an ark. After the flood receded, Yahweh allowed the previously prohibited sacrifice of animals, thereby giving humans the right to kill and eat many— but not all—of the beasts with whom they share the earth.

The original dogma of Creation, as set forth in the story of Adam and Eve, was that all animals possess a spirit which resides in the blood. This is why until the time of Noah it was forbidden to eat flesh. In return for the permission given Noah to sacrifice animals, the Hebrews had to obey strict laws regulating slaughter (followed to this day in kosher procedures): The blood must first be drained from the animal so that its spirit can flow into the earth. The myths of a fall from grace through eating a forbidden food, and the establishment between humans and animals of the relationship of predator to prey, are an attempt to account for the paradox of the various taboos against eating certain otherwise desirable foods. Such foods are not necessarily avoided because of cultural revulsion, as North Americans and Europeans avoid eating dogs, rats, and worms. The forbidden foods are usually animals and not plants—except most notably in Polynesia, where both are subject to prohibition, and where the word "taboo" itself originated. Prohibitions include fishes in many parts of Africa, the duck regarded as unclean in Mongolia, and the camel meat that makes the Ethiopian Christian who eats it subject to excommunication. Prohibitions are sometimes applied to the mixing of foods that are normally permitted. Jews are permitted to eat both milk products and many kinds of meat, but not at the same meal; some Eskimo groups prohibit mixing foods from the sea with those from the land. Almost without exception, prohibited foods are edible, nutritious, and likely to be considered a delicacy in other societies. In light of all this, are not food taboos irrational and indeed detrimental to the society?

Not at all—and a case in point is the prohibition on pork in the books of Moses, and subsequently endorsed for Moslems in the Koran. Of the many explanations that have been offered for the prohibition, one of long standing (dating back at least to Maimonides in the twelfth century) is hygienic. Pork is said to spoil more rapidly than other meats in the hot climate of the Near

East; pork is known to harbor trichinosis, an often fatal disease caused by a microscopic parasite; and the pig is considered filthy because it wallows in and even eats its own excrement. Temperatures in the Holy Land, though, are no higher than in many other parts of the world where pork is regularly consumed. The danger of trichinosis can hardly have been the rationale for the Mosaic prohibition, since the parasite, which was not even observed by scientists until 1821, was considered harmless to humans until 1860. Not only would it have been very difficult to establish a causal connection between pork and the disease, since the symptoms of trichinosis do not appear for several days after eating tainted meat, but there is in fact a strong possibility that trichinosis was unknown to the Holy Land in Biblical times. It may also be asked why Moses did not prohibit the meat of cattle, sheep, and goats, which are transmitters of several diseases, such as brucellosis and anthrax, that cause human death at about the same rate as trichinosis. The assertion that the pig is tabooed because it is a filthy animal likewise will not stand up. In the wild state, the pig is not filthy; it wallows in mud and excrement only when it has been confined in the barnyard, as a way of keeping its skin cool through evaporation, since it lacks sweat glands. If everyone had regarded the pig as filthy, it would never have been domesticated in the first place or be devoured as it is in many parts of the world.

The prohibition against pork does not appear in the Bible until after the Exodus from Egypt. Before that, Noah had been told that "every moving thing that liveth shall be meat for you" (Genesis 9:3). During their bondage in Egypt, the Israelites had resided near Tanis (called Zoan in the Bible), where an Egyptian cult worshiped swine as sacred animals. Accordingly, the Mosaic ban might reflect a desire to set the Israelites apart from their Egyptian masters, so as to bind the Israelites into a cohesive society. The difficulty with this explanation of cultural identity is not only that many of the same foods were prohibited both by Moses and by the Israelites' hostile neighbors, but also that the meat from cattle, sheep, goats, and other animals was in fact eaten by both. The Israelites might possibly have prohibited cooking meat with milk because this was a practice of nearby pagan societies—but at the same time they gave a central place to animal sacrifice, just as many of these same pagans did. The central question of why a taboo was placed on pork remains unanswered by any hypothesis involving cultural identity.

At the time of the Mosaic prohibitions the Israelites were pastoral nomads, moving through arid plains and hills, to which cattle, sheep, and goats are adapted, whereas swine are not. Swine require the shade and the large amounts of moisture that prevail in humid forests, but not in the arid Near East. This ecological explanation, though, still does not explain why the pig was forbidden rather than being simply ignored. After all, other animals of the Near East were not adapted to certain environments, but no religious taboos were promulgated against eating them.

The problem of the pork taboo can be solved if the symbolism surrounding the dietary and religious laws found in three of the books of Moses—Leviticus, Numbers, and Deuteronomy—is taken into account. In other words, Moses the Prophet should be taken at face value rather than being looked upon as Moses the Trichinosis Expert, Moses the Sociologist, or Moses the Ecologist. The crucial dietary prohibitions are in Leviticus, chapter 11, and they divide the beasts into clean, which may be eaten, and unclean, which "shall be even an abomination unto you; ye shall not eat of their flesh, but ye shall have their carcasses in abomination" (Leviticus 11:11). Yahweh then presents what amounts to a natural history of the animals of the land, sea, and air, telling which may be eaten and which may not, and sometimes giving a justification for the rules.

The central theme of the book of Leviticus is that the wholeness, completeness, and perfection of Yahweh are to be reflected in worship at the holy Temple. The animals offered in sacrifice there must be perfect and without blemish, and no one with a physical impairment could approach the Temple without first being ritually cleansed. Ideas concerning perfection permeated the entire religious life and culture of the ancient Israelites. Any kind of hybrid or confusion was therefore anathema. Diverse things must not be mixed; and so it was prohibited to plow with an ox and an ass together (Deuteronomy 22:10), to sow two kinds of seed in one field (Leviticus 19:19), and to let one kind of cattle breed with a different kind (Leviticus 19:19). In society as in eating, the social classes are to be kept separate, and the Israelites must not form a marriage union with pagans.

The animals fit to be eaten are therefore the domesticated cattle, sheep, and goats that had been blessed by Yahweh as complete, whole, and perfect when the pastoral Israelites first inhabited the Holy Land. Also permitted are certain wild animals similar to the domesticated ones that have cloven hoofs (walking on two toes, each of which is encased in a layer of horn) and that "chew the cud" (that is, are ruminants with several stomachs that regurgitate and chew again the food that has already been swallowed)—among them gazelles, antelopes, ibexes, and wild forms of sheep and goats. Other land animals are dissemblers, seemingly perfect but not really so. The hare and the coney (also known as the hyrax or rock badger) grind their teeth as though chewing a cud, but they do not have cloven feet. The pig and the camel have cloven hoofs, but are not ruminants.

The same sort of distinction between perfection and confusion is made concerning creatures of the earth, air, and water. Each animal must conform perfectly to its class; any that do not are regarded as unclean. Animals that live in water are expected to have scales and to propel themselves by fins as fish do; sea creatures such as the mollusks, which lack fins and do not move about, and the lobsters, shrimps, and crabs, which have the appendages of land animals, are therefore anomalies to be avoided. Four-legged animals are expected to hop, jump, or run; so such land animals as the mouse, the weasel, the shrew, the mole, and various lizards which seem to possess only two feet (the front limbs being like hands) are imperfect and thus prohibited for food. Birds are expected to inhabit the air; that makes an abomination of the ostrich, which does not fly, and of the swan, the pelican, and the heron, which spend most of their time in water. The "creeping things"—such as serpents, snails, and most insects—do not conform in their mode of locomotion with the fish in the water, the birds in the air, or the running mammals of the land; in other words, they are neither fish, fowl, nor flesh. Other anomalies are the owl that flies at night instead of during the day, the eagle and the vulture that feed on prey and therefore consume the unkosher blood, and the bat, a land mammal that flies as if it were a bird. Such a division of animals into edible and abomination meant that at every meal, and even during much of the day in preparation for mealtimes, the Israelites were forced to contemplate afresh the perfection and wholeness of Yahweh's world.

The pig is no more singled out in Leviticus for abomination than the coney or any other animal. Not a single word indicates that it is repugnant because of "unclean" scavenging habits, or is a threat to health, or is associated with pagan enemies. The Mosaic prohibition against it is mentioned only twice, once in Leviticus and again in Deuteronomy. Both references are brief and matter-of-fact: The pig must not be eaten because "though he divide the hoof, and be clovenfooted, yet he cheweth not the cud" (Leviticus 11:7). The pig is simply an anomaly, and in light of the Israelites' feelings about perfection would be expected to be prohibited. How then did swine achieve such notoriety as typifying the Old Testament dietary abominations? The answer is not to be found in the books of Moses but in the much later history of Judas Maccabeus, as it appears in the apocryphal books of the Old Testament. In the second century B.C., the land of Israel was under the domination of the monarch Antiochus IV, a notorious persecutor of the Jews, who desecrated the Temple of Solomon. He gave an order that swine were to be sacrificed there, and that Jews were to eat pork as an act of submission to Syria. He might just as well have forced the Jews to eat camels, vultures, coneys, or other animals prohibited in Leviticus, but he no doubt chose swine because they were readily available from pagan neighbors. By this edict he gave prominence to what had been only one of numerous dietary taboos.

In response to the persecutions by Antiochus, Judas Maccabeus and his family organized a guerrilla army that defeated an expedition sent from Syria to destroy them, captured Jerusalem, and in 165 B.C. reestablished the Temple (an event celebrated to this day by the Jewish feast of Hanukkah). The pork that Antiochus had made a token of submission was singled out for special anathema by the Maccabees; avoiding it became for the Jews an assertion of purity, of allegiance to the ancient Law of Moses, and of opposition to pagan rule.

Ideology, interacting with the cultural system and ecology, can similarly explain the Moslem prohibition against eating pork. Islam arose in the seventh century A.D., and its sacred book, the Koran, incorporated many Mosaic dietary laws, including this prohibition. In fact, the taboo against pork is much more forcefully stated in the Koran than in the Old Testament. Apparently to some extent a tactical decision on the part of Mohammed, it gave Islam a point of clear distinction from the Christians, who were its major adversary and who had no objection to pork; it also encouraged the support of its Jewish neighbors in the Near East. The possible conversion of the latter to Islam would have been encouraged by incorporating the taboo, in much the same way that Christianity had made Easter coincide with the pagan festivals of the vernal equinox.

Ecologically, it would have been maladaptive for Mohammed to allow his followers to raise swine. Ever since the time of Moses, the landscape of the Near East had been changing drastically as a result of intensive agriculture and pastoralism. Forests (in which pigs live easily enough) were converted to grassland and desert (in which pigs can survive only with human intervention). Under the arid conditions of Arabia, the raising of animals that do not eat grass and cannot be herded over long distances was uneconomic. Pigs compete with humans and with other domesticated animals for the same foods—grains, tubers, and nuts—and for the water, without providing secondary benefits. Pigs do not grow wool to be sheared nor do they give milk; they cannot pull a plow, carry loads, or be ridden. It was therefore imperative to forbid an animal that would have been an ecological and economic disaster if people had continued to breed it in large numbers.

Several points should be emphasized about the Jewish and Moslem abomination against pork. No evidence whatever exists that it was due to hygienic considerations, or that the environment of the Near East, the cultural separateness of Jews or of Moslems, or ideology in itself can explain it. Rather, at various times all three must have been in interaction. The priestly authors of the books of Moses and the Koran placed special emphasis upon dietary laws in part because foods can serve as badges that distinguish one people from another. If conditions had been such that it was ecologically rational to raise swine, then it can be assumed that the eating of succulent and nutritious pork would have been permitted. Indeed, the Koran specifically provides (in *The Bee*, 115) that the devout Moslem is permitted to eat the flesh of wild swine, which were scarce, and the hunting of which did not pose the same ecological threat as raising herds of domesticated swine would do. In modern Israel, where the ancient prohibitions on pork still prevail among Orthodox Jews, some agricultural communes have found it adaptive to raise swine, for the reason that the animals convert into flesh the refuse that might otherwise go unused.

In India today, where tens of millions of people are hungry, sacred cows wander without hindrance through the markets, helping themselves to the very foods that humans need so badly. Nearly two hundred million cattle—possibly a fifth of those in the world—inhabit India. In a largely vegetarian nation, they not only contribute little in the way of meat, but compete for food with starving humans. Nor are they worth their keep because they provide much milk; the udders of a scrawny zebu cow produce barely enough to nurse a single calf to maturity, and each year more than half of the cows of India produce no milk whatever. A North American farmer expects to get approximately ten thousand pounds from a milk cow, but in India perhaps five hundred pounds a year per head on the average is obtained—a scant return that does provide some valuable nutrients, but which hardly accounts for the huge numbers of seemingly worthless animals wandering almost everywhere.

The prohibition against eating beef is often pointed to as the supreme example of an irrational food taboo and as the ultimate triumph of religion over appetite. The Indians' reverence for all living things, except the hungry humans of their own country who might eat these cattle, is said to have existed for so many thousands of years that it is now ingrained. Historical actuality does not sustain this view. The Vedas, the sacred texts of Hinduism, dating back a little less than three thousand years, contain an occasional objection to the eating of beef, but elsewhere the texts approve the slaughtering of cattle. They make clear that the priestly Brahman castes ate beef, and were taught rules for carving and distributing portions of it at feasts. The Buddha placed a taboo on eating the flesh of humans as well as that of elephants, horses, lions, tigers, panthers, bears, dogs, hyenas, and serpents—but not cattle. Nor was the eating of beef specifically prohibited when King Asoka made Buddhism the state religion about 2250 years ago, even though cruelty and animal sacrifice were condemned in principle.

Somewhat less than two thousand years ago, the slaughter of cattle finally became a religious and civil offense—and the cow has been venerated in India ever since. Prayers are offered for cows that are sick, and garlands are hung about their necks on festive days. In some places, pigs are actually slaughtered and sacrificed to benefit the cattle. Gandhi preached veneration of the cow, finding in it a symbol around which he could rally the nation. When India finally became independent in 1949, the constitution included a bill of rights for cattle. Nowadays the police even round up stray cattle that have fallen ill and nurse them back to health.

Admittedly, a certain degree of hypocrisy prevails in India concerning the sacredness of cattle. Some farmers do cull their herds, as is clear from such statistics on cattle as those from the state of Uttar Pradesh, where there are more than two hundred oxen (male cattle) alive for every one hundred cows—a discrepancy that could exist only if farmers were systematically killing the cows. Nor does this always mean butchering a cow outright. The same effect is arrived at by other, slower, but equally certain methods: neglect, tethering an old or sick animal until it has starved to death, or selling an animal to a Moslem or Christian, who can be expected to slaughter it.

It has already been observed that no religious teaching can long survive if it is maladaptive. Whether a religious belief is rational or irrational is beside the point. If the people who follow it do not flourish, then obviously the religion itself cannot flourish either; in short, the reverence for cattle must have satisfied the stomach as well as the soul. Something did happen in India roughly two thousand years ago that might account for a religious and civil proscription against eating beef. An increase in population made parts of India among the most densely inhabited places on earth, with the result that lands that should never have been farmed were put to the plow—producing an ecological disaster that reduced India to the eroded and deforested semi-desert it is today. At this point, religious sanctions dealt with what had already become a necessity; they forbade the hungry villagers to kill the cattle that were needed for other purposes than as a supply of meat.

The ox and the male water buffalo are essential to Indian farmers for plowing their fields. The fact is that India suffers from a shortage of them rather than being burdened by an excess. Even a farm of less than ten acres needs a pair of them. A recent count showing that India has about 70 million such farms would mean that 140 million draft animals were needed to pull plows, whereas India has a total of only 83 million. Since in India all fields must be plowed at the same time, so as to coincide with the monsoon rains, neighboring farmers cannot share animals—and in so poor a country, tractors are of course out of the question. Oxen are also needed during the rest of the year for threshing grain and to pull the oxcarts that are the main means of transportation in rural India. Oxen thus serve as tractors, threshers, and trucks combined—and the factory from which all these must come is the sacred cow.

It is the cow that gives birth to a replacement for the time when one of a pair of oxen falls ill or grows old. Of course the cow is as likely to produce a female calf as a male one, but that is the chance the farmer must take. What makes the cow essential to the Indian farmer, therefore, is not the need for meat or milk or for an object of veneration, but as the only source for producing oxen. A farmer who loses his oxen, or who is forced to sell the family cow during hard times, will soon no longer be a farmer. He cannot borrow enough money to purchase replacements, and neighbors are not likely to loan him a pair of oxen. Every year numerous Indian farm families lose their land because of this lack. They may work for a while as laborers on someone else's farm, but sooner or later they will migrate to the cities, adding their numbers to the destitute and homeless millions already living there. It is no wonder that an Indian farmer can be seen crying over the death of a beloved cow, or paying for a religious service in behalf of one that is ill; a farmer who loses a cow has lost almost everything. A farmer would presumably rather eat a sacred cow than watch his family starve, but he knows, consciously or unconsciously, that the eventual penalty for slaughtering such an animal is that the family assuredly will starve.

This explanation of why India's cattle are treated as sacred was offered as long ago as the eleventh century, by a Moslem scientist, Al-Biruni. "We must keep in mind," he wrote,

> that the cow is the animal which serves man in traveling by carrying his loads, in agriculture in the works of ploughing and sowing, in the household by the milk and the products made thereof. Further, man makes use of its dung, and in wintertime, even of its breath. Therefore it was forbidden to eat cows' meat.

Granted this economic necessity, a well-intentioned Westerner might suggest the substitution of a superior breed that would produce large quantities of milk as well as give birth to oxen. It may be answered that the zebu, a native breed, has become adapted over thousands of years to the pattern of erratic rainfall that prevails in India—the torrential monsoon followed by long periods of drought. Zebu cattle can survive for weeks with virtually no food and water; they are highly resistant to diseases that affect other breeds of cattle in the tropics; and like camels, they store water and food in their humps and recover quickly when both are available again. A foreigner might also wonder why, if the cows are really so valuable, they are allowed to roam untended. The fact is that in this way the cows are being fed. During the dry months in particular, the cows maintain themselves by scavenging on clumps of grass along roads or railroad tracks and on the waste food at market stalls. Hungry cows may also be rounded up by the government as strays, to be reclaimed by their owners on payment of a small fine after the animals have been boarded and nursed back to health. The religious prohibition against eating beef is therefore a form of disaster insurance during the difficult dry months of the year, when Indian farmers would be most tempted to butcher their cows for food. This insurance is of benefit not only in restraining the small farmers from acting against their own best interests, but also indirectly to all of India, which must be fed from their seventy million farms.

Even when cows appear to be wandering untended, they are providing the dung which is used as fuel and fertilizer. Cow dung is actually the preferred fuel of India because it burns slowly, allowing farm families to work in the fields while food on the hearth is cooking. The cattle of India are estimated to produce eight hundred million tons of manure annually—the energy equivalent of nearly two hundred million tons of coal, which would cost billions of dollars in foreign exchange if it had to be imported. A study in West Bengal has shown that very nearly all of the dung is recovered. Cattle that have been allowed to stray are followed from place to place by the owners' children, who collect the dung.

It must be asked, finally, why the Indians do not slaughter and consume cattle that are too decrepit to pull loads, produce calves, provide milk, or even furnish much dung. This failure to slaughter demonstrably useless cattle for food, or to sell them to a slaughterhouse run by Moslems, is less irrational than it might appear. The survival into old age of some decrepit animals is, first of all, a small price to pay for the protection given to all cattle. Moreover, a farmer can never be certain that an animal has become totally worthless. An animal that appears beyond hope might nevertheless recover, whereas once a cow or ox has been killed the farmer will have destroyed his hope of surviving as a farmer. In any event, most of these decrepit cattle do provide meat eventually to members of the lowest-ranking castes, who dispose of the bodies of the twenty million cattle that die from natural causes every year. That they consume this meat, notwithstanding the teachings of Hinduism, is a fact known to every upper-caste Hindu. Little is said publicly about it, since strict enforcement of the prohibition against eating beef would oblige the high-caste people to find some other way of providing essential proteins to tens of millions of the lower castes.

When the conditions prevailing in the ancient Near East made it uneconomic to raise swine, which could provide no other benefit besides meat, a ban on the animal naturally followed. Given the social and physical environment of India—with its dense population, limited technology, eroded lands, and erratic rainfall—raising cattle for meat likewise became uneconomic. Whereas the problem presented by swine in the Near East was that people were tempted to divert their resources in order to raise them, the problem in India was to stop not the raising of cattle—which offered other benefits—but the slaughtering of them for meat. So in the Near East the pig became an abomination, but in India the cow became a sacred animal.

The proscriptions placed upon eating such foods as beef and pork raise one final problem. After a taboo develops for good ecological and cultural reasons and has been sanctioned by resort to the supernatural, how is it to be maintained? During the thousands of years in which taboos against pork and beef have been in effect, assuredly some Jews, Moslems, and Hindus have occasionally flouted divine prohibitions and consumed the forbidden flesh—without dire consequences. Why, then, have such taboos not been abandoned? In certain instances, indeed, they have been. Early in the nineteenth century, when the native society of Hawaii was disintegrating as a result of disease, foreign conquest, and an imposed Christianity, King Kamehameha II bravely decided to test the efficacy of his entire system of belief. He and other members of the royal family sat down to a meal that transgressed virtually every one of the most sacred taboos. No dire consequences having occurred as a result, that was the end of food taboos in Hawaii.

More often, enough consequences either real or imagined do ensue to sustain a taboo. Where the belief is widespread that eating forbidden foods will have an untoward effect, just such an effect becomes likely. In *Antony and Cleopatra,* Shakespeare has Octavius praise Mark Antony by saying, "On the Alps it is reported thou didst eat strange flesh, which some did die to look on"—a reminder that the mere sight of forbidden food may be dangerous. The punishment for breaking a taboo may be a self-fulfilling prophecy, as in certain Bantu societies: A deficiency disease affecting young children is said to be the punishment for a violation of the taboo against sexual intercourse between the parents of an infant before it is weaned. The taboo works because if intercourse does result in conception, the child will have to be prematurely weaned; lacking substitutes for mother's milk, the child will probably suffer from a deficiency disease, just as the taboo had forewarned.

Most people in Western societies have experienced vomiting and other physical reactions after the discovery that a reviled food has been unknowingly eaten, and the same thing holds true for people in non-Western societies. Melanesians brought up from birth to believe that the violation of a food taboo will be followed by illness can be expected to vomit after learning that they have unwittingly eaten meat from a tabooed stingray or bush pig. Members of the Wind Clan of the Omaha Indian tribe are forbidden to eat or even to touch shellfish—a prohibition that is explained to young people at their initiation as being a matter of physical fact. The consequence of such psychosomatic pressure is that a transgression may lead to paralysis, skin eruptions, and other ailments.

A study of violations of food taboos made two decades ago on Ponape, one of the Caroline Islands of the South Pacific, revealed physical reactions very similar to the diarrhea, hives, dermatitis, shortness of breath, and other allergic reactions that have been observed by physicians in Western societies. Almost everyone who ate a forbidden kind of fish broke out in hives that resembled the spots on the fish; those who violated a taboo against eating turtle meat were likely to suffer shortness of breath or a skin reaction. Even those "modern" Ponapeans who knowingly violated the taboos nevertheless often believed they were suffering the culturally appropriate symptoms. For example, one man who had violated a taboo attributed to that act a roughening of the skin on his face that appeared several years later.

Interestingly enough, many of the foods tabooed on Ponape are widely regarded by physicians as being allergenic, particularly certain species of fish and shellfish. Allergic reactions occur in response to eating or touching particular foods to which an individual has become sensitized. A person might be allergic to eggs but not to milk, to strawberries but not to cherries. But how can a reaction occur when there is a taboo on a broad category of unrelated plants and animals rather than on a specific one? On Ponape, for example, certain people are forbidden to eat the "runt" of any plant or animal, whether it be an immature coconut or breadfruit, a puppy or a piglet. It is significant that the violation of this taboo is supposed to cause not an allergic symptom but the birth of a deformed child. Enough children are presumably born from time to time with some physical defect or other to maintain the belief that one of the parents had violated the taboo.

Actual deaths because of the breaking of food taboos have been widely reported from virtually all parts of the world. It has been supposed that the deaths were due to poison secretly administered by witch doctors or shamans to maintain their powers. Sheer terror, though, is sufficient to account for such deaths. A devout man who has eaten a food prohibited in his society will feel a deepening sense of dread as he awaits the consequences, and this will be increased by his social isolation; such a man can expect no sympathy from kin and friends. The body's reaction to fear is to prepare for an emergency by producing increased amounts of sugar and adrenalin and by causing certain blood vessels to dilate. In the evolution of mammals, this was an extremely beneficial adaptation, providing the burst of energy necessary for either fight or flight. But if the physical activity for which his entire system has been prepared does not take place, at the same time that the dread continues to increase, the effects will be those of severe shock: a drop in blood pressure, reduction of oxygen in the blood, and coronary collapse. Until his fear is alleviated—as is unlikely so long as his society provides no channel for expiation—continued fear may simply kill him. All in the society will thereby receive confirmation that the taboo works.

"Bait shyness," a mechanism that has been studied in both animals and humans, suggests a way in which the physical effect of violating a food taboo might serve to prevent further violations. Animals that survive a harrowing experience connected with poisoned bait—observing the fate of another animal, or having themselves been made sick—thereafter avoid such foods. Rats that have recovered from a single episode of poisoning usually reject, for the rest of their lives, any food with the same taste as what made them sick. Bait shyness thus appears to be a special way of learning long-term avoidance from a single bad experience. This is quite different from classic Pavlovian conditioning, in which several pairings of stimuli are necessary to produce a conditioned response, and in which the response is gradually extinguished unless it is reinforced from time to time by repetition. The kind of learning seen in bait shyness must have evolved as an adaptation that saved mammals from having to carry around extra mental baggage to cope with the same experience each time it occurred. Humans, whose brains are so much larger and more complex than those of rats, would seem to have no need for this special kind of learning. Yet a study of the food avoidances of nearly seven hundred North Americans, ranging from young children to the elderly and including members of many ethnic groups, showed that a single pairing of the food in question with an upset stomach was sufficient to produce the aversion. Most of the aversions had begun in childhood, and some of them had gone on unabated for as long as fifty years.

The prevalence in every society of food taboos—which to outsiders appear foolish, uneconomic, and often meaningless—has long posed an intellectual problem. But, as this chapter has attempted to show, there really is nothing very mysterious about them. Taboos become established for very sound cultural, economic, and ecological reasons. They are then usually bolstered by divine sanctions, and continued repetition during the impressionable years of childhood is usually sufficient to inculcate a lifelong observance. Feelings of revulsion about certain foods are very much bound up with a person's own culture: Robinson Crusoe was filled with revulsion, and Friday with happy anticipation, at the thought of the same meal of human flesh. Sometimes, for one reason or another, individuals in the society will transgress a prohibition. If no consequences followed, the taboo would soon cease to operate. But usually something does happen: an upset stomach, an allergic reaction, or indeed any ill fortune that might be blamed upon the flouting of the taboo. Once a consequence has been paired with the breaking of a specific taboo, the evolutionary mechanism of bait shyness insures that the event will never be forgotten.

7

Foods for the Gods

BECAUSE FOOD is the human's most fundamental resource, offering food or abstaining from it are symbolic ways in all societies of showing devotion to supernatural powers. Although an offering might be considered the same as a gift, the two differ. First, an offering implies unequal status, the recipient being the superior party; and second, whereas gifts are almost always accepted, whether or not they are desirable or appropriate, an offering may not be found worthy by the supernatural. A more restricted kind of offering is the religious sacrifice, which means, as its name implies, the surrendering of something of value, a denial of it to oneself in favor of the supernatural. Most sacrifices consist of food, and meat is favored because it is more difficult to obtain than plant food. Those who sacrifice a cow, a goat, or a chicken appear to be saying that they know they cannot afford it, but that their loss will be overcome by the even greater benefits to be obtained from the supernatural.

Although Greek and Roman writers referred to human sacrifice as the practice of barbarians, in Homeric times the Greeks would occasionally kill a prisoner to placate an angry god, and the Romans from time to time sacrificed Greeks, Gauls, or Christians. In most instances, though, animal rather than human flesh was brought to the altar, ritually killed, cooked, and distributed to the faithful for a ceremonial feast. Animal sacrifice is mentioned in the Old Testament stories of Cain and Abel, of Noah, of the patriarchs—and, of course, the Israelites would not have been immune to the tenth plague in Egypt except through the sacrifice of the Paschal (Passover) lamb, whose blood they smeared on their doorposts so that Yahweh would recognize and "pass over" the Israelite households while the Egyptians were smitten by the deaths of their first-born. Animal sacrifice among the Israelites occurred not only on Passover but also at the Feast of Weeks (Shavuot) and the Feast of Tabernacles (Succoth), at the new year, on the first day of the new moon, as an act of repentance, and in fulfillment of vows. According to the first book of Kings (8:63), Solomon sacrificed 22,000 cattle and 120,000 sheep at the dedication of the Temple. Sacrifices continued to be offered until the Temple was destroyed by the Romans in A.D. 70; they were commonplace during the time of Jesus, who made no objection to them.

For the Bantu peoples of southern Africa, a sacrifice might consist of flour or beer, but is most usually a domesticated goat, sheep, or an ox. Wild animals are never offered as sacrifices because they are free gifts of nature and therefore lack the high value that a sacrifice is supposed to have. The Bantu make plain that a sacrifice is not the expression of "religious devotion" or "group emotion," as some divines have declared this kind of offering to be, but rather the equivalent of a complicated marketplace negotiation. Concrete demands are made of the spirits; the value of the sacrifice is calculated precisely so as not to be more valuable than the favor being asked; and acceptance of a sacrifice pledges the spirits to bestow that favor. The sacrifice of a prized animal on the occasion of a marriage, for example, binds the spirits to approve the newly established ties and obligations between the relatives of the married couple.

Sacrifices of food might seem at first thought to be extremely wasteful, especially for the Bantu peoples who often subsist on a diet deficient in protein. The truth is that in societies that stress animal sacrifice, there is little waste, since the frequency of sacrifice and the quality of the offerings both vary greatly according to what is available. When cattle are plentiful, a sacrifice will mark a rite of passage, or the arrival of either too little or too much rain, or an illness among either humans or animals, or the commemoration of various ancestors. In fact, so many potential occasions for a sacrifice can be found that one might be held on almost any day of the year. Once the animals have been sacrificed and the ancestral spirits have had their fill, the meat then of course becomes a great feast for humans. On the other hand, excuses can always be found for not offering a sacrifice at a time when animals are scarce.

Regardless of the occasion, the animals used for a sacrifice will be chosen with a prudent regard for economic loss. Among the Nuer, a cattle-complex people of southern Sudan, the herds are so small that each person owns an average of no more than two animals. The Nuer say that the sacrifice of a healthy young ox is fitting for an important occasion such as a wedding, a grave illness, or a severe drought. In actual fact, though, an old and virtually useless ox, or even a barren cow, is more likely to be sacrificed; if even such an animal cannot be afforded, the Nuer will substitute sheep and goats, which will nevertheless be referred to during the sacrifice as *yang* ("cattle"), in what amounts to a flagrant hood-winking of the supernatural. Should a Nuer not want to part with any animal at all, he can resort to the further expedient of finding a small cucumber that grows wild in abandoned fields and offering it as though it were an ox, calling it *yang* and ritually stabbing it with his spear. The cucumber is thus consecrated as if it were an ox, and for all ritual purposes an ox it is.

Entering into the calculations of the Nuer about any sacrifice is the extent to which a particular offering will place the spirits under an obligation to reciprocate with some desired benefit. Once a sacrifice has been made, justice is on the human side, and the spirit is the one at fault if the person making the sacrifice does not receive a benefit in return. The transaction is much like trade between the Nuer and Arab merchants. The Nuer do not think of the transaction as actually buying things from the merchants; rather, they are offering the merchant something as a favor, for which he is expected to reciprocate with a gift from his shop. Nor have the spirits been "bought" in the Western sense; they have simply been made aware of an obligation to repay the sacrifice with deeds. A bargain has been struck, a sacrifice has been made—and the spirits must now live up to their part of the bargain. The economic calculation involved in sacrifices was understood by Plato, who in his dialogue *Euthyphro* has Socrates speak of offerings as "an art which gods and men have of doing business with one another."

If the Nuer are not to suffer a decrease in the size of their herds and flocks, a homestead consisting of several huts cannot afford to sacrifice more than the one or two animals on an average born each month. This may not seem like much meat per capita, particularly when the sacrifice must be shared with other homesteads— but with other homesteads likewise sharing their meat from one or two sacrifices per month, a distribution of meat throughout the year is insured. Whatever the Nuer might say about the religious importance of sacrifice, it is a matter of economic survival to be flexible about what is offered on the occasion of a particular sacrifice. The size of the herds at the moment, the question of whether or not meat has been shared recently, the weather, the prospects for obtaining food, and numerous other considerations determine whether a Nuer herder will sacrifice a healthy young ox, some other animal, or a wild cucumber—or find an excuse not to hold a sacrifice at all.

Those who live in a more complex society might regard such attitudes toward sacrifice as immoral and in no way pertinent to their own experience. But who can swear never to have negotiated anything with the supernatural? In time of illness or danger, even the agnostic might silently vow, "Lord, if you do such-and-such for me now, I will do such-and-such later." And who is there even among the devout who has not once calculated the economic worth of a religious offering? Animal sacrifices might seem to be of little consequence because modern societies have substituted for the scarce resources of the Nuer such scarce attitudes as selflessness of the mind and heart. It must be pointed out, though, that the switch by modern religions from concrete food to abstract piety as the object of sacrifice has conveniently done away with an awkward problem: the enormous cost in resources if a ceremonial feast were to be made available to a large and dense human population. People in modern societies have been told that it is no longer important that a sacrifice be food fit for the gods; rather, it is the act of giving that matters.

This modern view of sacrifice—as a moral act that places high value on things of the spirit rather than upon subsistence resources that are in short supply—amounts to a major restatement of the traditional view that sacrifice entails a material loss. The economic calculation of modern religions is, upon analysis, little different from the prudent manipulations of the Nuer. As the founder of modern anthropology, Edward B. Tylor, observed more than a century ago, "Throughout the history of sacrifice, it has occurred to many nations that cost may be economized without impairing efficiency. The result is seen in ingenious devices to lighten the burden on the worshipper by substituting something less valuable than what he ought to offer, or pretends to."

A quite different way of expressing devotion to the supernatural is to deprive oneself of food by fasting. Fasting has been variously justified as cleansing the body of impurities, as atoning for sin, as a protest of inequities, and as fostering an appreciation of the hunger suffered by others. No matter what the reason, fasting would seem to be an irrational form of behavior in that it deprives the individual of essential nutrients; in fact, zealous fasting sometimes produces the same medical symptoms as are seen during famine caused by drought or war. Yet fasting has managed to persist in all the major religions, as well as in many local cults, regardless of its effect on physical well-being.

The reason for this is that fasting is usually not very harmful, because each religion offers ways to alleviate its deleterious effects. Each kind of fast has a provision that circumvents possibly harmful consequences. The fasting by Jews on Yom Kippur is a total one—but it lasts for only a day. For Roman Catholics, the Lenten fast covers the forty weekdays before Easter—but it involves only certain foods, for which substitutes are available. Moslems fast during the entire ninth month (Ramadan) of the Islamic calendar. Abstinence from nourishment is, though, restricted to the hours between sunrise and sunset; once the sun sets, any food not specifically forbidden in the Koran can be eaten, with the result that gluttony in the evening and before dawn is fostered. And those Moslems who might find fasting difficult are exempted: children, women who are menstruating, pregnant, or nursing an infant, people engaged in manual labor, soldiers, and travelers. Furthermore, fasting is sometimes adaptive for the society—as in Ethiopia, where fast days often correspond with the "hungry season" when food is in short supply anyway, thereby stretching out the scant supplies.

For the Hindus of India, fasting is an extremely complex matter; the kinds of fasts and their frequency vary according to caste, sex, age, and degree of orthodoxy. Devout Hindus might fast to appease a deity, to obtain a boon, to ward off evil, or to honor a particular god or goddess (each one of which is to be revered by fasting on a specific day)—in addition to such occasions throughout the calendar year as the new and full moons, the eleventh day after the new moon, the equinoxes, and the solstices. It is readily apparent that a year contains many more potential fast than nonfast days. Devout Hindus obviously could not survive if their many fasts consisted of total abstinence from eating—and indeed most fasts are only partial. Nor do the Hindus engaged in a fast suffer from any marked decrease in the amount of food consumed. Whatever foods they are allowed to eat are prepared in such quantity that on fast days a Hindu might actually eat more than on a nonfast day.

Most religions involve not only offerings, sacrifices, and fasts, but also the consumption of certain foods on specific occasions. As a result, those plants and animals that the religion has sanctified will be moved from place to place in company with the pious; the turmeric plant of India, for example, which is used not only as a seasoning but also in Hindu ritual, has in this way been spread throughout southeastern Asia. Jews and Christians have both placed a high sacramental value on wine made from grapes, thus encouraging the cultivation of the vine far beyond the Mediterranean. Christian monks brought it to many of today's wine-producing centers, all the way eastward to the Crimea. Later, Spanish, Portuguese, and French priests brought the European grape to parts of the New World. Jews returning to Palestine during the nineteenth century found that the ancient vineyards there had been uprooted by the Moslems, who forbid the drinking of alcohol. One of the first tasks they undertook was to establish grape cultivation to meet their ritual needs.

A less familiar example of the spread of a food for ritual use is the planting throughout the Mediterranean in Roman times of citrus trees, which are not native to the Mediterranean. The whole story of their introduction and spread is unknown. Plant geographers do not even agree about the exact place of origin of citrus, but it is believed to have come from the region between southern Arabia and western India. The first member of the genus to be carried to Mesopotamia and to the Nile Valley was the citron, which may have been singled out because its fruit is large (between four and eight inches across), and because the tree itself is striking in appearance, flowering throughout the year. Its cultivation in the Holy Land possibly dates to the reign of King Solomon. In any event, the Jews certainly must have brought it to Palestine by the time they returned from captivity in Babylon about 2500 years ago. It figured in the celebration of the autumn harvest festival variously known as the Feast of Tabernacles, the Feast of Tents, or Succoth, which traditionally called for "the fruit of a goodly tree," usually taken to mean the citron. By at least 2100 years ago, the citron had come into common use, and it was even proposed as a standard of measure, much as the carob seed had been used as a standard of weight. After the Jews rebelled against Rome in A.D. 66, they were dispersed to various Roman colonies. Because the Jews took the citron with them for use in ritual observances, many of the places where they went at that time have continued to this day to be centers of citrus production—including southern Spain, Italy, Sicily, Tunisia and Algeria, the Nile delta, Turkey, and the coasts of Lebanon and Syria.

The rabbis had laid down rigid specifications about the size, shape, freshness, and unblemished state of the citrons used for ritual purposes. Since to produce a single acceptable fruit probably hundreds had to be grown, a market had to be found for the rejected ones. That was not difficult because many Romans soon recognized the citron's virtues for food and also came to attribute magical and medicinal qualities to it. Pliny the Elder recorded in his *Natural History* that these "Palestinian trees," as he called them, were becoming naturalized in Italy, although he personally did not find the fruit to his taste. The citron nevertheless remained a luxury item, and in A.D. 301 the Emperor Diocletian set the maximum price for a citron at twelve times that for a melon.

The cultivation of other citrus fruits was apparently a by-product of all this. Jewish gardeners, who were in demand throughout the Roman world for their skill in fruit cultivation, had not overlooked the orange and the lemon, fruits with similar requirements for growth; they had in fact used the citron as grafting stock for other kinds of citrus, particularly the orange. The Talmud, in which the oral law of the Jews was codified during the early centuries of the Christian era, mentions what appears to have been the orange as "the sweet citron." After the fall of Rome, the market for oranges and lemons disap, eared. The cultivation of the citron alone continued without interruption simply because it was used ritually by Jews throughout the Mediterranean. Other kinds of citrus were not grown again in quantity until the tenth century, when they were once more introduced into Europe, this time by the Arabs.

All through the Old Testament—from Genesis through the Song of Solomon and in the stories of David, Samson, Job, Judith, Esther, and Ruth, to name only a few—eating scenes are as frequent as battle scenes. Everywhere in the ancient Mediterranean world, certain foods were associated with gods, spirits, and supernatural heroes. In Egypt, Osiris was the god of grain as well as the god of death and rebirth. The *Iliad*, the *Odyssey*, and other ancient sagas are filled with references to food, drink, feasting, and sacrifice. The early martyrs of the Christian Church included an extraordinary number who endured tortures and temptations concerned with eating, performed miracles involving food, or were killed by being boiled, broiled, roasted, minced, and served up at a meal.

The central mystery of Christian ritual centers around eating, and it was long a subject of contention.

The occasion of the Last Supper is described in the gospel according to Mark (14:22–24):

> And as they did eat, Jesus took bread, and blessed and brake it, and gave it to them, and said, Take, eat: this is my body.
>
> And he took the cup, and when he had given thanks, he gave it to them: and they all drank of it.
>
> And he said unto them, This is my blood of the new testament, which is shed for many.

No record exists of any great concern by the disciples whether Jesus' statement was to be taken literally or symbolically as meaning that Jesus' imminent death would be a sacrifice on behalf of all humankind. Paul made it an issue because of his desire that Christianity be acceptable to potential converts among Jews, Romans, Greeks, and pagans. He presented Jesus as the Paschal lamb offered up for sacrifice at Passover, thus identifying the Last Supper with the animal sacrifice of other Mediterranean rituals. Paul is also responsible for making Jesus' words into the rite known in Greek as the Eucharist (literally, "thanksgiving"). In the original Eucharist, members of the Christian community gave thanks as they ate bread from the same loaf and drank wine from the same cup, thus commemorating the sacrificial death of Jesus as he had asked them to do. This communion of the faithful was later incorporated into the Mass, during which those who had been baptized consumed the bread wafer or Host (its name taken, significantly, from the Latin *hostia,* "sacrificial victim").

The doctrine of the Church concerning the Eucharist was established in A.D. 1215, when Pope Innocent III summoned a council at which it was decreed as an article of faith that the bread and wine in the sacrament are truly the body and blood of Jesus, changed through transubstantiation. Eating the Host would thereafter no longer be a symbolic act. By this decree, Christianity made its most sacred ritual an act equivalent to the god-eating of certain pagan rites.

God-eating is rare in religious systems, but anthropophagy (better known as cannibalism) has been reported by people from Western societies in virtually all parts of the world. Accusing native peoples of such reprehensible acts gave the colonial powers a justification for conquest: It was necessary to end the barbarous practices of the heathens. After the Spanish conquistadors mispronounced the name of the Carib people in the West Indies as "Canibal," the word found its way into many European languages to designate those who practiced anthropophagy. Most native peoples were not cannibals. Certainly the hunter–gatherers were not; concerning them, the Europeans either concocted the notion that they were or else critically accepted the dubious testimony of their neighbors. The Walbiri of central Australia, for example, referred to their enemies the Lungga as eaters of human flesh; so did the Comanche Indians of the American Southwest in regard to the Tonkawas, and still other tribes declared that the Comanche themselves were not averse to the practice. The colonial powers also passed over the fact that cannibalism had once been rife in Europe. In France and Germany during the ninth and tenth centuries, for example, bands of professional killers roamed the countryside, attacked travelers, butchered the carcasses, and sold the meat in markets as "two-legged mutton." Cannibalism still persisted after the Middle Ages in central Europe and may account for the werewolf legends there.

No wonder, then, that any attempt to learn more about cannibalism meets with a confusion of rumor, legend, and self-serving reports. It is true that the eating of human flesh has been documented from all over the world—sometimes as a unique event in the face of starvation (such as the cannibalism practiced by the

Donner Pass survivors in California in 1847, or, more recently, the Uruguayan rugby team whose plane was wrecked in the Andes in 1972). Anthropophagy apparently was a practice of *Homo erectus,* whose fossilized bones dating from some half a million years ago have been recovered from caves near Peking. The bones had been fractured as though to obtain the marrow, and skulls were also found that seem to have been opened so that the brains could be eaten. Bones fractured in the same way appeared in the archeological record of many early humans, among them some of the ancestors of the American Indians.

The subject of anthropophagy is further complicated by the existence of several different kinds of cannibalism. Two of these are based on a social distinction: that is, whether the eater belongs to the same social group as the eaten (in which case it is known as endocannibalism) or is either unrelated or an enemy (exocannibalism). Endocannibalism is rare; its most notable known occurrence is among some South American Indians and some tribes of interior New Guinea. Other distinctions are made according to purpose: between gastronomic cannibalism, as a source of food, and ritual cannibalism, for supernatural ends. The cannibalism of highland New Guineans is primarily gastronomic; a more common intention, though, is to acquire the spiritual qualities or vitality of other individuals by eating them. This was the intent of the pre-Dynastic Egyptians, of the Scythians living around the Black Sea, and of the Chinese during the Ch'in, Han, and T'ang dynasties. The Iroquois Indians vied with one another for the privilege of eating the heart of a particularly brave enemy so as to acquire his courage. In some instances the purpose is both gastronomic and ritual. The Panoans of western South America regarded eating the flesh of relatives as a duty, in order to banish the spirit of the deceased, preventing it from reoccupying the body. But some Panoans also roasted the dead body like a piece of game, drinking the blood like wine, and even hastening the deaths of the old and the sick so they could be eaten while some nutrition was left.

Endocannibalism and exocannibalism both flourished in the eastern highlands of New Guinea until about 1960, when efforts by the Australian government to end the practices finally succeeded. The reason these New Guineans ate human flesh was frankly gastronomic: They needed it to stay alive. Cannibalism was for them also a customary way of disposing of the dead; as one anthropologist put it, "Their bellies are their cemeteries." Men, women, and children alike were eaten; whether the flesh came from an enemy or a relative made no difference. A few restrictions were placed on eating the corpses of certain kinds of relatives, but virtually every corpse served as food for someone. A woman did not eat her own children and a man did not eat his parents-in-law, and vice versa; a husband did not eat his deceased wife, although she would have no such qualms regarding him; a man would not eat his grandchildren, but he was entitled to the flesh of a deceased nephew or niece. When a child died, the mother usually sent word to her brother, who could come to her husband's village and obtain meat from the body.

A person who had died and been given proper mourning by kin might then be butchered in much the same way as a pig, or else buried and left until the flesh decomposed. In either case, the corpse was ordinarily dismembered by kin, who first removed its hands and feet, then cut open the arms and legs to strip out the muscles. The torso would be opened to remove the viscera, and finally the head was cut off and the skull fractured to extract the brain. Little was wasted. The marrow, viscera, and brain were all cooked and consumed together with the flesh; the bones were often pulverized and eaten with green vegetables, or small pieces of flesh might be cooked in a stew with ginger and vegetables. Even though the people of the eastern high-lands of New Guinea eat pork and other meat in a fresh state, they appear to have preferred human meat when it was decomposed. A corpse was usually left in a shallow grave until the process was well advanced. After it had been dug up, the maggots that had begun to feed on the flesh were collected and cooked separately as a delicacy.

The corpse of an enemy, on the other hand, presented an opportunity for the venting of anger and hostility. When warriors returned home with such a body, the villagers assaulted it and fought over the best portions of meat. Sexual abuse of these corpses was fairly common. A man not only got pleasure from copulating with the corpse of an enemy female, but he was also vicariously attacking the enemy once again. One man was seen to copulate with a young woman who had just been killed. His kinswoman impatiently began cutting out the corpse's belly while he was so intent on copulation that he did not notice how close the knife had come. Slicing into the belly and then hacking downward through the vagina, she cut off the tip of the man's penis, removed it, nonchalantly popped it into her mouth and ate it, with scarcely a pause in the process of butchering.

Although New Guineans did not practice cannibalism for ritual purposes—that is, to absorb the strength or power of the deceased, or out of fear of the deceased's spirit—they did nevertheless often believe human flesh to possess magical properties, the most important of which was that it promoted fertility, human as well as horticultural. To encourage the growth of gardens, pieces of human flesh were placed in nearby trees, and bones were buried in the ground. During the mortuary rites, the kin of the deceased took the body to a garden, where it was either buried temporarily or butchered. In either event, the deceased was said to have been "given to the ground," thereby encouraging it to produce crops. Dying men and women were heard to tell the surviving kin to eat their flesh so that the gardens would grow.

Among the Fore tribes in one small part of the cannibal region in New Guinea, which consisted of about 160 villages with a total population of 35,000 people, a disease occurred that caused perplexity to medical researchers. First observed during the 1950s, when Australian administrators and police entered the area, the ailment was aptly known as *kuru,* which in the Fore language means "trembling." A degenerative disease that affects motor coordination, it begins with tremors, jerkiness, and clumsiness. The afflicted person later loses the ability to walk, and eventually cannot maintain balance even while sitting. Death comes as a result of inability to eat, pneumonia, or simply rolling into the fire at night. About 1400 deaths were recorded between 1957 and 1964.

Two unusual things about the disease eventually led to a hypothesis about its cause. It had been extremely rare in adult males; and after the Australians increased their police patrols in the area and cannibalism was gradually eliminated, the number of cases declined, and the disease even disappeared completely in children. These two things would be accounted for if the cause was a virus transmitted through human meat, which acted slowly over a period of years. The exemption of adult males from the disease would be explained by the fact that in this particular area males did not practice cannibalism, believing that it robbed them of vitality and made them vulnerable to enemy arrows. Children born after cannibalism had been prohibited would then be free of the disease, whereas adolescents and adult women would be expected to show continued symptoms because they had previously eaten the infected meat. After years of patient research, the cause was indeed identified as a virus with a long incubation period, spread through the eating of brain tissue.

Before attempting to explain the motivations of New Guineans for the practice of both exocannibalism and endocannibalism, it is profitable to look into cannibalism by the Aztec Indians of Mexico. Hernán Cortés and the soldiers who overran the Aztec state in 1521 were a ruthless lot, toughened in battle against the Moors and the Indians of the Caribbean islands. Nevertheless, even they had been appalled by the evidence of human sacrifice on a scale that dwarfed their own bloody imaginings. Bernal Díaz del Castillo, the chronicler of the expedition, wrote of one Aztec city: ". . . in the plaza there were piles of human skulls so regularly arranged that one could count them, and I estimated them at more than a hundred thousand. I repeat again that there were more than a hundred thousand of them." The total number sacrificed annually may have been astronomical—as many as 250,000, according to one estimate— and that impression appears borne out by the 20,000 to 80,000 victims for just one event, the dedication of the pyramid at Tenochtitlán in 1487. No other society in history has approached these numbers. Why so many? The traditional explanation, that sacrifices were demanded by the bloody religion of the Aztec, fails to explain why such a religion should have evolved in the first place.

A more likely explanation can be found by asking what the Aztec did with all these carcasses after the hearts were plucked out and the corpses rolled down the steps of the pyramids. The answer given by Bernal Díaz is that they were eaten: "Moreover every day [in just one place] they sacrificed before our eyes three, four, or five Indians whose hearts were offered to those idols and whose blood was plastered on the walls. The feet, arms, and legs of their victims were cut off and eaten, just as we eat beef from the butcher's in our country." Confirmation comes from the Aztec nobles who dictated the ethnography of their people to Spanish priests after the conquest. They reported that the corpses were carried from the base of the pyramid to be butchered, and the skulls displayed on racks after the brains had been eaten. The body itself was dismembered and divided up, with three of the four limbs becoming the property of the warrior who had brought in the victim. He proceeded to give a feast, serving up the limbs in a stew with tomatoes and peppers.

Why the Aztec should have turned to cannibalism on such a scale has recently been explained in ecological terms, some unique to that people. All the ancient civilizations were similar in that their increasing populations soon outstripped natural resources and upset the equilibrium of the environment. Sooner or later, declining supplies of wild game and plants made domestication essential. In the Old World, wheat, barley, rice, and millet were all domesticated; in the New World, the plants were maize, beans, squash, peppers, and tomatoes, among others. But Middle America was unique in that it lacked the animal species—cattle, sheep, goats, and swine—that had proved so valuable in the Old World. Those species potentially capable of being domesticated had died out in the New World, as a result of environmental changes and probably also of overhunting, many thousands of years before the Aztec rose to power. (In the South American Andes, the guinea pig, the llama, and the alpaca were eventually domesticated, but these did not range as far north as Middle America.) The only animals that the people of the region had been able to domesticate were the dog and the turkey. But the dog, as a carnivore, competed with humans for meat and the turkey competed with humans for grain. Moreover, no animal provided any of the milk products that were so important to the Old World civilizations.

The Aztec population had been increasing rapidly right up to the time of the conquest by Cortés, even as its supply of animal protein from wild sources was diminishing, and almost no protein was available from domesticated species. The Aztec responded by intensifying agricultural production in a variety of ingenious ways, among them the chinampas or "floating gardens." These were narrow strips of land surrounded by marshy canals; they produced several crops a year, and the plots were kept fertile by scooping up the rich mud from the bottom of the canals before sowing. The Aztec also waged unrelenting warfare against other peoples in Middle America, forcing them to pay tribute every year in food as well as in sacrificial victims. Even so, five famines had occurred in the two decades before the Spaniards arrived.

The hypothesis that cannibalism was the reason behind the Aztec sacrifice has come under attack by some who say the chronicles and the ethnographies dictated by the Aztec nobles are not reliable. In light of their basic reliability about other aspects of Aztec culture, however, the charge hardly stands up. Nor does the further objection that examples of cannibalism known from elsewhere in the world have been for ritual purposes. Anthropologists familiar with New Guinea cannibals point out that the supply of animal protein there is similarly limited, since the forests offer little wild game and pigs are too scarce to provide much of the needed protein; and they conclude that the New Guineans waged unremitting war with one another because of their need to obtain human flesh. In fact, some cannibalistic groups there have been known to refer to weaker neighbors as their personal stockyards for providing meat.

A careful analysis of the size and body weight of cannibals in New Guinea shows that a typical group (somewhat less than one hundred people) might receive almost thirty-five percent of its protein requirements by eating the flesh of one man a week. Any such analysis can be only tentative because of the possibility that New Guineans have different nutritional requirements than North Americans and Europeans, as was discussed on page 37. Even if the members of such a group obtained no more than fifteen men per year, they would be receiving about ten percent of their protein needs from cannibalism. Virtually all of the groups in interior New Guinea suffer from a deficiency of animal protein. Some are fortunate enough to obtain as much as a quarter of their protein from pigs; for many other groups, this source provides less than seven percent. The rest of the animal protein was obtained by hunting, fishing, collecting reptiles and insects—and by cannibalism. Anthropophagy was thus, for many groups in New Guinea, the largest single source of animal protein—one that has tipped the balance toward survival in the protein-poor interior. Because anthropophagy had been eradicated in recent decades by the Australian government, meat from animals must now be imported to make up for the deficiency.

Can all this be applied to Aztec cannibalism? Possibly—although whereas the New Guineans ate every part, including the internal organs and bones of the victim, the Aztec are thought to have eaten only the limbs and brains. Some critics of the hypothesis regarding the Aztec have stated that anthropophagy on a large scale need not have existed because the Aztec had alternative sources of protein: fish and frogs, many kinds of waterfowl, armadillos, gophers, snakes, lizards, and insects—all of which, though, are small, often difficult to catch, and not sufficiently numerous to feed a huge population. The approximately one million people who lived in and around the Aztec capital could not possibly have received an adequate supply of protein from hunting, any more than the present-day populace of New York City could be supplied with meat from the Catskill Forest Preserve or that of London from Sherwood Forest. One recent estimate of the amount of protein contributed to the Aztec diet from wild sources comes to, on the average, about one slice of deer meat, two small fish, three-quarters of a duck, and a sackful of insects and worms in a year. The Aztec might, of course, have obtained their essential amino acids by eating maize and beans together. To obtain sufficient protein in this way, however, the two vegetables would not only have to be eaten at the same time, and in the correct proportions, but also in very large quantities.

The Aztec might possibly have gotten protein from sources that are no longer used. They were, for example, observed by the Spaniards to eat vast amounts of a green mud that was taken from the lakes, and sold in markets all over Mexico. The Spaniards identified this as a mineral. Having noted the strange custom the Aztec had in eating it, they then forgot about it, and it more or less disappeared as a food source after most of the lakes that once surrounded what is now Mexico City had been drained. The mud has recently been identified as consisting of a blue–green alga, *Spirulina*, which is extraordinarily nutritious. It is nearly seventy percent protein, and contains all the essential amino acids, along with seven major vitamins. This *Spirulina* offered a potential supply of the protein required by the Aztec.

If that had been insufficient, they might have obtained large supplies of protein from the amaranth, a plant domesticated in Mexico about four thousand years ago. Lists kept by the Aztec show that the quantities of amaranth paid to them as tribute nearly equaled those of maize and beans. Amaranth was clearly a staple of the Aztec diet before the arrival of the Spaniards—and rightly so, because it scores higher than other cereal grains in protein, fat, phosphorus, riboflavin, and ascorbic acid, being somewhat lower only in thiamine and niacin. The reason for the virtual disappearance of this major food crop from Mexico after the Spanish conquest is said to be that it was used in pagan ceremonies, being ground into a paste, mixed with blood from sacrificial victims, and then formed into idols. The Spaniards, regarding the practice as a travesty on the Christian communion, banned both the idols and the growing of amaranth. Cultivation of the plant lingered on, but it was eventually replaced by European grains, particularly wheat.

Were the Aztec, then, so needy of protein that they had to practice large-scale sacrifice as an excuse for cannibalism? Or did the sacrifices occur simply because of "a maniacal obsession with blood and torture," as Lévi–Strauss has asserted? Or is there still another explanation? The actual quantities of human meat resulting from sacrifice—if equally apportioned to every one of the millions of an Aztec citizens—could not have amounted to much for each and could not alone explain the way in which sacrifice and the cult of the dead so completely permeated Aztec society. The customs of a culture, though, do not depend on averages. Human meat was not equally distributed, but was apparently given as a reward to the nobility, and also to the warriors who made up about a fourth of the population. Bravery in combat was the only way an Aztec could obtain high office, which was not hereditary but was based on achievement. A warrior was also accorded other privileges, such as being allowed to wear cotton garments, to have concubines—and to eat human flesh. Warriors and their families thereby received animal protein, fatty acids, vitamins, and minerals, and gained an advantage in better health over those who were not so privileged. As food shortages grew more acute, the incentive presumably became all the stronger.

Once the whole gory system got going—priests calling for victims and ambitious commoners clamoring for war in the hope of being rewarded, obliging the priests to call for still more victims to propitiate the gods of war—it would have been impossible to stop. What might have begun as a simple ceremony to obtain human flesh in ways sanctified by the gods would have become more and more complex, so that by the time of Cortés it had grown into an exceedingly powerful cult that dominated the Aztec state. Though much about it may never be known with certainty, two facts at least are clear: To propitiate their gods, the Aztec engaged in human sacrifice on a scale unknown in any other society; and, following the sacrifice, at least some of the flesh was eaten.

As the only major human behavior in which everyone engages several times a day, every day, eating can become a way by which some people define themselves. Among these are the faddists who use eating to achieve non-nutritional ends, or who follow certain diets with such exaggerated zeal as to take on many of the aspects of a religion. Insofar as certain "natural" and "organic" diets encourage the consumption of fresh vegetables and fruits, whole grains, nuts, and dairy products, excluding or sharply decreasing consumption of refined sugar and salt, they are nutritionally beneficial. They can become maladaptive, though, when such things as yogurt, wheat germ, honey, ginseng root, or massive supplements of certain vitamins become the equivalent of sacred substances, health-food stores become tabernacles, and an organic farm becomes the next thing to Lourdes or Mecca.

Food fads are as old as Hippocrates, who believed that a certain kind of diet would lead to health and happiness, and they become established for the same reason: Food acquires emotional overtones beyond mere nutrition. The incentive for following a fad diet often is more psychological than nutritional. Those troubled by a complex world filled with uncertainties may try to impose some order by going back to "natural" (that is, simpler) foods. A faddist will insist on "natural" vitamins, even though a vitamin has the same chemical formula and acts upon the body in the same way whether it comes from a natural source or has been synthesized in a laboratory. They will pay a high premium for "organic" honey—even though such a thing can hardly exist, for the simple reason that bees foraging on flowers do not distinguish between those that have and have not been treated with chemical fertilizers or sprayed with pesticides.

Possibly the oldest of food fads is vegetarianism. Although the pejorative term "food faddists" does not properly include those vegetarians who are members of Asiatic religious groups, for whom vegetarianism is an ancient tradition with a storehouse of nutritional information, it does apply to many of the modern followers of a movement that began in England early in the nineteenth century. It influenced, among others, George Bernard Shaw and also Percy Bysshe Shelley, who in 1813 published a treatise arguing that the human body was not suited to the consumption of animal foods. The biological aspects of vegetarianism have already been discussed on pages 41–43, but any discussion of eating must not neglect the cultural aspects of the movement.

Vegetarians range from those who eat fish, eggs, and milk products (but not meat from mammals and birds) to those who eat only raw fruits and nuts. Very few vegetarians are motivated primarily by an objection to cruelty to animals or to depriving any creature of life. More often, vegetarians are motivated by the belief that people will lead a more contented and harmonious life if they can somehow eliminate their animal-like behavior—in short, an adherence to the Doctrine of Signatures already discussed on page 106. Gandhi, for example, experimented with many different diets before he eliminated all meat and milk products as a way to calm his spirit and to allay what he looked upon as animal passions. Claims have also been made that vegetarianism discourages crime, develops the intellect, and simplifies human character—none of which has been proved. Modern vegetarianism is only one of several such fad diets. Others developed in recent decades include the Zen macrobiotic, low-carbohydrate, high-protein, and megavitamin diets, and those promulgated by Adelle Davis, Gayelord Hauser, Carlton Fredericks, Robert Atkins, Nathan Pritikin, and Herman Tarnower (the "Scarsdale doctor"). The specific recommendations of each differ so greatly that sometimes they are directly opposed, but they do have in common a claim that the control over food intake is the key to happiness and well-being. For the organic-food movement, this control begins with the selection of seeds and continues through gardening, harvesting, food preparation, mastication, behavior during meals, and finally proper bowel movements for the elimination of wastes.

The faddists eventually establish a religious fellowship whose orthodoxy in matters of eating sets it apart from the population at large. Followers of health-food teachings usually regard as suspect the wide range of nutritional and health information that is available to everyone else from scientists and physicians, government agencies, and established publishers of books and newspapers. As they develop their own network of communications, the faddists gradually extend their beliefs about food to other avenues of life, until in time they arrive at a full-blown ontology or world view, encompassing religion, government, economics, environment, and sex and the family. The nutritional value of food, once the central issue, becomes almost secondary—a ritual obligation dutifully carried on day after day. The faddists believe they have liberated themselves from the metaphorical associations that food has for everyone else, yet they have their own metaphors for eating behavior that differ little in essence from those of other groups and societies around the world.

8

The Feast and the Gift

PROBABLY NO SOCIETY is without those unifying events known as festivals, whether they honor the nation, pay homage to divinity, or bless the crops. At each of these a limited number of distinctive foods are eaten: in the United States, hot dogs and barbecue on July Fourth, a turkey at Thanksgiving, a roast goose or ham at Christmas. In Britain, mince pie has been a traditional Christmas food; its spicy ingredients symbolize the gifts brought by the Magi to the infant Jesus, and the latticework of the top crust is supposed to represent the hayrack above the manger. In Europe during the Middle Ages, a special bread was prepared at the time of the winter solstice that was circular like the sun but twisted at the center into the form of a cross, so as to represent the four seasons. It was called a bretzel; today's pretzel retains much the same shape but has lost the symbolic connection. Whatever the particular celebration, the foods that are eaten often have in common that they take time to prepare, are scarce, and are expensive.

In simple societies the most common religious occasion is a communal feast, whose function is to maintain the unity of those who participate in it. In Java, such feasts are known as *slametan*. The kin, friends, and neighbors who come together to eat at such a gathering are said to be joined by dead ancestors and supernatural beings as well. The occasion for a slametan can be almost any event the giver wishes to honor, sanctify, or endow with well-being: having reached the seventh month of pregnancy, birth, circumcision, marriage, illness, death, moving into a new dwelling, or winning the support of a particular spirit, to list a few. The emphasis is slightly different for each occasion, and special kinds of food are usually provided at each.

Men are invited to a slametan by a messenger only five or ten minutes before it is about to begin; they are expected to stop whatever they are doing and to gather immediately. This almost everyone does, since an invitation has been awaited; it is hardly possible in a small village to keep the preparations secret. Once all have arrived and formed a circle around the platters of food, the host briefly states his reason for celebrating a slametan; he calls upon the spirits to join them; a prayer is offered in Arabic, which few of those present are likely to understand. Each participant (except the host, who does not eat) is then given a stiff banana leaf on which he places samples of the special meat and fowl, along with rice colored and molded in various patterns and shapes for each occasion. The host then bids the guests, and the spirits as well, to eat. Food, rather than prayer, is the heart of the slametan. The spirits are said to feed on the aroma of the food, leaving its substance for the human diners. After briefly sampling the food the guests one by one ask the host's permission to leave, taking with them the uneaten food, which they will share with their families. Upon their departure the slametan has ended, a mere ten or fifteen minutes after it began.

Outsiders might regard a slametan as too brief, haphazard, and even irreverent to have much ritual efficacy. But it is, as one anthropologist has described it, "a kind of social universal joint" that can be made to fit a wide variety of occasions. Protection is obtained from the spirits; social harmony in the village is promoted, since everyone present is treated the same; most important to the Javanese is that it confers what is known as *slamet*, a state of physical and mental equanimity during which everyone feels that nothing upsetting will happen. The Javanese do not seem to be consciously aware that in addition to ritual, social, and psychological purposes a nutritional one is also being served: With everyone in the village providing a slametan or even several of them throughout the year, food is constantly being redistributed, so that everyone in the village eats approximately the same diet.

Feasting was of great importance to many North American Indian groups, but nowhere more than in the potlatches (from a Nootka Indian word, *patchatl*, "to give") held by those along the Northwest Coast from Oregon to southern Alaska. By the time anthropologists began studying the potlatch late in the nineteenth century, it had become an orgy of conspicuous consumption at which food was wasted to a degree unknown in any other society, past or present. Kin groups competed with one another in giving ever more lavish feasts, in providing more food than at the last one—in short, to make the guests eat until they were bloated, were forced to stagger off and vomit up what they had eaten, and then return to eat more. To dramatize how niggardly a rival chief's previous feast had been, the host group would load down the guests with food and gifts to take home. At one potlatch given by Kwakiutl Indians, the guests consumed the meat from fifty seals, and among the gifts they received were six slaves, eight canoes, fifty-four elk skins, two thousand silver bracelets, and thirty-three thousand blankets. If it was believed that a rival group had not yet been humiliated, food and wealth almost beyond belief would be destroyed in the flames. This extravagance belonged to a time when the societies of the Northwest Coast had become the beneficiaries of the surplus wealth pumped into their economy by North Americans engaged in fishing and the fur trade. Since the Indian populations at the time had been plummeting as a result of disease, fewer people were available among whom to divide the wealth, and so the survivors had grown rich beyond their own imagining.

Numerous attempts have been made to account for the origins of such a wasteful system: that it grew out of competitiveness between rival groups; that it was really the occasion for building up peaceful relations with neighbors, substituting rivalry at feasts for armed conflict; that its true function was to validate the rank of hosts and guests, each guest being served according to a precise tallying of status; that it was meant to confirm the strength of the society. The potlatch undoubtedly was all these things. Beyond them, what made it crucial to the adaptation of the Northwest Coast Indians was the unreliability of their coastal environment. Though their environment has been described as an abundant one, providing food from the sea, the rivers, and the forests at all times of the year, this was not true in a consistent or dependable way. Deer, for example, were to be found mainly in certain burned-over areas; a dry spell meant that the forests would not produce their usual quantity of berries and nuts; the salmon on their migrations upstream could be taken only at certain places, and their numbers varied from one year to another. Such wide fluctuations occurred throughout the region. The supply of fish taken by the Southern Kwakiutl of British Columbia varied annually from thirty-five percent to two hundred percent of the average. Although the Indians of the Northwest Coast could have easily survived on the *average* annual bounty, a limit was put on their numbers by what was available during periods of scarcity.

In many simple societies, this "law of the minimum" sets a limit to population growth far below what might be sustained during a bountiful year or season. The Northwest Coast peoples did, of course, attempt to counteract the law by storing a supply of nuts from the forest or by drying fish and preserving it in oil. Storage bins, though, were not always sufficient to provide food during the lean years. One other way of surmounting the law of the minimum was to put aside a surplus in the form of obligations on the part of others. If, for example, one group whose subsistence was based on obtaining seals from the sea enjoyed a year in which the animals were abundant, this group might then give a potlatch for another group whose rivers had failed to produce many salmon. The guests would be feasted for a few days and would go home loaded down with presents of food that would help get them through a lean time. The river people would undoubtedly have been shamed. But in the following year the situation might be reversed; the salmon in the river might be plentiful, and the seal hunters hungry because they had been kept from the open sea by fog and rough water. Now it would be the turn of the river people to hold a potlatch, thus humbling their former benefactors—and at the same time repaying the debt of last year by becoming this year's hosts.

Competitive feasting has the effect of offering a margin of safety in the event of shortage. It keeps people extracting food from the environment at high rates of productivity in order to prepare for the next potlatch. It equalizes the differential productivity of villages that occupy the diverse environments of forests, rivers, and coastline. The potlatch thus provided a setting in which groups who recognized no common economic authority could meet to exchange resources. The investment made in a potlatch was secure, and would eventually be returned with interest. Competitiveness, rivalry, and prestige were therefore—if this explanation is correct— not the reason for the potlatch but simply a means of keeping the system in motion.

Competitive feasting similar to the potlatch, but without its extravagance, is found in societies around the world that lack any other mechanism to redistribute resources. The rise to prominence of the feast-giver, who is also the redistributor of surpluses from local groups, is seen in those inhabitants of the islands of Melanesia known among anthropologists as the "big men"—also referred to as "men of renown," "generous men," "great providers," or "center-men." The last term seems most apt because it connects a cluster of followers gathered around a pivotal personality. Whatever such a man is called, he is the entrepreneur, the man who combines statesmanship with a reputation of working hard for the general welfare. Big men do not inherit previously existing positions of leadership, nor are they installed in any office. They create the office by their deeds and then see to it that no one else fills it. The primary way these things are done is by sponsoring a feast.

A big man starts his career early, often while he is in his teens, and his first leap toward high status cannot be taken without the efforts of his own household and kin. He encourages his wife to cultivate larger yam gardens; having increased their production, he can enlarge his domestic working force by taking more wives. The economic importance of having many wives was stated in pidgin by one Papuan: "Another woman go garden, another woman go take firewood, another woman go catch fish, another woman cook him—husband he sing out plenty people come *kaikai* [that is, come to eat]." He borrows pigs from his kin and breeds them to increase the size of his own herd. His neighbors and kin are impressed by the diligent labor of his wives and children, his flourishing gardens, his large number of pigs. Realizing that this man can bring them wealth and prestige, they increase their own productivity to add to his surplus. In this way he draws on the circle of his relatives and friends for additional labor, and is ready to begin the expansive phase of his aspirations.

He sponsors his first feast "to build his name," as the Melanesians put it. To make it memorable, those who have become his followers work almost around the clock to erect a fine house for the accumulated bounty he is to display: fish, yams, bananas, all piled as high as possible to overwhelm the guests. At one such feast, given on Guadalcanal several decades ago, an aspiring big man offered his guests three hundred pounds of fish, three thousand cakes made of yams and coconuts, nineteen large bowls of yam pudding, and meat from thirteen roasted pigs. The big man himself ate sparingly and not until after the feast was over. For such a man, once his career has begun, the feasting never ends. He must immediately go to work to prepare for another, bigger feast; he must worry about other big men who might shame him by topping his feast with a more lavish one. So he spurs on his followers, flushed with their first victory, to increase their production. He becomes miserly, consumes less food than anyone else, and works harder to set an example. Prestige, not a higher standard of living, is his reward.

The aspiring big man must now make careful calculations against losing all by a blunder. Deciding to challenge an established big man whose reputation is greater than his, he invites this big man to his next feast. It is a grander one than the first, thanks to additional supporters who, impressed by his first effort, are now contributing their productivity. The challenged guest must reciprocate in a reasonable length of time with a feast still more lavish. If he is unable to do so, he will be humiliated and no longer considered a big man. His followers will desert him to become supporters of the new big man—who is less able than before to rest on his past achievements. His own ambition, calculation, and self-deprivation having enabled him to become a successful big man, he now lives in fear that the same route will be followed by some equally enterprising rival. So he constantly goads his relatives and supporters to work hard in preparation for a challenge. One thing that makes them willing to do so is being able to bask in the aura of prestige that surrounds their "center-man." Another is that because they now produce more food than before, they are living better than they ever did.

The way the big man goes about setting himself above his followers and becoming the ruler of an incipient chiefdom may offer a clue to the manner in which complex society might evolve out of a relatively simple horticultural economy. His consuming ambition becomes the means whereby a small, fragmented society may surmount its divisions and evolve to a higher level of cooperation. Before the European colonial governments outlawed warfare in Melanesia, a big man not only got his followers to produce more food, but also got them to go to war for him. The big man both intensified food production at home and became a raider against the food supplies of neighboring groups.

Melanesians speak of him as "the great provider," but for economists he is a redistributor. In most societies based on foraging and simple horticulture, everyone is approximately equal in status, everyone eats the same food, and no one works so hard as to exploit all of the available resources. In a redistributive system, on the other hand, many different kinds of food, each produced by a household or a kin group that more or less specializes in it, are brought to a central place for distribution—one may bring yams, for example, and return with supplies of fish. Redistribution is obviously a much more efficient use of resources, permitting a larger and denser population, than is the simple sharing of hunter–gatherers—but it works only when a powerful individual, a redistributor with a large following, can coordinate the efforts.

Competitive feasting increases production and thus makes available to the redistributor both the food to be distributed and the social occasion for doing so. In the early stages of what is on the way to becoming a complex society, the redistributor consumes less than everyone else, but sooner or later egalitarianism gives way to selfishness. The redistributor demands, and receives, certain benefits for himself and his kin: a larger share of food, higher rank, and hereditary status. To sustain his position, though, he must continually find new sources of production, either by increasing yields or by making raids against neighbors. These developments must have taken place in the chiefdoms of the Northwest Coast, Polynesia, and elsewhere. Competitive feast-giving by ambitious young men would eventually have led to political states with their large and dense populations, social classes, intensive production, and frequent warfare.

As societies grow more complex, the privilege of levying taxes, rents, and tributes from those of lower status is accompanied by the privilege of eating very much better than the great mass of the population. In medieval England the tables of nobles were so laden with every sort of food that they became known as "groaning boards," and a knight might put away a dozen dishes during a single sitting. The menus for royal banquets in the fifteenth century list as many as forty dishes, although it was considered proper merely to sample rather than gorge on them. The purposes of these opulent feasts were social and political, a display of the control a noble had over both people and sources of supply. The seating arrangements were a reflection of social rank. Members of the lesser nobility were obliged to share a serving with one or more others; those belonging to the lower classes were not allowed even to look at what was served to their superiors. Youths of high birth sent to the court of a noble were similarly distinguished according to rank and social status while they were being educated in the etiquette of entertaining guests.

Serving food in an important household was an avenue for social and political advancement; most of the knights of the medieval courts began their careers in this way. Each server had his own title and rank. The most exalted was the carver, who was expert in the use of an extraordinary number of butchering utensils, along with technical terms and social rules. He had to know, for example, that only the left wing of a capon was suitable for the lord and that the kidney of a fawn was the delicacy served first. The panter (his title derived from *pain,* French for "bread") was schooled in the use of a variety of knives, such as the one for smoothing the edges of trenchers, hard squares of bread that served as plates upon which meat was heaped (whence the word "trencherman" to describe a hearty eater). The butler had responsibility for the butts or casks of wine and ale.

In most societies, certain foods are associated with the ruling classes. These include camel stuffed with goat and fowl in the Near East, venison and game birds in northwestern Europe, and dog in aboriginal Hawaii. In medieval times certain spices were scarce, being either imported to order or brought as a gift by an ambassador—and so a particular aroma could be an affirmation of power and status. Most often, though, prestigious foods are animal, and they are limited in supply and usually expensive. Those not rare in nature are made artificially exclusive by the practice of denying them to the common people. This was done in medieval Europe and Elizabethan England with venison and other game, which could be hunted only by the nobility. When the Pilgrims celebrated their first Thanksgiving, venison became a spectacular substitute for the chicken, hare, and pigeon meat that filled the "flesh pies" they had eaten in England. In Europe, deer were kept in preserves for the pleasure of the nobles and their friends, and venison was not sold or bartered. Accustomed only to fowling pieces, the Pilgrims lacked both the guns and the skills necessary to shoot deer that first Thanksgiving. Because the culinary status symbol of seventeenth-century England was ordinary food to the Indians, Chief Massasoit presented five carcasses of deer for the occasion.

Restrictions upon what certain people are permitted to eat, known as sumptuary laws (from the Latin *sumere,* "to consume"), go back to antiquity, and were common in medieval Europe. In 1363 Edward III of England directed sumptuary edicts at members of the servant class, whose expectations had risen with the shortage of labor resulting from the Black Death, in an attempt to limit both what they ate and what they wore. In France, six different edicts in the period between 1563 and 1577 alone tried to limit the number of courses served to three, even at festivals, and to forbid the serving of meat and fish at the same meal. Whoever ignored these edicts, whether host or guest, was subject to large fines, and the cook who had prepared the meal was to be imprisoned for fifteen days on bread and water. The failure of Edward's legislation, and the need for edict after edict in France, attest to the difficulty of enforcing sumptuary laws. If they had been enforced, vegetables would have come to play a more important role in the traditional diet of Europe. As long as animal foods could be obtained, Europeans disdained all vegetables except cabbages, onions, peas, and certain herbs. Such plants as radishes, spinach, lettuce, parsnips, turnips, carrots, and beets were known but were rarely eaten until an increased population and dwindling supplies of meat made doing so a necessity.

Most people are likely to take pride not only in having the food they serve reflect their social status, but also in having important people as their guests at table. In some societies, though, this is exceptional behavior. The highest compliment that the Bemba can pay to a man is not to have him as an invited guest—but rather to send a gift of porridge, relishes, meat, and calabashes of beer to be eaten privately in his hut. The least hospitable thing would be to invite a guest to share one's own meal. Feasting among the Bemba, rather than being an occasion for conviviality or conversation, is a symbolic way to offer respect. A man who is sent food to eat in privacy is complimented by being treated like the chief who eats alone; but to ask a man to share a meal would be to treat him like a dependent.

Hindus in India, possibly more than any other group in the world, have made eating the insignia of status. In fact, the hierarchy of the caste system is embodied in what is eaten, with whom, and by whom the meal is prepared. Food categories and social categories thereby become one; a person acceptable for the table is acceptable also for the marriage bed. The rejection of an offer of food is a gesture of superiority, and also an implicit refusal to give female relatives in marriage. Accordingly, the focus of the marriage ritual in India is commensality. As the bride and groom publicly exchange pieces of food, they are reinforcing the structure of the caste system.

Besides its great masses of Hindus, India has minority populations of Moslems, Jains, Sikhs, Zoroastrians, and Christians—and also of about 150 tribes with their own ritual practices. Some Hindu beliefs, such as those concerning ritual purity and the veneration of various animals, were adopted from the tribes and incorporated into the Hindu system of ethics. Almost all tribes set themselves apart by the foods they eat and avoid. Even within a single tribe, members belonging to different subdivisions of it eat separately. Once such distinctions are made, the judgment will follow that some ways of eating are superior to others, and that so are the people who practice them. Inevitably, a hierarchy of social status based on eating will be established. One division of the Kamar tribe, for example, considers itself superior because its members do not eat snakes, crocodiles, and monkeys, as those of another division do; and the Yanadi of Kerala will have nothing to do with tribes whose members eat frogs.

The numerous castes in a Hindu village compose a hierarchy ranging from high to low. A study of several villages in northern India showed the basis of social rank to be the foods prepared and eaten by each caste, though the reasons for the placing of a particular caste were often vague. Hindus in general rank all foods according to four categories: raw, superior cooked, inferior cooked, and garbage. The highest rank is given to raw foods, which are the only ones suitable for a Brahman or anyone else belonging to the highest castes. Less valued are cooked foods, but of these certain ones are considered superior if they contain ghee, a clarified butter from which the water has been removed. The costliest of fats, ghee is prized in India as tending to build health and virility. Inferior cooked foods include barley cakes, pickles, and cheap curries, all of which lack ghee. Garbage, the bottom-most of the four categories, includes not only waste, but also the abominated beef and pork—and even any raw or superior food that has become polluted through contact with people from lower castes.

Logic would require the ranking of various castes to follow these categories, but among the thirty-six castes in one village t...at was studied, no consistency in ranking was found. Meat (that is, "garbage") was eaten not only by members of the two lowest castes, but also by people belonging to another caste that was considered to be among the highest in the village. How was it possible for the members of this caste to rank high, yet be consumers of meat from the sacred cattle? It was learned eventually that what members of each caste thought about members of other castes depended not so much on who ate what as on who took food from whom. If members of caste A habitually gave food to those of caste B, then caste A was considered to be higher; and because members of castes X and Y exchanged food with one another's members, they were ranked as equal. The ranking became more complex when many castes were involved in food transactions. If A gave food to both X and Y—whereas B gave only to X and not to Y—then A was considered higher than B because of having given to more castes.

Such distinctions might appear irrelevant to people brought up in Western society; but in village India food is closely bound up with the economy, since it is the traditional payment for artisans and servants. Members of caste 34 will ordinarily not accept even raw grain as payment from a member of caste 35, but they will accept it from a member of this lower caste who threshed it while in the employ of a landowner belonging to a higher caste. Similarly, flour ground by a low-caste woman in her own house will be regarded as inedible by the high castes, whereas flour ground by the same woman as an employee of a Brahman household will be quite acceptable. Since the government of India is now attempting to modernize the country's economy, it might be supposed that such distinctions would soon die out. For a number of reasons, though, the entire system of food transactions is inherently conservative. Any change of attitude by one caste is likely to affect the relative standing of many others. Accordingly, the reasoning goes (except among the members of the lowest caste, who have nothing to lose by change), better to stay where you are than to risk falling lower. Moreover, some castes are of equal rank because they use food as payment to one another, which would make it difficult to change the rank of one of these without changing the rank of the others as well. But above all, any attempt to modify the traditional food transactions between castes would bring economic chaos to the village.

Because food is essential for all human beings, offering it to someone is usually considered to be a "pure gift"—not trade, not barter, no strings attached. That attitude is ingrained in much everyday behavior. Panhandlers really want money, but they are practical enough to dress up a request for it by saying they need it to buy a cup of coffee or a sandwich. International relief organizations employ the same tactic when they appeal for contributions by showing a child with an empty food bowl rather than the tractor on which the money is more likely to be spent.

That a gift of food entails not simply charity or generosity, but is a complex transaction, can be clearly seen in simple societies where the giving of food is an obligation. When the Arctic explorer Peter Freuchen was given meat by Eskimos with whom he had been living, he thanked them, as he had been trained to do at home. An old man promptly corrected him:

> You must not thank for your meat; it is your right to get parts. In this country, nobody wishes to be dependent on others. Therefore, there is nobody who gives or gets gifts, for thereby you become dependent. With gifts you make slaves just as with whips you make dogs.

Thanking anyone for food is a serious breach of etiquette among hunter–gatherers because it implies both that the giver is not generous as a matter of course and that he is not a good enough hunter to afford to give away meat. More important, by his thanks the recipient seems to deny the obligation to repay at some future date. A hunter shares because it is the appropriate thing to do in his society; he later expects to receive, and this is his right. The well-brought-up recipient in a hunting–gathering society praises the giver for his hunting prowess but never for his generosity.

The exchange of food, or a symbolic representation of it, marks the beginning and the end of sociability—the establishment, maintenance, or severing of the social bond. Accordingly, in most societies a restraint is placed on selling or exchanging food for other kinds of goods. In those indigenous societies possessing rudimentary forms of currency—such as certain groups in Melanesia, and the Pomo and other Indians in California—currency could not be used to obtain food. In such a society, the social value of food within the group is too great to be given a market value. The Salish Indians of the Northwest Coast, for example, described a category of their possessions—canoes, shell ornaments, tools, and baskets—as "wealth." Food, on the other hand, was described as a "holy thing" that ought to be given and not be exchanged for wealth. In many other simple societies, food does serve as a sort of payment to someone equal in status who helps out in gardening or building a canoe. Some economists regard such payments as wages and as revealing incipient capitalism. But if the payments represent any incipient tendency, it is one toward socialism. The giving of food to those who provide labor for household tasks is a metaphorical extension of the household economy to a wider circle. Rather than serving as a means of exploiting the labor of others, its function is to give more people a claim on the productive fortunes of a household other than their own.

A gift is usually defined as a voluntary transfer of some good without any stipulation of payment. Such a transfer, though, is almost never entirely free. Social pressures may force someone to give gifts to kin on birthdays; social benefits may be anticipated as a result of a gift when it is made to someone of higher status, or the giver may calculate that something of at least equal value will be given in return. This ambivalence about gifts appears in the New Testament. Matthew (10:8) quotes Jesus as high-mindedly admonishing the disciples: "Freely ye have received, and freely give." But in Luke (6:38), Jesus points out that gifts will bring recompense: "Give, and it shall be given unto you . . . For with the same measure that ye mete withal it shall be measured to you again."

The New Testament thereby attests both to common wisdom and to anthropological fact that however selfless gift-giving may appear to be, some balance in reciprocity is expected. One person might continue giving to another at Christmas for a few years before there is any reciprocation—but when that occurs, it is expected that the reciprocated gift will be lavish and approach the cumulative value of the previous gifts. Is not such a system at the mercy of freeloaders who always take but rarely give? Not usually. In simple societies, such a thing is so unthinkable that freeloaders are taken for witches and may be banished or killed. The Bemba in fact define a witch as someone who comes to a hut looking for a handout of food. Even in Western societies, a person who invites another for several dinners in a row without a reciprocal invitation feels exploited; word sooner or later gets about, and the freeloader will pay a penalty in being shunned socially.

Artful ways to avoid reciprocating do nevertheless exist. Bemba housewives attempt to dodge reciprocal obligations by hiding their beer at the approach of a relative, and then saying that they are poor and, alas, have nothing to eat. The Maori of New Zealand sometimes avoid reciprocating by falling back on the distinction between raw and cooked food, of which only the latter is given to others. So to avoid obligations they often eat food unprocessed or underdone—as is stated in their adage, "Broil your rat [a favorite Maori dish] with its fur on, lest you be disturbed by someone."

Ambivalent attitudes about sharing and freeloading are seen in the Gurage of Ethiopia, whose anxieties about food have been described on pages 91–92. Those with a reputation for generosity in giving food are the people with the highest prestige and authority in all spheres of Gurage life. There is nevertheless anxiety about retaining enough of a supply to be able to give at a future time. With such contrary motivation prevalent, it is no wonder that two patterns of behavior have developed. Publicly, the giving of food is part of normal social relations; but these occasions are more a matter of etiquette than of nourishment, and are about as filling as a coffee break would be. Privately, late at night, the family eats its main meal in the seclusion of its dimly lit hut.

In the face of ambivalence, how can such a system continue to operate? It can because reciprocity makes possible new social obligations beyond those of close kin. The offering of highly valued foods—such as an antelope steak among the San, or in North America an aged Smithfield ham from Virginia, lobsters from

Maine, or caviar from the Black Sea—elevates the new fellowship as a matter of importance. But even food that is not particularly valuable can be given in ways that foster and maintain social relations. Food is offered to visitors even though they have just eaten elsewhere. Visitors who refuse, or who accept and then do not eat with a show of enthusiasm, are considered to have committed a breach of etiquette. In some Melanesian societies, the same food will be given and regiven in a round of gifts so many times over that it becomes decayed or bruised. That it no longer has much utilitarian value does not matter; what does matter is that it continues to circulate, and is always accepted graciously. The giving and regiving of inedible food stands for friendly social relations, and the transaction as a whole serves to keep everyone aware that mutual obligations have been incurred.

This section of the book has been concerned largely with the avoidance of certain foods because of their symbolic aspects, with the religious sanctions placed upon food, and with the social controls operating at occasions at which eating occurs. The next section will concentrate on a narrower aspect of these general topics: the numerous preferences and avoidances that have little to do with individual taste, yet are so firmly ingrained as to be characteristic of a whole culture.

Part III

THE PATTERNS
OF EATING

9

Taste and Distaste

HUMANS will swallow almost anything that does not swallow them first. The animals they relish range in size from termites to whales; the Chinese of Hunan Province eat shrimp that are still wriggling, while North Americans and Europeans eat live oysters; some Asians prefer food so putrefied that the stench carries for dozens of yards. At various times and places, strong preferences have been shown for the fetuses of rodents, the tongues of larks, the eyes of sheep, the spawn of eels, the stomach contents of whales, and the windpipes of pigs. Italians symbolically cannibalize the most respected figures in their culture by eating such things as "nun's thighs," "the Pope's nose," and "nipples of the Virgin." Nor has there been a shortage of unusual combinations, such as the Scottish haggis—a cow's lungs, intestines, pancreas, liver, and heart, seasoned with onions, beef suet, and oatmeal, all cooked together in a sheep's stomach—or the favorite dish of the Roman Emperor Vitellius whose ingredients were the tongues of flamingoes, the brains of peacocks, the livers of pikes, and the sex glands of lampreys.

People in every society regard their own preferences as sensible and all deviations from these as perverse or

197

even loathsome. The witches in *Macbeth* boiled in their cauldron foods that outraged the sensibilities of the audience, thereby making clear the enormous gulf between the hags and proper Elizabethans:

> Fillet of a fenny snake,
> In the cauldron boil and bake;
> Eye of newt and toe of frog,
> Wool of bat and tongue of dog,
> Adder's fork and blindworm's sting,
> Lizard's leg and howlet's wing . . .

Most North Americans and Europeans are revolted by hearing that certain Mexicans eat fried grubs, that dog flesh has been esteemed in China since antiquity, and that the fox was once considered a delicacy in Russia. Yet our tastes are often regarded with equal repugnance by others. Perhaps a third of humankind would rather starve than consume the bacon, ham, and sausage that are relished in North America and Europe, and many would be nauseated by the milk that is drunk in such large quantities.

De gustibus non est disputandum—"There is no arguing about taste"—runs the Latin proverb. But taste did not just happen. Cultural, historical, and ecological events have interacted to cause frogs, for example, to be esteemed as a delicacy in southern China but to be regarded with revulsion in northern China. Even though much remains unknown, tastes cannot be dismissed as inarguable or illogical; an attempt will be made here to discover why, as Lucretius put it, "What is food to one man may be fierce poison to others."

Among the approximately thirty million tribal people of India, a total of 250 animal species are avoided by one group or another. Most of these people will not eat meat from a tiger or any of various snakes, particularly the cobra. Although they say they feel a kinship with these animals, it is obvious that both are highly dangerous and that hunting them systematically would be foolish.

Monkeys are avoided, probably because of their close resemblance to human beings; in these tribes, cannibalism is viewed with extreme horror. A reluctance to eat the females of edible species of animals has been attributed to veneration for the maternal role, but it could also be due to a policy of allowing the females to reproduce and provide more edible young. Many tribes avoid eating any animal that has died of unknown causes, an intelligent attitude in view of the possibility that the animal might have died from an infectious disease that could spread to humans. Animals that consume excrement or garbage are similarly avoided, an adaptive step that prevents contact with parasites, and that might explain why members of one tribe eat any of twenty-one different species of rats, but not the house rat.

Because of the wide variety of tastes and preferences displayed in societies around the world, it is extremely difficult to put together the menu for a meal that would please most people. One nutritionist posed the problem: What dinner could be served that would be acceptable to a cross section of all the peoples in the world? He finally came up with a menu of chicken, rice, squash with chili sauce, tea for a beverage, and a banana for dessert. No society has ever been known to approach its food supply scientifically, by analyzing all the potential foods in the environment and then giving preference to those that were most nutritious. Even in the case of cultivated plants, little correlation can be found between nutritional value and the amount consumed. Broccoli, for example, has a greater concentration of nutrients—including ten vitamins and minerals—than any other plant used for food in the United States, but ranks twenty-first in the amount consumed; on the other hand, the tomato, the most commonly eaten vegetable or fruit, comes in sixteenth as a source of vitamins and minerals.

Even the San, who much depend on hunting and gathering for all of their food needs in the arid environment of the central Kalahari, regularly hunt only a dozen or so of the forty-eight wild animals they consider edible; and of the eighty-five kinds of plants they regard as food, they concentrate most of their efforts on only a handful because of abundance, reliability, ease of preparation, and cultural considerations. The same is true in more complex societies. Only certain cuts of meat from a very limited number of animal species are for sale in even a large supermarket in the United States. The reason for this is often economic: It would be expensive to collect and process large quantities of such animals as rattlesnakes and gophers for their meat. But the primary obstacle is still cultural prejudice. Californians do not harvest the snails that overrun their gardens, though these could be obtained with little effort and are of the same species that are imported from Europe as expensive *escargots*.

What has been said so far about food choices should make one thing clear: People in exotic societies are not necessarily starving when they eat what North Americans and Europeans would deem repulsive. The foods eaten today in some simple societies may have been resorted to as a result of poverty, but the situation would have been different under aboriginal conditions. Many such people have now become displaced persons, pushed into the least hospitable parts of the earth first by the spread of agriculture, later by colonialism, and most recently by industrialization. The San have been deprived of game by the expansion of the cattle-keeping Bantu into their lands; Eskimos no longer hunt all the various animals of the sea that used to sustain them; the forests that once yielded abundant pine nuts for the Shoshonean Indians have been cut for timber and their hunting grounds have been overgrazed by cattle. Even so, these people have shown a remarkable ability to put together a nutritious diet out of what was available.

Instead of believing that indigenous peoples around the world are the victims of irrational food choices, North

Americans and Europeans should look at some of their own prejudices, such as the taboo against eating meat from the sacred dog. Like the sacred cattle of India, dogs are given the freedom of the streets; there are so many of them that in places special sanitary ordinances have been passed to prohibit littering sidewalks with their excrement. Like the sacred cattle, dogs may be given affectionate names, are often decorated with bows, share the family meal, and sleep with their owners. Inoculated against diseases, cared for when ill, their eating preferences catered to, these pets live out their lives untroubled by any risk of being eaten by their owners or sacrificed to the gods. Unlike sacred cattle, though, these millions of dogs perform few services beyond barking at intruders, occasionally flushing game for sportsmen, and, in a few places, herding cattle and sheep.

The idea of keeping a large population of nearly use-less animals, which compete with humans for protein yet are not themselves eaten, would appall traditional Chinese, Melanesians, Hawaiians, American Indians, and Africans—many of whom not only use the labor of dogs but also eat them. The Chinese have bred dogs of certain kinds, such as the chow, primarily for culinary purposes; roasted puppy hams and suckling pups have been features of their cuisine. For many North Ameri-cans and Europeans, eating dogs is taboo as being equivalent to endocannibalism, since dogs are part of the human household. The justification, though, is not really consistent. North Americans and Europeans of-ten treat calves, rabbits, and pigs as pets, giving them affectionate names and even sometimes nursing them from a bottle—but are able to master their qualms about eating them eventually. In many other societies where dogs are also regarded as household pets, no distaste is connected with using them later for food. The fact is that the societies in which dogs are eaten, whether or not they are pets or are useful in providing security and aiding in the hunt, are those that lack other sources of meat from large herbivores. But where huge industries already exist to produce cattle, sheep, hogs, and poultry, all of which are herbivores, the carnivorous dog is almost useless as a source of meat, and instead must be treated as if sacred.

Even more surprising than the status of the dog is the repugnance felt toward eating horsemeat at many times and places throughout North America, Europe, the Near East, and southern Asia. Horseflesh is nutritionally as valuable as beef; in fact, an industry already exists to produce horsemeat—for dogs. Horses not only are easily raised, but also can provide ten to fifteen years' work before they are slaughtered for food, which is not true of swine or beef cattle. The eating of horsemeat goes back tens of thousands of years, and even continued down to historic times in the immense region stretching from eastern Europe to Mongolia. Pastoral economies there have been centered around the horse; it was used for transporting humans and for carrying loads, while the hide went into various manufactured items, the meat was eaten, and the milk was fermented into the liquor known as *kumiss*.

The practice of eating horseflesh spread from central Eurasia to many parts of the continent. It was favored in the court of the Emperor Tamerlane at Samarkand, and was once widespread among the Germanic tribes of northern Europe; the Japanese still eat horsemeat and it is often an ingredient in sukiyaki. Sooner or later, though, the major religions turned against the practice. The Jews declared the horse to be an abomination because it did not satisfy the requirements of chewing the cud and being cloven-hoofed; the Buddha specifically prohibited eating horseflesh; and the prophet Mohammed personally avoided horseflesh, although he did not forbid it to others. With the spread of Christianity, an attack was launched upon the consumption of horseflesh, ostensibly because of its association with the worship of pagan deities; in A.D. 732 the practice was finally forbidden to Christians by Pope

Gregory III. Being forced to give up hippophagy made pagans such as those of Iceland reluctant to convert.

In declaring the horse to be an abomination, all of the faiths were applying religious justification to what had become an ecological necessity. Horses are of value when extensive grazing lands are available, as they are in central Eurasia and even in Iceland, or so long as their usefulness for transportation, warfare, or agriculture is not outweighed by their consumption of domestic grain, as it came to be with industrialization in Europe and elsewhere. With the rapid growth of human numbers in the Mediterranean region, the scarcity of forage made raising horses for food an extravagance. The same thing was true in India, where the sacred cow was a much better choice for pulling plows and other transport, and for providing fuel in the form of dung and food in the form of milk. The attacks on hippophagy by most major religions were therefore ecologically rational positions that provided benefits for the followers of those faiths—and, of course, ultimately for the faiths themselves. The prohibitions against horseflesh consequently became ingrained as a repugnance in much of Europe and in some other parts of the world influenced by the colonial powers.

Hippophagy nevertheless persisted, and indeed horses were prized for food in places in Europe where forage was available. In Switzerland, Christian monks were eating horseflesh in the eleventh-century, despite the ban placed on it four centuries earlier. The Irish likewise continued to eat it; horsemeat feasts took place in sixteenth-century Denmark; in Spain, young horses, known as "red deer," were commonly eaten and the meat was used to feed the navy. Hippophagy was openly practiced around the time of the French Revolution, and by 1836 large quantities of horseflesh were being consumed in Paris. Toward the end of the nineteenth century its sale was legalized in France, Germany, Austria, and Scandinavia. The siege of Paris by German forces in 1870–71, during which time Parisians consumed at least 70,000 horses, had much to do with overcoming the prejudice against it. In France, around 1960, as many as 3500 butcher shops were specializing in horsemeat.

Since then the consumption of horsemeat has once again declined rapidly throughout western Europe. A new wave of revulsion against it has been blamed on an outbreak of salmonella in 1967, but much more probably the decline has to do with ecology and economics. When, over the past few decades, armies stopped purchasing horses for cavalry and for transport, they did away with a major incentive for the raising of horses, which were already becoming a luxury with the mechanization of farms. Virtually the only use for a horse in western Europe nowadays is recreation, and that is insufficient to justify breeding horses in large numbers. Most of the horsemeat eaten in western Europe in the past few decades has therefore had to be imported; but transportation and related costs have raised the price to about that for beef and veal, further discouraging a horse industry. Because horses compete for grass and grain with other herbivores, which are superior to them in fertility, tractability, and the amount of meat produced per pound of animal, horsemeat will probably not again become an important food in western Europe.

In North America, where horseflesh never was a major source of food, beef is now the most important meat. Each person in the United States consumes, on an average, nearly 125 pounds of it a year—twice the consumption of pork, the second most popular meat. A whole lexicon of beef cuts has developed, including such items as rib roast, rib eye, porterhouse, sirloin, filet, tenderloin, T-bone, shoulder cut, brisket, flank, and ground round. Among the world's foods, beef in North America has been unusual in being at once widely eaten and prestigious. Roast chicken is esteemed less highly than roast beef and no cut of pork matches the prestige of the psoas muscle of a castrated bull, more commonly known by the elegant French name of filet mignon. Steaks, the most desirable and expensive cuts of beef, retain their prestige value even though they are more plentiful than the low-prestige organ meats (each animal, after all, has only one tongue, one liver, or one brain). Little difference in nutritional value can be discovered between the various cuts of steak, and the cheaper cuts cost less simply because they are less prized.

The preeminence of beef in North America is a cultural phenomenon arising out of peculiar ecological and technological conditions. Pork had been, year after year, more popular than beef in the United States until the beginning of this century, and in occasional years since then; ham in particular had long been esteemed, probably because the curing process had once been an art demanding time and skill. The long predominance of pork is still entrenched in the everyday vocabulary of the United States. People speak of "bringing home the bacon" rather than "bringing home the steak"; government appropriations that confer benefits locally are known as "pork barrel"; affluence is described as "living high on the hog." The source of these expressions is easy to understand. The pig's status for centuries as the primary food animal for much of the continent had been maintained because it is one of the most efficient converters of plant food into flesh in the entire animal kingdom, producing about twenty pounds of meat from each hundred pounds of feed—three times the average for cattle and twice that for poultry. Pigs bear more young than cattle, and their habit of rooting about for nuts and plants on the forest floor enabled them to forage for themselves as long as extensive tracts of woodland remained. Moreover, a surplus of maize grown in the United States every year was fed to the hog and thereby converted into meat—which is why the Corn Belt and the Hog Belt overlap from Ohio to Iowa.

One trait of cattle eventually made them more valuable than pigs. As cud-chewing ruminants, they can digest the tough cellulose of which grass is composed, whereas pigs cannot. As the boundaries of the United States shifted westward, an immense empire of grassland was opened, in which cattle but not pigs could be fed. Just as the eastern forests had once given free forage to pigs, the rangelands now gave forage to cattle. Before the market for western beef could be extended to the populated urban centers of the eastern states, however, three things had to occur. First came the development of railroad transportation; the second was refrigeration, with which railroad cars began to be equipped by the end of the nineteenth century; the third was the end of ecological competition from the once vast herds of bison, which was accomplished by their near extermination. Few obstacles then remained to providing the eastern markets with fresh beef at a price lower even than pork.

The reign of beef cattle, though, is fated to be short. With urbanization, highway development, and the degradation of rangelands because of overgrazing, the open land available for raising cattle has decreased. As a result, cattle production is now an expensive operation that consists largely of force-feeding grain to penned calves, using up enormous amounts of fuel and petrochemicals in the process. Beef, as a result, has lost its cost advantage over pork and especially over poultry, fish, and milk products. Ecological and market conditions that brought beef to prominence several decades ago are now decreeing that it will no longer be a cheap, easy way to obtain animal protein. The chances are that people in North America will begin to lose their taste for big steaks just as they have begun to lose their attachment to big cars.

Humans everywhere use the same facial movements to express disgust as a reaction to certain foods—including closed eyes, narrowed nostrils, a downward curl of the lips, and extending the tongue. Probably such muscular contortions are inborn in the human species, having evolved as a warning to others about toxic substances. The cultural occasions for their use, though, appear to be learned; children do not exhibit such expressions until some time between the ages of two and four, when they have learned from their culture what foods are considered repugnant. In North America, the disgust reaction will be elicited by even the mention of eating human flesh, an ape or a monkey, a dog, a snake, a spider, or feces. Some people also respond in this way to the sight of raw or putrid meat, viscera, or a fish with the head and scales left on. In view of all this, the presence in the human diet of quite a number of unpalatable foods becomes difficult to explain. Among the most sought-after products in the world are such things as black pepper, chili peppers, ginger, coffee, and alcohol, which are either extremely bitter or irritating to the sensitive membranes of the mouth. In consuming foods that are unpalatable the first several times they are tried, humans are unique among omnivorous mammals.

The widespread use of chili peppers (which are botanically unrelated to black pepper) is particularly striking. This is the flavoring used most widely in almost all nonindustrialized societies, and it is frequently used in industrialized societies as well: About a quarter of the adult human population of the world is estimated to use it regularly. Its fiery taste is due to the irritating substance known as capsicin. One cookbook published in the United States recommends putting on rubber gloves to handle chili peppers, and taking care not to touch the face or eyes with the gloves. South American Indians were able to repel Spanish invaders with the extremely irritating smoke from burning chilis. Nevertheless, archeological excavations in Mexico indicate that chili peppers were eaten at least nine thousand years ago and were among the earliest plants domesticated in the New World. In the centuries since Columbus brought them back to Spain, they have been planted in most of the tropical and subtropical regions of the world.

Several reasons justify the widespread use of chili peppers, and many other strong spices as well. Chili peppers surpass almost all other plants as a source for vitamin A; they are also a rich source of vitamin C and the B vitamins. Although they cannot, of course, be eaten in large quantities, even a small amount is important to nutrition in certain tropical and subtropical societies where the intake of vitamins is often marginal. Chili peppers also have the advantage of lowering the body temperature, since capsicin in even small quantities quickly produces sweating (and consequently evaporative cooling). Chili also facilitates the digestion of starches, increases gastric secretions, and stimulates the appetite—all of which are important because the staple plant foods eaten in the tropics and subtropics are often bland. Some evidence also exists that chili and certain other spices inhibit the growth of bacteria. A portion of Ethiopian *chow,* consisting primarily of chili but containing up to fifteen other spices, has been shown to inhibit almost completely staphylococcus, salmonella, and other microorganisms that cause intestinal disorders. The classic explanation for the use of spices, that they mask the taste and smell of spoiled food, is open to question, since so many people do not attempt to mask rotted foods but in fact pay a premium for such things as "high" venison and, in Southeast Asia, sauces made from fermented fish.

Coffee, like chili peppers, is initially unpalatable, and a taste for it must be acquired. Like chili also, it originated in a small geographical area (Ethiopia and Arabia), and contains at least one pharmacologically active substance, caffeine. One difference is that people do not become addicted to chili peppers. The wide acceptance of coffee in many places is particularly surprising in light of such adverse effects as difficulty in falling asleep, bad dreams, an increase in urination, and anxiety. Even so, wherever coffee is drunk, people go out of their way to train their offspring to accept it. Young people gradually become habituated to its bitter taste by drinking it diluted with milk and sweetened with sugar, and by encountering its flavor in candies, milk-shakes, ice cream, and commercial yogurt.

In many places where drinking coffee is not a custom, people seek out other plants that contain caffeine. In parts of the Orient and Europe, people are addicted to tea (which is equally bitter and which, contrary to the usual belief, contains nearly the same amount of caffeine as coffee). South American Indians drink maté; East Africans chew kola nuts; and, of course, even in remote corners of the world people now drink cola beverages. It is remarkable that the human species now prizes such bitter substances that its physiological system evolved to reject—and that it will consume the caffeine which, if it were a newly synthesized pharmaceutical product, would no doubt be restricted by government regulation or have its use prohibited altogether. Caffeine is addictive: Habitual users eventually develop a tolerance to it and suffer withdrawal symptoms if they abruptly stop taking it. Contrary to the notion that coffee can sober up a drunk, for some people it hastens the loss of sensory and motor control. Recent experiments have shown that laboratory animals given coffee after imbibing large amounts of alcohol perform less well on tests than they did under the influence of alcohol alone. This indicates that many of the people who follow alcohol with coffee at a party may be further impairing, rather than improving, the ability to drive home safely—simply because coffee sometimes has a euphoric effect on those who have built up a tolerance to it.

In light of these facts about coffee, and also other substances containing caffeine, some explanation must exist for their incorporation into many of the world's cuisines. Coffee was first used in Ethiopia, and even today the crushed beans, molded into a ball with fat, provide a day's ration for nomads who need quick energy. This is obviously adaptive. Equally understandable is the use of coffee beans among the Moslems of Arabia, where it was quickly adopted as a consciousness-altering substitute for the alcohol that is forbidden by the Koran. Although it is difficult to account for the original acceptance of coffee and other bitter drinks, their continued use is understandable because they have become enmeshed in particular cultures.

Coffee plays a role in North America similar to that played by tea in Britain. People who move into a new neighborhood are usually invited over for a cup of coffee or tea, which presumably the newcomers are competent to brew for themselves. What they do need is the neighborliness that coffee and tea now symbolize, and which were once symbolized by the breaking of bread. In North America, residents are presented with a quandary about how to behave toward newcomers. A high value is placed on social nearness between those residing physically close to one another, yet a distinction is made between a neighbor and a friend. One way out of this quandary is to initiate a new social relationship by offering coffee to newcomers. The offer stops short of extending the same relationship to the newcomer's children, since coffee is the North American's one nonalcoholic beverage that is acceptable to nearly all adults but almost never to the young children who must be taught how to drink it.

Humans eat and drink a wide variety of substances that disorient the mind, interfere with the ability to walk upright that took millions of years to evolve, and produce personality changes counter to the sociality that has been a hallmark of human existence. Alcohol is the most widely used of these substances. Indigenous societies in nearly every part of the world, aside from the South Pacific and most areas of North America, developed their own alcoholic drinks. So pervasive is the use of alcohol that in some languages, including English, "to drink" also connotes the drinking of alcohol. In every society, the use of intoxicating beverages has its own etiquette and its own relation to the supernatural.

(As A. E. Housman wrote in *A Shropshire Lad*, "malt does more than Milton can/ To justify God's ways to man.") The drinking of alcohol has also become the focus of symbolic behavior. The commuting worker mixes a cocktail at home to mark the transition from the work day in the city to the relaxation of suburban life. Similarly, an Orthodox Jew recites a blessing over the wine which is drunk at the end of the sabbath, as marking the passage from the holy day to the rest of the week.

For the Jívaro Indians in the headwaters of the Amazon, beer is a greater necessity than solid food. Adult males drink from three to four gallons of it a day, adult females from one to two gallons, and a nine-year-old child will down half a gallon. Even though almost all of the protein in their diet must be obtained by going out to hunt, Jívaro hunters will often abandon the pursuit of prey and return to the settlement because the supply of beer is about to run out. Since women produce the beer, a man finds it desirable to acquire at least two wives so as to be able to entertain many guests and thus become known for his generosity. The Bemba also regard beer as equivalent to our notion of solid food; on days when beer is drunk, very little other food is eaten. The Bemba's high regard for beer as a major food is justified, because the sorghum from which it is made provides a number of B vitamins in which the rest of the diet is deficient, as well as a number of important minerals. A foreigner who sees Africans drinking beer, knowing that they are short of food, will usually condemn it—not realizing that beer is both a nutritional and a social necessity. If a man cannot give a beer party, even a small one, from time to time, he loses standing in his society. For the Bemba, providing beer is the most important way to repay social obligations, to honor kin, or to offer tribute to a chief. It rewards people who have given aid, and it is offered to deities. Tribal councils, marriages, and initiation ceremonies cannot take place without it. No wonder that the Bemba work hard at cultivating the land needed to produce enough grain for brewing.

Beer is similarly important in many modern societies; a pint of even a weak European beer provides nearly a tenth of the calcium and phosphorus needed daily, and about a fifth of the B vitamins, in addition to carbohydrates and several other vitamins and minerals—in effect serving as a liquid bread. In British villages and city neighborhoods, the pub is the focus for social life. It has long been the place for exchanging gossip, for the public airing and settlement of disputes, and for the reinforcement of friendships. A small village that loses its only pub loses much of what held the community together.

The alcoholic content of the beer made by the Bemba and in most other simple societies is usually less than four percent. This was probably true also of the beer made in antiquity. No one knows for certain how far back in history fermented liquors go, but Sumerian tablets dating to nearly five thousand years ago mention nineteen different kinds of beer. Although the brewing of beer could not have taken place until cereal grains had been domesticated and were being grown in quantity, intoxicating drinks must have been known long before the development of agriculture. Ways of preparing them probably were developed independently in many places, and might easily have been learned by accident.

Many of the wild fruits collected by modern hunter–gatherers have a high enough sugar content to be fermented into an intoxicating drink, and presumably that was true in the past as well. Almost any culture would thus have been able to produce its own fermented drinks out of native plants. Canadian Indians made a liquor from maple syrup, Mexicans made pulque from the agave plant, South American Indians made beer from manioc, the Chinese and Japanese made wine from rice. One food which prehistoric cave paintings show to have been much sought after—

honey—would probably have been collected and stored. Because it is nearly pure sugar, it ferments readily and probably formed the basis for intoxicating drinks in many societies. Mead, made from fermented honey and water, was considered an acceptable offering to the gods by the ancient peoples of the Mediterranean region. Wine from grapes, on the other hand, was made only in Europe for centuries after Moslems destroyed the vines of the Near East.

With the drinking of alcoholic beverages customary in so many societies throughout the world, it might be supposed that all human beings react to it in much the same way—but they do not. The Japanese, the Chinese, and the Indians of North America tend to become drunk on very little alcohol, whereas various other peoples around the world can consume enormous amounts of it without exhibiting signs of intoxication. The Japanese seem to radiate a drunken glow even before the saki has had time to reach the stomach. Anecdotal evidence ever since the pioneers has indicated that North American Indians respond to alcohol with more rapid behavioral changes than do people of European ancestry. Scientific evidence for possible genetic differences, though, is ambiguous. One study, comparing alcohol metabolism by Canadian Ojibway Indians and Canadians of European ancestry, showed significant differences between the two groups; another, comparing the Pima and Papago Indians of Arizona with whites, showed virtually no differences.

One obvious explanation for the conflicting results is that American Indians are not a single homogeneous population but consist of many groups, each with its own genetic makeup. Another complication is the difficulty of separating genetic predispositions concerned with alcohol from the matrix of social, economic, and psychological traits of the various American Indian populations. The Canadian Ojibway, for example, inhabit a cold and moist environment, have traditionally been hunter–gatherers, were nomadic, and have a history over the past several centuries intertwined with rivalries between the English and the French and with the rise and fall of the fur trade. On the other hand, the Arizona Indians inhabit a hot and dry environment, are horticulturists descended from sophisticated irrigation farmers; they are sedentary, and have a history connected with rivalries between Spain and the United States. Any of these and other variables might influence the Indians' response to alcohol. Such differences aside, genetic differences do seem to exist in the way alcohol affects various human populations. Controlled experiments comparing subjects of Asiatic ancestry (Chinese, Japanese, and Korean) with those of European ancestry have shown that Asiatics respond to alcohol with an intense flushing of the face, an increased pulse rate, and a loss of coordination more rapid than in those of European ancestry, even when the latter were consuming more alcohol per unit of body weight than the Asiatics.

Until recently the Camba Indians of eastern Bolivia, numbering about eighty thousand, probably consumed more alcohol than any other people on record. The undiluted distillate of sugar cane, containing 89 percent ethyl alcohol (making it 178 proof), which they took in such enormous quantities was probably the most potent alcoholic drink ever habitually used by any group of humans; it brings tears to the eyes of even a seasoned drinker. The Camba attributed no ill effects to it except an extreme burning sensation in the mouth and throat. Readily admitting a dislike of the taste, they profess to have enjoyed the drunkenness it produced. Camba males began drinking about the age of twelve, engaging in bouts that lasted an entire weekend. During that time a drinker generally passed out a few times, recovered, and drank himself back into a stupor.

Why did the Camba consume large quantities of a drink they disliked? The explanations usually given for alcoholism are anxiety, sexual dysfunction, and aggression—none of which is applicable to the Camba. That the Camba never got drunk alone and that a number of them usually shared a single glass make it clear that the drinking bouts had a social motivation for a people virtually without any channels for the expression of community interests. Nuclear families were geographically dispersed and independent of one another; kinship ties were tenuous; the sense of identification with the neighborhood or the church was almost completely absent. Fiestas were held nearly every weekend, and became the occasion for the intense social interaction that was otherwise lacking. These things still do not explain why the Camba drank until they passed out. Part of the answer is simply miscalculation: The high concentration of alcohol in even a single toast could easily make the difference between exhilaration and stupor. Another is that it becomes hard to refuse one more drink, lest suspicion be aroused about a man's willingness to be sociable.

The description given here of the bouts is in the past tense because the consumption of alcohol has decreased sharply since the early 1960s. About that time the Camba began enthusiastically joining *sindicatos* or "peasant leagues" aimed at land reform and a restructuring of the feudal order that had hitherto prevailed. United by social and economic ideals as they had not previously been by the Catholic Church or by any political organization, national or local, they now attended frequent meetings and demonstrations at which they referred to one another as *compañeros* ("companions"). The peasant leagues now serve as the unifying social mechanism that previously had been substituted for by heavy social drinking.

The former drinking habits of the Camba might appear unusual, but in fact those typical of North America and Europe are the exception. Even in those simpler societies characterized by the frequent consumption of large amounts of alcohol, drinking is rarely solitary, nor do the drinkers suffer withdrawal symptoms if they are deprived of alcohol. Striking differences can, of course, be seen between one Western society and another. Whenever people lift their glasses, much of what takes place has already been ordained by their culture: the kind of drink it is, the amount that will be consumed in a given unit of time, and the occasions on which the drink will be appropriate. Cultural expectations largely determine whether a drinker remains sober or passes into a stupor, behaves good-naturedly or aggressively, and whether the mood is one of guilt or good cheer. Cultural attitudes toward drinking differ markedly among the numerous ethnic groups of the United States, with those of Irish and of Scandinavian descent at one extreme, and at the other those of Jewish and of southern Italian origins, among whom alcoholism has traditionally been rare.

The causes of the differences between ethnic groups can be found in their European backgrounds. The long association of the Irish with alcohol has become a part of their social fabric. No one knows for certain when the distilled spirits originally called *aqua vitae* ("water of life") were first used in Ireland, but they were in evidence when the English invaded Ireland under King Henry II in 1171. Since spirits were then administered as a treatment for various physical and mental disorders, their taste, which most people find unpalatable at first, gradually became acceptable. By the nineteenth century, when large numbers of the Irish began to migrate to the United States, drinking had been incorporated into all social events, from the baptism to the wake. At the rousing party following a christening, the family's reputation was at stake and any stinginess in the amount or quality of the whiskey had to be avoided. Strong drink became synonymous with hospitality, and was almost never associated with the offering of food, as in virtually all other European cultures. The many religious fasts observed by the Irish throughout the year were from food and not from drink; anyone who felt hungry from fasting was permitted alcohol.

A long history of uncertain food supply and occasional severe famines has also contributed to heavy drinking in Ireland. Almost as a protective measure, the Irish developed a culture characterized by a tendency to eat irregularly, a willingness to fast, and feelings of shame about not having food good enough to offer as a form of hospitality. Alcohol, in these circumstances, provided the social and psychological satisfaction, as well as the caloric energy, that people elsewhere obtain from food. Most of the people of Ireland, far from condemning alcohol, have long considered it to be of genuine medicinal value and a protection against the chill and damp of their climate. It is thus no wonder that overconsumption of alcohol was looked upon with tolerance, and that even drunkenness was condemned only when it threatened the family's resources.

Whereas in Ireland drinking has been largely convivial rather than for ritual purposes, the situation was just the reverse among Orthodox Jews. Wine was specified as a libation in the Temple service (as in, among other places, Numbers 15:5–10 and 28:7–10), but drunkenness was depicted as shameful (as in the stories of Noah and Lot). Among the Jews, strictures were applied to drinking as well as to eating, so that, even though Jews may drink as frequently as the Irish or any ethnic group in the United States and Europe, they have an extremely low rate of alcoholism. These strictures were woven not only into everyday life, but also into the traditional Jewish rituals connected with the cycle of holy days and festivals, with rites of passage, and with the observance of the sabbath.

People in the United States who trace their ancestry to southern Italy also have a very low rate of alcoholism, even though it is somewhat higher than in Italy itself. The per capita consumption of alcohol in Italy is very large; indeed, drinking habits are nutritional habits, and wine is regarded almost as though it were a food. Italians are convinced that wine is good for adults, and in small quantities even for children, to drink along with a meal. They therefore use it as a substitute for milk, which is generally avoided because of the milk-borne epidemics that were common in the past. The drinking habits of fifteen hundred Italians were examined by the Yale University Center of Alcohol Studies; virtually none of them looked on wine as providing escape or relaxation, and only one out of the fifteen hundred expressed any real fear that drinking wine at meals might lead to alcoholism. Cultural attitudes clearly affect what, how much, when, and with whom people drink—and these cultural attitudes have been transported along with the Irish, Jews, and Italians when they migrated to other countries.

In any accounting for tastes, notice must be taken of differences in the inherited abilities of individuals to detect the tastes of foods. A chemical known as PTC (phenylthiocarbamide), for example, seems extremely bitter to certain people whereas for others it has no taste at all. Genetic studies have shown that these traits are inherited. Most American Indians are in the category of those able to taste PTC; in some groups nearly a hundred percent of the people can taste it. "Tasters" are also more numerous in many parts of Africa, in eastern Asia, and in the Near East, but very much less so in Europe and in India. (Tasters probably have more food aversions than nontasters, a trait that can be adaptive, since it prevents the consumption of possibly toxic foods.) Similarly, it appears that the tendency to taste the artificial sweetener saccharin as sweet is genetic. For many other people it tastes bitter because of two dominant genes that allow them to detect its bitter components. An experiment that determined the sensitivity of volunteers to the tastes of thirty-one different substances showed that no two volunteers had taste profiles that were very similar, except for pairs of "identical" twins—but even for them the profiles were not exactly alike. Differences of this sort are what make each human biochemically unique and could account for the food preferences peculiar to each person. But even though taste profiles might explain why one North American has different sensitivities from another's, they cannot explain why North Americans in general like hamburgers and apple pie.

Each species of animal chooses what it eats and drinks out of basic biological needs and the adaptation it has made over an immense stretch of evolutionary time. Yet the nutritional composition of one animal diet, from a biochemical standpoint, is very much the same as any other. All animals must obtain from their diet about forty or fifty substances needed by the cells to live and function. As a species evolved, it must have selected foods from what was available within its own niche that met its criteria for palatability in regard to taste, odor, texture, color, and shape. For humans, the two kinds of food that are most palatable are those having the texture and savory taste of meat, and those with the odor and the vivid colors typical of fruit. In addition to food from these two categories, neutral-tasting foods—leaves, roots, seeds, and shoots—provided the evolving humans with nutrients but did not supersede the special attractiveness of the other two. Combined, food from the three categories provided the ancestors of humans with all the protein, carbohydrates, fats, vitamins, and minerals they required. When proto-humans ate what they liked, they therefore must at the same time have been eating what they needed.

All this, though, does not explain why various groups of humans chose exactly as they did among these three categories, and among the particular kinds within each category. The differences in diet are to be explained in terms not simply of palatability or of ecology, but also of economics and cultural history. People in the United States, for example, drink coffee instead of tea as a consequence of the boycott of tea in the Colonies as an act of defiance against English rule. Not all tastes are so easily accounted for, though. Many of the tastes and distastes that prevailed during the T'ang Dynasty in China (seventh to tenth centuries A.D.) would seem strange today even to many Chinese. For example, the stomach contents of the water buffalo, roasted and served with spices, were considered a great delicacy in the southern part of the country—a preference that was adaptive because of the vitamins synthesized by bacteria in the process of fermentation. The meat of frogs, wild dogs, horned goats, and white-headed black oxen were avoided, apparently for no reason other than that the pharmacology of the time regarded these as poisonous. Other customs—such as the avoidance of any food that a dog had refused to eat—were more practical, the functional equivalent of the miner's canary.

The earliest impressions of childhood can have a strong influence on the preferences of adult life. Human infants are extremely sensitive to aromas: At the age of six weeks an infant can distinguish the breast of its mother from that of any other woman by its odor. The associations made in childhood of tastes and aromas with emotional experiences last into adult life; this fact was the point of departure for Marcel Proust, who recorded in *Remembrance of Things Past* how the taste of a madeleine cake set off a chain of recollections. Aroma can also have a cumulative effect; the more familiar it has become to a child through repeated exposure, the more pleasure it evokes. This is recognized by people in simple societies. During the ceremony following a birth among the Gadsup of New Guinea, the father's brother places food on the infant's tongue and intones: "We give you these foods from our gardens so that you will want these foods and work hard to grow them." Immediately after they are weaned, children are willing to eat almost anything that is offered to them. The familiar and the unfamiliar apparently become defined during this explorative early phase of eating. Once that phase has ended, the unfamiliar is rejected, and children develop their well-known finickiness. This is not to say that early experiences alone can account for the likes and dislikes typical of whole societies. Human children are not imprinted, as are many kinds of animals, with a permanent and irreversible attachment to certain foods. For humans, as omnivores who depend upon a changing array of foods from their environment, such imprinting would be maladaptive.

Nevertheless children become familiar from birth with certain flavors that are characteristic of their culture. The distinctive cuisines of the world are based not so much on the character of rice, maize, potatoes, bread, pasta, manioc, and other staples in themselves as on the "flavor principle"—a sensory experience produced by the mixtures of specific flavoring ingredients that are customarily added to a staple during its preparation. For example, a characteristic flavor in Mexican cooking is chili pepper and tomato; one in Chinese cooking is soy sauce and ginger root—and the same rice or chicken will taste Mexican or Chinese according to the flavors used. Some of the flavor principles to be found in the distinctive cuisines of the world are:

JAPANESE: soy sauce, saki, and sugar (sometimes also ginger root)

KOREAN: soy sauce, garlic, brown sugar, and sesame seeds

INDONESIAN: soy sauce, garlic, molasses, and peanuts

SZECHWAN: soy sauce, brandied wine, ginger root plus sugar for "sweet" dishes, vinegar for "sour," peppers for "hot"

CANTON CHINESE: soy sauce, brandied wine, ginger root, peanut oil (sometimes also sugar and garlic)

INDIAN: a basic curry mixture containing garlic, cumin, ginger, turmeric, coriander, cardamom, and pepper (plus mustard seed, saffron, cloves, coconut, or vinegar, depending upon whether the particular dish is "sweet," "sour," or "hot")

IRANIAN: yogurt with dill or mint

MIDDLE EASTERN: lemon, parsley, and garlic

GREEK: lemon and oregano (plus sometimes dill or cinnamon)

SOUTHERN ITALIAN AND SOUTHERN FRENCH: olive oil, tomato, and a mixture of herbs (thyme, basil, oregano, often with garlic)

FRENCH: butter, cream, wine, chicken or meat stock (often with the addition of cheese, herbs, and mustard)

EAST EUROPEAN JEWISH: chicken or goose fat and onions

RUSSIAN AND SCANDINAVIAN: sour cream with dill or caraway

CENTRAL AMERICAN: lime, chili peppers, and coriander (or garlic, scallion)

MEXICAN: tomato, chili peppers, and cumin

A list like this reveals something about the traditions that people in each society maintain for the enhancement of taste. Nearly everywhere, foods that are high in fats (such as pork, lamb, goose, and duck) are almost never prepared with sauces that are also high in fats (cheese, cream, eggs), but rather with a sauce based on fruit-wine or sugar, as in duck à l'orange, glazed ham, or lamb with mint sauce. On the other hand, foods that are low in fat (chicken, veal, shellfish) are often flavored with cream or butter sauces. The combination of low-fat fish with low-fat fruit is rare (except in Holland, where the combination is sauteed in oil), as is the combination of two high-fat foods (an exception being the North American ham-and-cheese sandwich). The basis for such practices in combining flavors is apparently a chemical one: The acids in fruit or wine break down the high fat content of certain meats, whereas fatty sauces enhance the flavor of bland foods such as chicken.

Although cultural influences are paramount, taste and distaste may stem from inherited predispositions. Anthropologists and nutritionists alike were long perplexed by the strong preference for milk in some societies and the strict avoidance of it in others. In the aboriginal New World, only two domesticated mammals were suitable for milking—the llama and the alpaca of the South American Andes. Apparently no attempt was made to obtain milk from either; instead, they were used for transportation or as a source of wool, and sometimes for meat. Numerous domesticated mammals of the Old World—cattle, water buffalo, yak, goats, camels, reindeer, and horses—provided milk, yet people in many societies failed to milk them; those who did often transformed the raw milk into cheese, butter, ghee, and various forms of yogurt.

It might be supposed, out of ethnocentric prejudice, that people anywhere in the world would want to drink milk if they had it. But this is far from true. North American relief agencies have sent powdered milk to the starving of the world—only to have the people of Colombia and Guatemala use it as whitewash, and the people of Indonesia take it as a laxative. The Navajo Indians simply threw it away, and so did the Kanuri of West Africa, who were convinced that it was a food of evil spirits. Throughout large areas of the Old World, a belief is ingrained not simply that milk is to be avoided, but also that it should not be taken from the animals, since to do so is to steal an essential food from nursing young. Sizable numbers of the world's population are nonmilkers, including all the Indians of the New World, along with the people of China, Japan, Korea, Burma, all the Indochinese countries, Malaysia, Indonesia, the aboriginal Australians, and others. In Africa, nonmilking peoples inhabit about a third of the continent, from the Guinea Coast and Congo River Basin on the west across East Africa to Mozambique and southward into Angola.

It used to be said that the reason for avoiding milk was simply ecological: that large areas in Africa, Asia, and elsewhere were unsuited to dairying. It is true that in many places good pasture lands are scarce, that tropical grasses are often deficient in nutrients, and that diseases are prevalent among domesticated animals in tropical environments. It is also true that dairying cannot be incorporated easily into many traditional economies. On the other hand, dairying has been successfully introduced into some such areas of Southeast Asia by migrants from India and Pakistan who are traditional users of milk products.

During the mid-1960s, scientists discovered significant differences among various populations of the world in the ability to digest lactose or milk sugar, a carbohydrate that is broken down into simple sugars by the enzyme lactase. Although the young of almost all mammals produce this enzyme at birth, around the time of weaning they gradually lose the ability to manufacture it. The same thing is true for many humans; after early childhood, drinking no more than a cup of raw milk may produce cramps, diarrhea, flatulence, and sometimes vomiting. The loss of the enzyme is obviously an evolutionary adaptation for mammals, humans included: Its absence prevents adults from competing with infants, who can digest only milk. All hunter–gatherers develop an intolerance of milk about the time of weaning, and the sharp decrease in the production of the enzyme prevails for the rest of their lives. The situation began to change just under ten thousand years ago, when domesticated animals made milk and its products available to adults as a new food source.

Studies of many milking and nonmilking cultures have revealed that a deficiency or a sufficiency of the enzyme in the population parallels the cultural acceptance or rejection of milk. Wherever milk is valued as a food, the adults are equipped to manufacture lactase, and the consumption of dairy products has a long history. This is true of northern Europe, of the pastoral regions of the Near East and Africa, and also of the Caucasus, Central Asia, Pakistan, and parts of India. Numerous individuals from lactose-intolerant populations who have migrated to areas in which milk-drinking is common (such as the Chinese now living in Australia or the United States) have gradually accustomed themselves to drinking small amounts of raw milk. They cannot, though, consume large amounts of it because of the genetic limitation upon their production of the enzyme.

When some human groups started to milk domesticated mammals, nine or ten thousand years ago, they were perhaps motivated by a desire to provide milk offerings to a mother goddess. Humans who sampled this milk themselves would have experienced the gastric distress connected with an inability to digest it. A genetic mutation in some individuals would have permitted the enzyme to be produced, enabling them to digest milk as adults. These individuals would have had an advantage in being better nourished than those who could not make use of a nutritious new food; they would have survived in greater numbers and have produced more surviving offspring, who would have inherited the same advantage. In time, according to the Darwinian theory of natural selection, the enzyme-producing individuals would have supplanted those who lacked this trait.

Calculations have shown that if adults capable of manufacturing the enzyme were able to produce only one percent more surviving offspring in a generation than those who did not, and did so over four hundred generations (approximately the number that have lived since milk-producing mammals were domesticated), the prevalence of the inability to digest milk would have declined from ninety percent to about sixteen percent of the population. This range of percentages is very close to the actual range of tolerance for milk now found throughout the populations of the world. And the theory of natural selection is supported by the correspondence of those cultures in which milk is regarded as a desirable food with low percentages of lactose-intolerant individuals. There are a number of exceptions—notably the Greeks, Arabs, and Near Eastern

Jews, among whom many individuals are intolerant of milk despite a long history of dairying. But dairying is not synonymous with drinking raw milk; in all of these societies, milk is mainly processed into cheese, yogurt, and butter, which are low in lactose. Everything that has been learned in recent years about lactose intolerance supports the conclusion that Asiatics do not avoid milk because they do not wish to deprive infant mammals of it, that Africans do not fear it because of evil spirits, and that the Chinese are not perverse in finding a thick milkshake repugnant. These attitudes were undoubtedly adopted as rationalizations to explain the already-existing intolerance of milk.

Other attitudes about food preferences that may seem contrary to reason might similarly have a biological component—such as the difficulty that certain peoples, notably in Britain and in western India, have in digesting wheat, because of an inherited sensitivity to its gluten. These areas mark the outer boundaries, west and east, of wheat culture in Eurasia, and possibly the inability to digest the cereal has a natural-selection explanation similar to that of milk. Genetics alone cannot explain tastes and distastes, but obviously it cannot be ignored. Together with ecology, cultural history, economics, and childhood experiences, it is one more contribution to the network of influences that go into explaining why various people eat what they do. All of these, plus still other variables, act together to form what is known as "cuisine"—the subject of the next chapter.

10

The Wisdom of Cuisine

HUMANS are virtually the only creatures in the world that observe rules about what is eaten, how it is prepared, and with whom it is to be eaten. The only other animals that do anything remotely approximate are the Japanese macaque monkeys, among which strong food preferences have developed, along with traditions about preparation unique to each band. For example, some bands wash potatoes in the sea, whereas others do not—a trivial distinction as compared to the complexity of the human pattern of eating. Four components make up this pattern. The first is the very limited number of foods selected from what the environment offers—usually on the basis of availability and on the yield of nutrients in proportion to the energy required to obtain them. The second component is the manner of preparation; the third is the society's traditional principle of flavoring staple foods; and the fourth consists of rules: the number of meals eaten each day, whether they are eaten alone or with others, the setting aside of foods for ceremonial use, and the observation of taboos.

These four components make up what is called a "cuisine." The meaning of the word as used here encompasses not merely the artistic presentation of food, but everything concerned with eating. Many small choices about eating, made over the centuries or indeed through the millenia, eventually produce a distinctive cuisine. This is as true of the Mexican's chili-seasoned tortillas and beans as of the enormously subtle range of French *haute cuisine*. A cuisine is basically as conservative as religion, language, or any other aspect of culture. Iranian peasants today eat essentially what their Persian ancestors ate more than six thousand years ago; the basic Mexican diet dates back to about five thousand years before the arrival of the Spanish; the combination of spices known as curry has distinguished the cooking of India for thousands of years. The reason for this conservatism is the limited number of foods regarded as being edible—a selection that is passed on through the generations as part of the accumulated wisdom of society. The flavor principle of each society tends to be identified with what is edible, whereas unfamiliar flavors are by definition associated with the ways of strangers. People of Chinese ancestry living in North America often grow vegetables from Asia, even though North American vegetables very similar in taste and texture are available. Even while braving a totally new experience as pioneers in space, the astronauts needed the security of familiar foods, and so they chose to take with them those with the tastes of beef and gravy, fried bacon, chicken, corn flakes, and fruit cakes.

The fear of new foods (neophobia) has been documented in other mammals, including primates, and undoubtedly it has been advantageous for survival: Foods previously eaten without difficulty are safe; new foods are a possible danger. Neophobia may have played a part in the rapid expansion of fast-food restaurants with extremely limited menus, to which families return with the assurance of familiarity. Stress seems to strengthen neophobia, and may be the reason why humans who are ill shy away from all but familiar foods. Notwithstanding the conservatism of all cuisines, some new foods are constantly being added to them. In Hawaii, the preferences of immigrant ethnic groups have been added to the original Polynesian cuisine of roast pig, sweet potato, and coconut: vegetable dishes from China; pickled vegetables from Korea; raw fish and seaweed from Japan; curries from India; pastries, bread, frankfurters, and steak from the mainland United States. Asparagus has recently been accepted as a food by the Chinese on Taiwan, but only after being prepared with the traditional flavoring of soy sauce, brandied wine, and ginger root.

The origin of most cuisines is lost in the unrecorded past. In China, though, both archeological evidence and written records go back thousands of years. During the period of the Shang and Chou dynasties, between about 2200 and 3800 years ago, eating became a preoccupation virtually throughout the society. Confucius, who lived during the Chou Dynasty, found nothing incompatible with being a sage in knowing the minutiae of preparing food; for many other Chinese, a knowledge of food and drink marked one as educated. Of the 4000 persons who tended the Shang royal palace, 2271, or nearly sixty percent, were concerned with various aspects of preparing and serving meals. These included the 162 master dietitians who made out the menus, the 128 chefs who cooked for the royal family plus 128 others who cooked for guests at feasts, the 335 specialists in plant foods and 70 in meat, and the 24 who had charge of preparing turtles and shellfish—not to mention, among others, 450 who prepared and served wine, 170 who served other beverages, 94 icemen, and 62 specialists in pickles and sauces.

From such statistics, the ancient Chinese would appear to have been more deeply involved with all aspects of eating than any other people in history. It was not only that the Chinese cooked an enormous number of dishes, utilized a great variety of foodstuffs, devoted much time to their preparation and consumption, and spent enormous amounts of money in the process. In addition, numerous customs, beliefs, and rituals were tied up with eating. And much of the day appears to have been spent in thinking about the meal that had just been completed and the one to be eaten next.

By the time of the Chou Dynasty, most of the foodstuffs, techniques of preparation, and utensils that would later characterize the fully developed Chinese cuisine were already in use. Under the Chou, nearly all of the twenty different methods of cooking known in China today were practiced—with the notable exception, however, of one that is now most characteristic. That method, stir-frying for a brief time over high heat, was soon to evolve as a means of conserving the supply of fuel (wood having become scarce as the forests were cut down and the cleared land produced crops for an increasing population). By using the stir-fry method, it became possible to cook small pieces of meat or vegetables in only a few moments by exposing a maximum surface area to the high heat. The small pieces of food used, together with the scarcity of tables in China, made necessary a utensil that would require the use of only one hand while the other held the bowl of food. For this, chopsticks amounted to an extension of the thumb and forefinger of one hand, allowing delicate manipulation without dirtying the fingers.

The Chinese under the Chou Dynasty had already developed other hallmarks of their cuisine: an emphasis on the mincing and flavoring of foodstuffs before they are cooked, and the use of a single staple in a variety of ways. In a land where population was increasing and where drought and other calamities periodically caused the people to go hungry, everything that was potentially edible had to be used—including rats (known euphemistically as "household deer"), snakes ("brushwood eels"), and grasshoppers ("brushwood shrimps"). The soybean typifies the diversity of ways in which a single resource might be used. The beans are first simmered and reduced to a purée, from which the "milk" is strained off. This milk is then dried to make the nutritious and easily digestible bean curd that is used in many Chinese dishes. The purée itself is put in a cool, dark place to ferment, after which it is soaked in brine for a few weeks. This liquid, after straining, becomes soy sauce; and even the residue in the strainer is used to make a thick, flavorful "cheese." In addition to curd, sauce, and cheese, the soybean yields an oil for cooking and a flour with a high protein content; or the bean can be sprouted and eaten raw.

In the thirteenth century, toward the end of the Sung Dynasty, Marco Polo traveled to China from Venice, the most cosmopolitan city in Europe, and he was enormously impressed by the Chinese cuisine. By then it had become, with minor exceptions, what it is today: a cuisine emphasizing variety of preparation, short cooking time, a mixture of small pieces, and the use of whatever resources are available. Every scrap of meat from the slaughterhouse was utilized: Soups and other dishes were made from the blood, heart, kidneys, lungs, entrails, and even the caul surrounding a newborn animal. One contemporaneous source listed 234 dishes, apparently all well known at the time, that could be made from flesh, fowl, and fish and from vegetable imitations of these. By the time of Marco Polo, three of the great regional styles known today had likewise already developed: northern (Peking), southern (Shanghai), and Szechwanese. The northern cuisine was bland, the meat used was usually lamb, and both wheat and millet went into a variety of dumplings, noodles, buns, and cakes. Southern cooking was more highly seasoned; it used pork and fish in large quantities, and its staple plant was rice. As is still true today, Szechwanese cuisine in many ways resembled the southern but was much spicier, making use of peppers and a fiery kind of pea. A fourth regional style, the Cantonese, has since been developed. It is midway between the bland dishes of Shanghai and the spicy ones of Szechwan, uses more grease than the northern, and emphasizes the blending of flavors, such as those of pork and salted fish.

During the Sung Dynasty, people looked on eating as an expressive act, which revealed not only where the diners came from and what their social position was, but even indicated their religious and moral beliefs. To travel meant not so much to see sights as to encounter different kinds of food; staying at home was almost as good because of the variety of foods available with each new season. Virtually every important event was in some way connected with eating. Worship included the ritual offering of food to dead ancestors or the gods. Eating involved such intellectual pursuits as combing ancient documents for forgotten recipes; philosophical and moral statements often used the metaphors of eating.

The earliest restaurants of which we have knowledge originated during the T'ang Dynasty (A.D. 618–907). By the time of the Sung Dynasty, which succeeded the T'ang, restaurants were providing food from every region of China; they were a place to find sociability and companionship, a drinking partner, and sex. In fact, the Sung restaurants served sex as much as they served food. Expensive restaurants lined the Imperial Way through the center of Hangchow; some of them were several stories high, with as many as 110 private dining rooms, to which one of the several hundred prostitutes associated with the restaurant could be invited. Somewhat less elegant establishments specialized in particular styles or categories of cooking, such as vegetarian dishes prepared according to Buddhist principles. There were also laborers' restaurants, which usually sold only noodle dishes or soups. Even today, the Chinese possibly eat out more than people in any other society. At least half of the inhabitants of Canton eat breakfast outside their homes; Shanghai alone has some 12,000 restaurants; in Peking, numerous restaurants are open twenty-four hours a day so that workers on night shifts can eat out.

Everything about the way the Chinese have traditionally eaten illustrates with particular clarity the major characteristics of a cuisine: the combined influences of the environment (the availability of certain foodstuffs), culture (the technology for producing and preparing food as well as the social and economic systems), and ideology (the body of beliefs about food and its place in society). In addition, a cuisine that endures must be adaptive in providing adequate nutrition. In this respect also the history of Chinese cuisine revolves around the attitude that food and health are inseparable. Good health is not simply an absence of disease; it involves the maintenance of vital energy by a harmonious balance of different foods and drinks. A proper diet will taste good, provide diversity, and be eaten in moderation. In other words, to the Chinese an elegant diet is also a healthful one.

The cuisine of the United States differs greatly from that of China simply because its history is so entirely different. For at least 20,000 years, and possibly for as long as 40,000, the ancestors of the American Indians developed a diversity of cultures based on a wide range of foods obtained from the coasts, rivers and lakes, forests, plains, and deserts. The soils in most areas were extremely fertile, and on them the native Americans grew maize, several kinds of beans, squashes, peppers, and many other plants. The European colonists took advantage of the variety of conditions the continent offered. The coastal Carolinas provided excellent conditions for the cultivation of rice, which became a staple there; sugar cane was grown in the southern states, and in New England the native maple trees were tapped for sugar. And all along the coast the colonists could harvest the abundance of the sea: fishes everywhere, turtles in the south, and in the north the many codfish that had already given their name to Cape Cod.

As soon as a group of colonists made a settlement, they planted a garden, with various kinds of squash as the mainstay, and a field of maize, with beans growing among the stalks. These native crops, grown with techniques taught the colonists by the Indians, were easy to cultivate, easy to prepare, and easy to store in dried form. The first settlers were mostly poor farmers, and if they could not make a living in one place, they found it easy to pack their few belongings and move farther west. They could not rely on wheat as a grain crop because it took too long to mature and was difficult to cultivate; but a crop of maize could be grown in only six weeks on a patch of land near the cabin, without the need for a plow and horses. Even at that time, Americans who were on the move relied on "convenience foods." Pioneers took with them a few sacks of dried maize. If it was winter, they made a bean porridge, frozen with a string run through it so it could be hung out of the way of animals; pieces could afterwards easily be broken off, thawed, and eaten. Another convenience food was johnnycake made of cornmeal, which kept for a long time without spoiling. (The name of this bread possibly began as "journey cake," from being taken along while traveling.) Many travelers also brought with them "pocket soup," an aspic made from concentrated meat soup that was the predecessor of the bouillon cube.

Swine and chickens, both of which could forage for themselves, were easily raised for meat, and were supplemented by the wild foods of the land and waters. The passenger pigeon, until the last wild one was shot in 1899, had been possibly the most abundant bird ever to have existed on the planet; in 1810 the ornithologist Alexander Wilson reported a flock a mile wide and 240 miles long. Flocks of as many as a hundred wild turkeys, each weighing up to forty pounds, abounded in the woods. Pheasants, partridges, quail, ducks, and geese were plentiful. Such wild game provided meat for the eastern cities well into the nineteenth century. Fishes of many kinds were taken in large quantities with nets and seines, but the oyster was the easiest of the foods from the sea to harvest. Lobsters were enormous: Some were caught in New York Bay measuring five feet in length.

This primeval abundance affected the emerging cuisine of North America. It established the tradition of plenty that has continued to this day and that made overeating by North Americans a problem from the first, as Benjamin Franklin observed in *Poor Richard's Almanac:* "I saw a few die of starvation but hundreds [die] of eating and drinking." Abundance made a virtue of large portions simply served. Except in the slave states, the high cost of labor and the lack of domestic servants until the middle of the nineteenth century ruled out foods that required painstaking preparation. North Americans from the beginning took pride in offering food that was as forthright and without subtlety as the pioneers who have been so extolled in literature, films, and folklore. It was simple and nutritious, its essential flavors unmasked by sauces and garnishes that might confuse the palate. The carrot is an honest root, beef an undisguised slab of meat. The ingredients are kept separate from one another—the beef, the baked potato, the peas, the head-of-lettuce salad—all in proper place, like the plain-spoken sentences so valued by North Americans. None of the delicate modulations and shadings of French cooking are to be found—and indeed, despite the early and major influence of French culture on North America, its cuisine was resisted until the present century. Democratic enthusiasm made a virtue out of simple and often tasteless food; any catering to the delights of the palate was scorned as a sign of Old World decadence. In the presidential campaign of 1840, for example, the Whigs boasted that their candidate, William Henry Harrison, lived on wholesome salted beef while his aristocratic opponent, Martin Van Buren, lived on such effete luxuries as strawberries, celery, and cauliflower. Harrison won, but his frontier diet did not prevent him from catching pneumonia at his inauguration; he died after only thirty-one days in office.

After the abundance of the continent, a second major influence on the development of North American cuisine was the diversity of cultures. The Indians contributed not only the crops that would become staples, but also ways of preparing them. They gave the colonists green beans, potatoes, onions, the sunflower, peanuts, plums, many kinds of berries, and maple syrup; they taught the colonists how to prepare succotash, hominy, and the dish that would later be known as Boston baked beans. Various European groups brought Old World recipes with them and then adapted these to what they found in North America. The British contributed, among other things, chicken pie, apple pie, and plum pudding. The French influenced the making of soups, the use of the tomato (a native plant that the colonists long ignored), fricassees, and chowders. From the Spanish came sugar cane, the oranges planted in Florida by Ponce de León, and wine-growing in California. The Spanish also introduced barbecuing, a technique they learned from Caribbean Indians; they gave to it the word *barbacoa,* which referred to the grid of sticks on which the meat was roasted.

The Dutch added crullers and cole slaw, among other items, to the cuisine; the Scotch contributed oatmeal and barley broth; the Irish brought the potato back to its native New World soil; Germans contributed various kinds of sausages, Bohemians certain cakes made from prunes and poppy seeds, Italians various pasta dishes, and East European Jews bagels and gefilte fish. Foods brought from Africa with the slaves included okra, watermelon, and grain sorghum. These contributions from immigrant groups had in common the thrifty use of various parts of plants and animals that might otherwise be thrown away—as, for example, in the scrapple invented by the Pennsylvania "Dutch" (who were really Germans, their name a corruption of *Deutsch*), containing scraps of pork shoulder and pork liver, fried together with cornmeal, onions, cloves, and herbs. The recipes of the immigrants were often further adapted by the slaves who left their imprint on many dishes.

A third major characteristic of North American cuisine has been a willingness to experiment and to borrow from other cultures. Thomas Jefferson introduced macaroni to the United States, served French-fried potatoes, used vanilla as a flavoring, and experimented with ice cream. The cosmopolitanism of North American cuisine may be seen in the constituents of a hearty American breakfast. It usually begins with fruit, such as an orange (domesticated in the Mediterranean region) or a cantaloupe (domesticated in Persia). This is followed by a bowl of cereal made from grains (domesticated in the Near East if wheat, in China if rice, and in Middle America if maize) or by pancakes or waffles (both Dutch) with butter (originally a Near Eastern cosmetic). The breakfast might also include an egg (from a bird domesticated in Southeast Asia) and bacon (from an animal domesticated in the same region, salted and smoked by a process invented in northern Europe). It also includes a hot beverage, usually coffee (from Ethiopia by way of Arabia), tea (from Southeast Asia), or chocolate (from the Spaniards, who learned how to make it from the Aztec).

Yet another major aspect of the North American cuisine is the primacy given to certain staples. Much as Japanese cuisine relies upon rice and seafood, or that of southern Africa upon grain porridge with relishes, the North American cuisine has traditionally emphasized meat and maize. Very few other societies in the world give such prominence to meat as North Americans do, and far fewer regard meat as the focus of the meal and the other dishes as peripheral. In Japan during the seventeenth century, the only meat available was from wild game. Meat was also a luxury food in China during the same period; even the mandarins were content with only a few mouthfuls of pork or chicken. The same was true of the Near East: According to one estimate, the average amount of meat consumed by one person in Istanbul was between one-third of a sheep and a whole sheep—in an entire year.

The emphasis on meat in the North American cuisine can be traced to Europe, where at the time of settlement the diet included large amounts of it. From the Middle Ages onward, European tables had been loaded with meat, because of the vast areas, except around the Mediterranean, suitable for pasturage. But as the population increased during the seventeenth century, the stock-raising that had become an integral part of agriculture there began to decline along with the lands that might provide fodder for the herds. By then, though, the carnivorous tradition was already entrenched in North America. It was bolstered by the conditions of life on the frontier, which made killing wild game for food a necessity. The frontiersman entered the North American mythology as a symbol of masculinity, the crack shot who could always put meat on the table.

In the South and West in particular, pork was eaten, until as recently as early in this century, at least once a day and sometimes at all three meals. Harriet Martineau, an English traveler who visited the United States in the 1830s, complained that she found "little else than pork, under all manner of disguises." The monotony of this diet did not cause concern; until late in the nineteenth century, all foods were thought to have the same nutritional value—to be, according to the prevailing conception, part of the same "universal aliment" that kept the body in good repair and that differed only in taste, texture, and the quantities that could be digested at a single meal. The pig was the ideal meat animal for the colonists; it needed little care, foraged for itself in the woods and forests, and prospered on the surplus maize that was grown. When butchered, it provided a large number of dishes. Choice cuts of meat were smoked and pickled; the ribs were roasted or cured into bacon; the liver, tongue, and brain were often eaten fresh; what might otherwise have been wasted parts were made into sausage and headcheese; excess fat was rendered into lard; even the large intestine was used to make chitterlings.

Equaling the pig in the variety of uses to which it could be put is maize, the plant staple of United States cuisine. Like the pig, it is adaptable, and grows in all the contiguous states and northward into Canada. It could be roasted fresh in the shuck; after drying, it could be ground into meal to make porridge, griddle cakes, waffles, and a great variety of breads. Cornbread in its simplest form is a baked cake or "pone" made from meal, salt, and water. Variations on this basic recipe included the addition of milk, shortening, or eggs to make corn dodgers, hoe-cakes, corn muffins, and egg bread. Maize was also converted into hominy, made by soaking the kernels to remove the outer layer, after which they are boiled and eaten as a vegetable, or dried and ground into a coarse meal to make the thick porridge known as grits.

Much of what has been said here about North American cuisine has had to be in the past tense because of radical changes in recent decades. Agribusiness now spends billions of dollars speeding up the production and processing of food, developing new chemical additives to give it a character the original produce never had (plus preservatives so that after weeks or months on the grocery shelf it can still turn a profit) and packaging and advertising it—in short, exerting almost total control over what North Americans eat. It has had to be written in the past tense also because the cuisine that has emerged out of the bounty of a continent must now cope with deficiencies. Increasing numbers of the elderly, the poor, and the uneducated are undernourished, while even those belonging to the educated middle class sometimes eat so unwisely that they are malnourished. To the characteristics of North American eating must now increasingly be added inadequate nutrition.

Every cuisine is based to some extent on staple foods that are available in abundance. The cuisine of southern China would be unimaginable without bland rice to soak up the flavors, as would an American supermarket without foods derived from maize or a European diet without bread. Such staples almost always are the primary source of calories, and their production occupies a major part of the time allotted to providing food. They almost always are interwoven into religion, mythology, and history. The foods most extolled are those that also represent psychological security. When Hawaii was threatened with a shipping strike some years ago, people of Chinese and Japanese ancestry hoarded rice in preference to any other kind of food. For mainland North Americans, the equivalent is milk; troops returning home after World War II often asked for fresh milk as soon as they disembarked.

North American and Middle American Indians made the maize–beans–squash triad the cornerstone of their cuisine, yet they might have fastened upon numerous other plants that could easily have been domesticated (and indeed, some were). Fossil remains of the maize that was domesticated in Mexico seven thousand years ago show that the wild plant was no more conspicuous than many kinds of weeds growing today along roadsides; its ear was no larger than the filter tip on a cigarette, certainly too small to excite much interest as a source of food. Beans and squash in the wild state would similarly have been useful to the ancestors of American Indians only when little else was available. The flesh of wild squash is bitter and dry; wild beans are thick-skinned and bland. The wild forms of all three are today used in Mexico only as starvation foods. Why, then, were these particular ones selected?

Maize, beans, and squash offered certain advantages

that the ancestors of the Indians must have recognized: They were easily stored, they were tolerant of habitats disturbed by humans, and they responded readily to efforts to increase their yield through cultivation and artificial selection. In other words, the three were not so much desirable foods in themselves as they were plants that lent themselves to domestication, permitting an increased yield while not increasing very much the energy expended to grow them. This was particularly true for maize, which spread from Mexico (and possibly also from an independent place of domestication in Peru) throughout the tropical and temperate regions of the Americas—and later, of course, throughout the world. In the course of domestication, maize underwent a greater change than any other of the world's major crops, and it also made a wider adaptation to geographical conditions. Maize is today so thoroughly domesticated that it cannot reproduce without human help in scattering its seeds, owing to the tough rachises that hold the kernels to the ear.

Descendants of the wild ancestors of maize still grow abundantly as weeds on soils that have been disturbed. Hunter–gatherers returning to a campsite they had cleared the previous year would probably have found clumps of them flourishing. If so, no conscious act of domestication would have been needed at first. The cultivation of beans and squash must also have begun around the same time, as excavations in Mexico indicate; wild beans and wild squash grow in disturbed soils of the same sort as wild maize, with the beans even twining around the stalks for support. In focusing their attention on maize, beans, and squash, the domesticators thus merely had to copy a natural model. Both in their habits of growth and in the nutrition they offer, the three plants complement one another. Beans, like other legumes, enrich the soil for the maize and squash by means of nitrogen-fixing bacteria that are supported by their roots; the spreading leaves of squash plants shade the soil against loss of moisture and suppress the growth of weeds. Maize is deficient in the amino acid lysine, without which the human body cannot utilize the plant's protein, whereas beans have a high lysine content. Thus the two foods eaten together provide a much more nutritious diet than either one alone.

Hunter–gatherers, even though they do not plant, also have their abundant, reliable, and nutritious staples. The wild mongongo nuts gathered by the San are as reliable as any cultivated crop, and an abundant supply is produced year after year. The San consume millions of mongongo nuts during at least eight months out of the twelve; even so, the nuts are so abundant that millions more are left on the ground to rot. Their nutritional value surpasses that of most cultivated staples. As compared even to the nutritious peanut, mongongo nuts contain considerably more protein, about three times as much calcium, double the potassium, and almost exactly the same amount of iron, along with large amounts of vitamins and minerals. Although the diet of the San includes about eighty-five species of plants, the mongongo alone provides, on the average, about forty percent of their daily energy requirements.

Plants, being unable to flee from the animals that seek to devour them, have been under continuous evolutionary pressure to develop protective toxins. Humans have nevertheless been ingenious enough to overcome these defenses and convert a number of toxic foods to their own use. A white potato of average size contains ninety parts per million of the poison solanine—a concentration that can increase rapidly if it is exposed to the sun after being dug. Eating only four or five of them could produce symptoms of poisoning. Among other common foods, spinach and rhubarb contain significant quantities of the toxin oxalate, which lowers the concentration of calcium in the body and consequently causes acute nephritis, nervous disorders, and a reduction in the ability of the blood to coagulate. Dogs, horses, and cattle allowed to feed freely on onions have developed symptoms of anemia within a week. No society is known in which it is customary to eat onions, spinach, or rhubarb in quantities large enough to produce poisoning. The same thing was true also of the white potato under aboriginal conditions in South America; it was after potatoes became a staple food in several parts of the world, notably in Ireland, that they began to be consumed in large quantities, and cases of poisoning began to be reported in the medical literature.

A still more toxic plant is manioc or cassava, the root crop that is eaten by perhaps 250 million people, primarily in South America and West Africa. The importance of manioc as a staple is easy to understand. It yields more calories per unit of land than any cereal grain, requires less labor, and can grow in a greater variety of soils, including those that have been depleted of nutrients. Mature tubers can be left in the ground for as long as two years before they spoil, thus becoming a reserve against hunger. Manioc frees tropical people from agricultural labor and allows them to devote more of their energy to obtaining protein. Until it is processed, though, manioc is toxic because of its large content of cyanide, and this must be removed by a complicated series of steps that involve peeling, grating, crushing, and rinsing. Once the cyanide has been removed, virtually all of the plant is utilized: The leaves are fermented with peppers to make a relish that is rich in vitamins; the flour is used for bread and cakes; manioc starch goes into the bland pudding known as tapioca; the stock is used in soups; and the tuber is used to make beer.

Since the process of making manioc and other toxic plants edible is so difficult, the question naturally arises: How did humans ever determine in the first place which plants were safe to eat? A partial answer comes from the Tonga of Zimbabwe who were resettled by the Rhodesian government for political reasons. Their experience with strange foods in a new environment was probably similar to what happened through the centuries in the region from which they had been forced to move. People already inhabiting the new location represented an important source of information about which of the unfamiliar plants might be eaten safely and about ways in which the toxins might be removed from others. The information was not always reliable, though, because a number of deaths from poisoning occurred almost immediately; the Tonga in the future avoided these and also several shrubs whose fruit caused stomach upsets. They further tested the safety of new foods by allowing their dogs to eat them first. By such methods, the Tonga eventually developed a repertory of new foods and processes for preparing them. Much the same thing must have occurred in the past.

Among the important societal rules that represent one component of cuisine are table manners. As a socially instilled form of conduct, they reveal the attitudes typical of a society. Changes in table manners through time, as they have been documented for western Europe, likewise reflect fundamental changes in human relationships. Medieval courtiers saw their table manners as distinguishing them from crude peasants; but by modern standards, the manners were not exactly refined. Feudal lords used their unwashed hands to scoop food from a common bowl and they passed around a single goblet from which all drank. A finger or two would be extended while eating, so as to be kept free of grease and thus available for the next course, or for dipping into spices and condiments—possibly accounting for today's "polite" custom of extending the little finger while holding a spoon or small fork. Soups and sauces were commonly drunk by lifting the bowl to the mouth; several diners frequently ate from the same bread trencher. Even lords and nobles would toss gnawed bones back into the common dish, wolf down their food, spit onto the table (preferred conduct called for spitting under it), and blew their noses into the tablecloth.

By about the beginning of the sixteenth century, table manners began to move in the direction of today's standards. The importance attached to them is indicated by the phenomenal success of a treatise, *On Civility in Children,* by the philosopher Erasmus, which appeared in 1530; reprinted more than thirty times in the next six years, it also appeared in numerous translations. Erasmus' idea of good table manners was far from modern, but it did represent an advance. He believed, for example, that an upper-class diner was distinguished by putting only three fingers of one hand into the bowl, instead of the entire hand in the manner of the lower class. Wait a few moments after being seated before you dip into it, he advises. Do not poke around in your dish, but take the first piece you touch. Do not put chewed food from the mouth back on your plate; instead, throw it under the table or behind your chair.

By the time of Erasmus, the changing table manners reveal a fundamental shift in society. People no longer ate from the same dish or drank from the same goblet, but were divided from one another by a new wall of constraint. Once the spontaneous, direct, and informal manners of the Middle Ages had been repressed, people began to feel shame. Defecation and urination were now regarded as private activities; handkerchiefs came into use for blowing the nose; nightclothes were now worn, and bedrooms were set apart as private areas. Before the sixteenth century, even nobles ate in their vast kitchens; only then did a special room designated for eating come into use away from the bloody sides of meat, the animals about to be slaughtered, and the bustling servants. These new inhibitions became the essence of "civilized" behavior, distinguishing adults from children, the upper classes from the lower, and Europeans from the "savages" then being discovered around the world. Restraint in eating habits became more marked in the centuries that followed. By about 1800, napkins were in common use, and before long they were placed on the thighs rather than wrapped around the neck; coffee and tea were no longer slurped out of the saucer; bread was genteelly broken into small pieces with the fingers rather than cut into large chunks with a knife.

Numerous paintings that depict meals—with subjects such as the Last Supper, the wedding at Cana, or Herod's feast—show what dining tables looked like before the seventeenth century. Forks were not depicted until about 1600 (when Jacopo Bassano painted one in a Last Supper), and very few spoons were shown. At least one knife is always depicted—an especially large one when it is the only one available for all the guests—but small individual knives were often at each place. Tin disks or oval pieces of wood had already replaced the bread trenchers. This change in eating utensils typified the new table manners in Europe. (In many other parts of the world, no utensils at all were used. In the Near East, for example, it was traditional to bring food to the mouth with the fingers of the right hand, the left being unacceptable because it was reserved for wiping the buttocks.) Utensils were employed in part because of a change in the attitude toward meat. During the Middle Ages, whole sides of meat, or even an entire dead animal, had been brought to the table and then carved in view of the diners. Beginning in the seventeenth century, at first in France but later elsewhere, the practice began to go out of fashion. One reason was that the family was ceasing to be a production unit that did its own slaughtering; as that function was transferred to specialists outside the home, the family became essentially a consumption unit. In addition, the size of the family was decreasing, and consequently whole animals, or even large parts of them, were uneconomical. The cuisines of Europe reflected these social and economic changes. The animal origin of meat dishes was concealed by the arts of preparation. Meat itself became distasteful to look upon, and carving was moved out of sight to the kitchen. Comparable changes had already taken place in Chinese cuisine, with meat being cut up beforehand, unobserved by the diners. England was an exception to the change in Europe, and in its former colonies—the United States, Canada, Australia, and South Africa—the custom has persisted of bringing a joint of meat to the table to be carved.

Once carving was no longer considered a necessary skill among the well-bred, changes inevitably took place in the use of the knife, unquestionably the earliest utensil used for manipulating food. (In fact, the earliest English cookbooks were not so much guides to recipes as guides to carving meat.) The attitude of diners toward the knife, going back to the Middle Ages and the Renaissance, had always been ambivalent. The knife served as a utensil, but it offered a potential threat because it was also a weapon. Thus taboos were increasingly placed upon its use: It was to be held by the point with the blunt handle presented; it was not to be placed anywhere near the face; and most important, the uses to which it was put were sharply restricted. It was not to be used for cutting soft foods such as boiled eggs or fish, or round ones such as potatoes, or to be lifted from the table for courses that did not need it. In short, good table manners in Europe gradually removed the threatening aspect of the knife from social occasions. A similar change had taken place much earlier in China when the warrior was supplanted by the scholar as a cultural model. The knife was banished completely from the table in favor of chopsticks, which is why the Chinese came to regard Europeans as barbarians at their table who "eat with swords."

The fork in particular enabled Europeans to separate themselves from the eating process, even avoiding manual contact with their food. When the fork first appeared in Europe, toward the end of the Middle Ages, it was used solely as an instrument for lifting chunks from the common bowl. Beginning in the sixteenth century, the fork was increasingly used by members of the upper classes—first in Italy, then in France, and finally in Germany and England. By then, social relations in western Europe had so changed that a utensil was needed to spare diners from the "uncivilized" and distasteful necessity of picking up food and putting it into the mouth with the fingers. The addition of the fork to the table was once said to be for reasons of hygiene, but this cannot be true. By the sixteenth century people were no longer eating from a common bowl but from their own plates, and since they also washed their hands before meals, their fingers were now every bit as hygienic as a fork would have been. Nor can the reason for the adoption of the fork be connected with the wish not to soil the long ruff that was worn on the sleeve at the time, since the fork was also adopted in various countries where ruffs were not then in fashion.

Along with the appearance of the fork, all table utensils began to change and proliferate from the sixteenth century onward. Soup was no longer eaten directly from the dish, but each diner used an individual spoon for that purpose. When a diner wanted a second helping from the serving dish, a ladle or a fresh spoon was used. More and more special utensils were developed for each kind of food: soup spoons, oyster forks, salad forks, two-tined fondue forks, blunt butter knives, special utensils for various desserts and kinds of fruit, each one differently shaped, of a different size, with differently numbered prongs and with blunt or serrated edges. The present European pattern eventually emerged, in which each person is provided with a table setting of as many as a dozen utensils at a full-course meal. With that, the separation of the human body from the taking of food became virtually complete. Good table manners dictated that even the cobs of maize were to be held by prongs inserted in each end, and the bones of lamb chops covered by ruffled paper pantalettes. Only under special conditions—as when Western people consciously imitate an earlier stage in culture at a picnic, fish fry, cookout, or campfire—do they still tear food apart with their fingers and their teeth, in a nostalgic reenactment of eating behaviors long vanished.

Today's neighborhood barbecue recreates a world of sharing and hospitality that becomes rarer each year. We regard as a curiosity the behavior of hunters in exotic regions. But every year millions of North Americans take to the woods and lakes to kill a wide variety of animals—with a difference, of course: What hunters do for survival we do for sport (and also for proof of masculinity, for male bonding, and for various psychological rewards). Like hunters, too, we stuff ourselves almost whenever food is available. Nibbling on a roasted ear of maize gives us, in addition to nutrients, the satisfaction of participating in culturally simpler ways. A festive meal, however, is still thought of in Victorian terms, with the dominant male officiating over the roast, the dominant female apportioning vegetables, the extended family gathered around the table, with everything in its proper place—a revered picture, as indeed it was so painted by Norman Rockwell, yet one that becomes less accurate with each year that passes.

Epilogue

Hunger in the
Social and
Human Body

THE THESIS of this book has been that to know what, where, how, when, and with whom people eat is to know the character of their society. The validity of such a thesis would be tested by what occurred in the absence of eating—the most extreme examples of which are the famines that have struck on all continents throughout recorded history. Over the past two thousand years, famines are believed to have occurred every two or three years, on an average, in western Europe, about as frequently in Africa, and nearly every year in China. Starvation affects every system in the human body: It produces diarrhea and other disturbances of the digestive tract; hypertension and eventual collapse of the circulatory system; a sharp decrease in the intake of oxygen by the respiratory system; a decrease in strength and control over limb movements governed by the neuromuscular system; and increasing vulnerability to changes in temperature as the thermoregulatory system fails. The disruption of the biological system is such that it seems hardly possible for the body to survive without food for any length of time. Yet in 1920 Terence MacSwiney, the mayor of

Cork, Ireland, began a hunger strike against the British, during which he swallowed nothing but water, and lived for seventy-four days. The explanation of his survival is that during starvation fewer and fewer of the nutrients in the body are eliminated in the form of waste. It is for the same reason that people trying to lose weight find the first pounds easier to shed than later ones. If the weight is reduced by twenty percent, for example, the body can still function on a diet providing only half the calories needed to maintain the original weight.

The biological body responds to the stress of a shortage of food in ways that allow it to remain alive for a time—but what of stress on the social body? The narratives of explorers, reports of relief workers, and wartime documents all attest to the disruption of the social fabric when seeking food becomes the primary activity. After hurricanes struck the South Pacific island of Tikopia, in 1952 and again in 1953, two anthropologists who had known the society in normal times made a study of the famine that ensued. From their documentation of the ever-worsening states—biological, behavioral, and social—caused by starvation, together with reports of other famines, it is possible to identify three stages of response to the shortage of food: alarm, resistance, and finally exhaustion.

At the onset of famine, contrary to what might be supposed, people are not lethargic; rather, they intensify their activities. The search for food brings people together, particularly with their own kin. The Tikopians responded to the damage of the first hurricane by increased cooperation, with families pooling their food resources ("linking ovens," they called it). At the same time, political unrest developed. Some of the hungry people of Tikopia blamed an aged chief, declaring that the hurricane had been unleashed by a deity whom the chief's weakness had offended. The chiefs, on the other hand, argued that the laziness and dishonesty of their subjects had brought on the famine.

During the second stage, that of resistance, the immediate threat of starvation becomes the focus of everyone's attention. People turn away from social cooperation to providing for their own immediate families. Taboos are generally ignored, because almost everything potentially edible is sought. During the siege of Paris by German forces in 1870, for example, the dinner menus listed brochette of dog liver, roast leg of dog, saddle of cat, horse broth with millet, ragout of rat, and plum pudding made from horse marrow. On Tikopia, people began hoarding food, and riots occurred whenever the leaders attempted to distribute supplies from storehouses. The traditional food gifts to chiefs ceased, as did the custom of holding feasts in honor of visitors. Anyone who arrived was now greeted with the statement that the dwelling was without food, whether or not this was literally true. Visiting quickly became suspect as merely a subterfuge for getting food.

Competition and aggression increased: Even brothers set up boundaries between their garden plots. Neighbors accused one another of moving boundary markers at night, and theft from gardens and storehouses became so common that many people gave up working the land altogether. Eventually nearly everyone was stealing and nearly everyone was being robbed. Almost the only people who did not steal were the chiefs, who of course had more land and more stored food to support themselves than the rest. Ritual observances were suspended, since any kind of ceremony on Tikopia, no matter how minor, involves the exchange of foodstuffs. As the desperation grew, the family itself ceased to function as a food-sharing unit. The death rate increased fourfold, and was greatest among those least able to obtain food for themselves, the very old and the very young.

As the final stage, that of exhaustion, is reached, social interactions all but cease to occur. Members of the same household now compete with one another for food. People sit silently at home. Social, political, and religious institutions no longer function; whatever energy remains is taken up with satisfying one's own hunger. In Ireland during the Great Hunger of 1845–49, in Russia following the Bolshevik Revolution, in Europe during the many peasant famines, and year after year in China, the picture was the same. On Tikopia, relatives stole from one another, as well as from the orchards and gardens of the chiefs. Most people stopped going to funerals, even those of close kin, because the shame of being absent was less than the shame of arriving without the traditional gifts of food. When, after one death, none of the deceased's kin had food to spare and so not one of them came, the ritual of burial had to be performed by strangers.

Even so, the social fabric of Tikopia did not disintegrate entirely. Mourning for the dead did continue through the worst of the famine, and token amounts of food were exchanged among close relatives. There was no gouging, no selling of food to the highest bidder. The most hallowed food taboos, those against eating bats and certain birds, were still observed. Cannibalism seems never to have been a serious possibility. Although obligations to chiefs and to ritual were frequently ignored, no one denied the existence of such obligations. Since the values of their society had been maintained, it was possible for the Tikopians to return to normal once food was again available. The way in which at least the skeletal structure of their cultural system was preserved, despite the extreme stress of famine, is a tribute to human adaptability, the product of millions of years of evolution—as well as evidence of the intimate linkage of food with culture and society.

Emergency shipments of food across great stretches of ocean eventually saved many of the people of Tikopia from dying of starvation before they could plant new gardens. Other people all over the world, though, have not been so fortunate, and the situation is expected to worsen. At the contrary extreme, the people of North America, Europe, and Japan today face the problems with overeating and the quality of what is eaten. ... than seventy percent of the deaths in the United ... es each year are caused by illnesses such as high blood pressure, stroke, coronary disease, adult diabetes, and colitis, which are linked in one way or another with bad eating habits. If these causes of death were eliminated, the average life expectancy for an infant would increase by eighteen years—as compared to the mere two years that would be added by the elimination of all deaths from cancer.

Statistics on changes of diet in the United States during this century present the spectacle of poor nutrition in the midst of abundance. Although the per capita consumption of calories is now actually lower than it was early in the century—a beneficial change in itself—there has been, deplorably, an increase by about twenty-five percent in the proportion of calories derived from fat. Most of the carbohydrates consumed in the United States once came from complex starches (whole grains, vegetables, and fruits), but they now come from refined sugar (primarily in soft drinks, but also in virtually every kind of prepared food, from baby foods to breakfast cereals, some of which contain more sugar per ounce than a candy bar). Nowadays fewer calories than ever before are obtained from unprocessed meat, fresh fruit, and fresh vegetables, and more from processed, frozen, and canned products. Despite America's boast of a healthful and varied diet, increasing numbers of people subsist almost entirely on prepared foods—sugary snacks, a TV dinner, or something out of a can. Today variety often consists of deciding on one of a dozen brands of breakfast cereals, all nutritionally very much the same, from a supermarket shelf.

As more sugars and fats, and more foods in processed form, are consumed, the quantity of vitamins and minerals available grows less. A diet high in fat and refined carbohydrates, combined with sedentary habits, also has meant a marked rise in obesity, a disease that is rare in people living in simpler cultures. Fully a third of North Americans are significantly overweight. Scientists disagree about the reasons for obesity. Some assert that certain individuals are genetically programmed to be obese, others that obesity is the result of a learned behavior: the indulgence in eating for social, cultural, or psychological purposes rather than purely for nutritional ones. Both causes are probably involved. A very small number of people are, of course, subject to glandular and metabolic disorders that make them store fat no matter how little they eat. Heredity may indeed be part of the reason why overweight parents tend to have overweight children, but a more likely explanation is behavioral—as is borne out by the fact that adopted children and pets in the households of fat people also tend to be fat.

A predisposition toward putting on fat might have been an evolutionary tendency whose ill effects were manifested only after agricultural technology made possible an abundant supply of food. Throughout almost all of human evolution, the availability of food, and particularly of meat with its high caloric content, must have been unreliable. Under such conditions, a selective advantage would have been attained by those people who ate whenever they could obtain food, whether or not they needed it. They did little harm to themselves in this way because such bonanzas occurred at irregular intervals; any weight they put on would have been lost during a subsequent period of scarcity. A continual overabundance of food became available for the privileged classes under the agricultural adaptation, and for much of the population under modernization. In these circumstances, obesity was made to appear culturally desirable—the plump and presumably healthy baby, the expansive girth of the plutocrat. But parents who stuffed their infants like steers or geese penned for fattening were condemning them to an obese adulthood. Obese children have more and larger fat cells than do children of normal weight. If such a child later loses weight, the size of the fat cells will decrease but not their number, leaving open the prospect of becoming obese again as an adult.

The plethora of fast-food restaurants such as McDonald's typify the recent change in eating habits. That they are antiseptic, depersonalized, a gastronomic atrocity, as critics have complained, is basically true. What is not true is the assertion that the food served there consists only of empty calories, and fails to provide adequate nutrition. A single hamburger at a fast-food restaurant typically supplies between one-third and three quarters of the Recommended Dietary Allowance of protein for an adult woman. It also provides at least a quarter of the RDA of thiamine, riboflavin, niacin, B_{12}, phosphorus, zinc, and iron. Furthermore, the amount of sugar is quite low (in fact, it is almost nonexistent if the sauces are left off). The fat content, though, is high, and so is the content of sodium.

The growth of fast-food restaurants has been phenomenal. By 1979 there were about 140,000 of them in the United States, and they had come close to supplanting traditional eating habits in many places. Attempts to explain this rapid development have centered on such things as accessibility, quick service, and relief from having to cook at home; on reliability, knowing that a Big Mac will be the same whether it is ordered in London, England, or New London, Connecticut; and on the considerably lower cost of eating there than in a conventional restaurant. Some critics have declared that the fast-food restaurants have caused changes in eating habits, but it seems more likely that they simply reflect the fundamental changes that have taken place in society as a whole. Traditional social rituals have declined, and the new rituals that are replacing them—rituals based on automobiles, television, technology, and efficiency—cut across previous religious affiliations, ethnic loyalties, and class allegiances.

A meal at McDonald's can be looked upon as having

some of the character of a social or religious ritual. Rituals occur in designated places, marked by distinctive emblems such as the cross above a church, and at prescribed times, such as the sabbath. For a patron of McDonald's, the eating rituals occur under the Sign of the Double Golden Arch and at the prescribed times of breakfast, lunch, and dinner. Ritual is also characterized by words and actions that have been prescribed by people other than the current performers of the ritual and that have been codified in some revered text, such as the Pledge of Allegiance or the Bible. The employees of McDonald's who take the orders and deliver the burgers, fries, and shakes display a behavioral uniformity that is prescribed by the originators of McDonald's and codified in the 360 pages of its standardized *Operations Manual*. Those responsible for carrying out the ritual have been trained at the McDonald's analogue of a seminary, known as Hamburger University, in Elk Grove, Illinois.

Ritual is also repetitive and stereotyped, of limited range, adhering to a largely invariable sequence. Day after day, year after year, burgers are sold at McDonald's with virtually the same catechism of requests and replies: "I'll have a Big Mac." "Will there be any fries with that?" "Thank you, have a nice day." The transactions at McDonald's express values esteemed by the modern North American society: technological efficiency, cleanliness, service, and egalitarianism. At a McDonald's, people find exactly what they have come to expect. They know the liturgy, and what pecuniary dues they will have to pay; they have found the comfort, the security, and the reassurance there will be no surprises that are among the benefits of any ritual.

As additives and adulterants are put in and nutrients are taken out, bread, rice, and potatoes become smoother and whiter, and canned fruits and vegetables become softer. Refining processes remove, among other things, fiber, whose lack is associated with certain chronic diseases of the digestive tract, cancer of the colon, and diverticulitis. Storage, freezing, and rapid transportation have made a greater variety of foods available throughout the year, but at a cost. Processing, by its very nature, must cause some loss of nutrients. For example, the first step in the preservation of vegetables by canning, freezing, or dehydration is blanching by immersion in hot water or steam, a process that in itself can destroy from ten to fifty percent of such water-soluble nutrients as thiamine and vitamin C as were originally present. Poultry that has been precooked and then frozen may lose forty percent of the thiamine it once contained. The heat used to process the grain in packaged breakfast cereals has a detrimental effect on protein, and in particular on the amount of lysine, which is low to start with. Evaporating milk destroys protein, enzymes, and certain vitamins (as much as sixty percent of the content of vitamin B_6).

Wheat has been milled, at least to some extent, for thousands of years, as is plain from the reference to "fine flour" in Leviticus (5:11). But with the invention of new kinds of equipment in the 1870s, millers were able for the first time to produce a white flour entirely devoid of the germ—thus removing the most nutritious part, which now goes into fodder for barnyard animals. Most of the vitamins and minerals found in wheat are contained in the germ, which supplies nutrients for the initial growth of a new plant. Modern white bread, as compared to wholemeal bread, is poorer in vitamin B_6 by about seventy percent, in pantothenic acid by fifty-eight percent, in folic acid by forty-seven percent, in potassium by sixty percent; and there are comparable losses of other vitamins and minerals. The only increases as a result of chemical additives ("enrichment") are in calcium, which is beneficial, and in sodium, which can be deleterious to health. (A detailed comparison of the nutritional values in wholemeal and white bread is given in the Reference Notes on pages 302–03.)

For thousands of years white bread and white rice have been regarded as high-status foods. The development of this apparently maladaptive preference came about because of the problem of spoilage. If flour is not milled, it cannot be stored for very long before the large amounts of fat in the whole grain become rancid, especially in the hot climates where wheat and rice are staples. (Rapid spoilage of the fatty part of the grain is the reason why a jar of wheat germ must be kept in the refrigerator.) The removal of the fat through milling therefore allows grains, which are harvested only at certain times of the year, to be stored between harvests. In other words, the loss of a great number of nutrients through milling is a price that is paid to avoid losing all nutrients. The eating of white bread did not become maladaptive until recent centuries. Up until then, people who could afford this luxury food presumably obtained the nutrients lost to milling from a variety of other foods. Only when the refinements of technology began to produce in quantity a white bread that is at once inexpensive and lacking in even the nutrients it once contained, did it begin to be accountable for dietary deficiencies.

No less distressing than what is taken out are the hazards to health as a result of what is now put into foods. As many as 2500 adulterants are regularly added to food as coloring agents, synthetic flavors, preservatives, thickeners, or thinners, and to prevent separation of the ingredients, as well as to replace lost nutrients. Some of the latter are advantageous. Iodine, added to common table salt, prevents goiter. Artificial sweeteners and such low-cholesterol items as margarine and egg substitutes entail some risks, but do lessen the dangers from obesity, diabetes, and various coronary disorders. But in too many instances the adulterants do no more than make food commercially appealing.

Adulterants include not only artificial substances, but natural ones as well: sugar and other sweeteners, salt, nitrites, caffeine, and natural colors. Among natural sweeteners, honey, a favorite of natural-food enthusiasts, sometimes contains cancer-causing substances that were present in the pollen of plants. The harmful effects of sugar, by far the leading food additive in the United States, have already been mentioned. Salt, the second most common additive, is even more dangerous to health. It is a major cause of high blood pressure (hypertension), which afflicts about twenty-five million people in the United States, and leads to kidney failure, stroke, and heart disease. Studies of the surviving hunter–gatherers show that they eat no salt except what occurs naturally in their food; they apparently never develop high blood pressure, even in old age.

Until modern times, salt was a desirable commodity, to be bartered or even fought over, because of its usefulness in preserving meat and fish for periods of need. The ancient Greeks spoke of desirable slaves as being "worth their weight in salt," and the English word "salary" is derived from *sal*, Latin for salt. Today salt so pervades the diet that each North American, on the average, consumes nearly five teaspoonfuls of it a day—even though the human body needs no more than a quarter of a teaspoon to provide the necessary sodium. Most people are aware of the high salt content of such things as anchovies and olives, but large amounts are also hidden in a wide variety of foods not usually considered salty: breakfast cereals, bread, puddings, pancake mixes, bouillon cubes, tomato juice, and virtually all canned soups and vegetables. An average portion of peas from the garden, for example, contains only two milligrams of sodium; canned peas have more than a hundred times that amount. The excessive intake of salt has become maladaptive because it interferes with the mineral balance of a human body that evolved in a world where sodium was scarce but where potassium, a common ingredient of fresh fruits and vegetables, was abundant. In the modern diet the situation is reversed. The available amount of potassium, which is needed for proper contraction of the muscles, including those of the heart, now tends to be scant in relation to the increased sodium in the diet. An imbalance of the two minerals causes an accumulation of water, bringing increases in blood volume, blood pressure, and heart rate. The processing of foods worsens this situation because it both increases the amount of sodium and decreases the amount of potassium.

Nitrites constitute another natural additive that is used in quantities far beyond what the human body can cope with. The primary use of nitrites today is to preserve frankfurters, bacon, ham, and other cured meats, and to impart the red color that consumers tend to equate with freshness. The penalty exacted for these uses, though, is a high one, because nitrites are carcinogenic. Many components of a normal and varied diet (such as lettuce, spinach, beets, carrots, and celery) contain nitrates, which are converted into nitrites by the action of bacteria in the digestive tract—but in quantities that are quite small as compared to the amounts used to cure meats. There is also some evidence that the vitamin C in these vegetables may block the conversion of the nitrates into cancer-causing substances.

Coloring agents are added to food simply to improve its marketability, not to provide any benefits as either a preservative or a nutrient. Since the color of fruit often fades quickly after picking, food processors add vivid colors to simulate freshness and wholesomeness. The dyes used by the food industry were formerly extracted from natural sources; but since these have the drawback of fading in the sun and tending to rub off the foods they are supposed to color, chemists have synthesized more stable dyes for the purpose. Virtually all of the ones used in recent years either are carcinogenic in themselves or else break down to form carcinogenic substances. The risks might be justified if the dyes provided benefits to the consumer, as nitrates do in protecting sausages against botulism along with the cosmetic benefit of adding color. But no such benefit accrues from adding dye to make grape juice look purple.

In addition to these adulterants, antibiotics are routinely fed to animals raised for their meat, so as to accelerate growth and improve their chances of surviving the crowded and unhygienic conditions of their pens. A total of nearly three million pounds of antibiotics are fed to livestock and poultry in the United States every year. Some of this quantity is excreted by the animals, some is metabolized—but some is simply deposited in animal tissues that are later consumed by the humans who eat the meat. Physicians usually exercise caution in prescribing antibiotics to their patients, since microorganisms tend to develop resistance to them, but they have no way to prevent the ingestion of constant doses from eating meat. In the 1970s about ninety percent of the cattle slaughtered in the United States were raised on feed containing a carcinogenic hormone, diethylstilbestrol (DES). This means that virtually everyone in the United States had been ingesting DES at a low level, year after year, until it was finally banned by the Food and Drug Administration at the end of 1979.

Any one of a great number of products might be singled out as typifying what has happened to our everyday foods, but a good example is the common white potato. Grown for thousands of years by South American Indians and for centuries in North America and Europe as well, it is a very desirable food, easily cultivated and providing a wide range of nutrients. Nowadays only about half of the commercial potato crop of the United States is shipped as raw tubers—and even these, seemingly unprocessed, have not only been chemically treated to prevent sprouting, but may also have been colored and waxed. The rest, including those destined for frozen dinners and French fries, are subjected to a great number of chemical processes and treated with both natural and artificial substances. About a fifth of the crop is used for potato chips, which involve still other treatments, despite some claims for "naturalness"—including the use of gases to prevent the darkening in color (an enzymatic process having no effect on taste or nutritive qualities) that occurs normally after peeling and again after cooking, and the addition of oils, salt, and often flavorings and preservatives. The final product of all this tampering is almost devoid of nutrients, not much more than a paper-thin blotter for soaking up the fats and salt used in its manufacture—in short, expensive junk that is possibly deleterious to health.

Many people nowadays are wary of chemicals in their food, and carefully study the labels on products in a search for "natural" foods. They would not be likely to buy a product whose contents were listed in this way:

Water, triglycerides of stearic, palmitic, oleic, and linoleic acids, myocin and actin, glycogen, collagen, lecithin, cholesterol, dipotassium phosphate, myoglobin, and urea. This product may also contain steroid hormones.

Yet this is a food eaten in huge amounts, by all but vegetarians, in North America. It is beefsteak, and in comparison to most common foods, it is a rather simple collection of chemicals. Milk, for example, consists of about a hundred chemicals and potatoes of about a hundred and fifty. Even natural foods consist of chemicals, and a considerable number of these are toxic—as can be seen in this well-balanced and tasty dinner that would win the approval of most nutritionists:

Smoked Salmon
Ham
Lima Beans   Cauliflower
Salad of Lettuce with
Radishes and Carrots
Compote of Strawberries,
Peaches, and Pears
Coffee

Were this meal to be judged under the current laws concerning safety in processed foods, every item in it would be prohibited for sale because of potential hazards to health. Smoked salmon, for example, contains small amounts of polynuclear aromatic hydrocarbons; their status as carcinogens has been confirmed in parts of northern Europe where smoked foods are consumed in large quantities and where cancer of the stomach is much more common than elsewhere. Ham would, of course, be eliminated because of nitrites. Lima beans contain glycosides, which break down during digestion to yield the poison hydrogen cyanide. Cauliflower contains a thiocyanate that causes enlargement of the thyroid. The salad would have to be eliminated because the nitrates in lettuce and radishes are converted into nitrites in the digestive tract, and because carrots contain carotoxin, a nerve poison, and the hallucinogen myristicin. Nor would the compote win approval under present laws against hazardous chemicals in foods, because all three fruits promote goiters. Strawberries also contain coumarin, which gives them a pleasant aroma, but which can interfere with the clotting of blood and may consequently produce uncontrollable bleeding from what would otherwise have been a trivial injury. Finally, coffee would have to be ruled out because it contains oxalates as well as caffeine, an addictive drug which may also cause birth defects.

The conclusion to be drawn from such an analysis of a meal is not to stop worrying about additives because (as argued by some apologists for commercial processing) all foods, whether natural or not, contain dangerous chemicals. Rather, cause for concern does exist because even natural substances are nowadays being eaten quite unnaturally. Ever since the early hominids began to walk on two legs on the African savanna, the human diet has apparently included hazardous chemicals. Until the modern adaptation, though, the risks were less because the same foods were usually not eaten day after day, and the variety of the diet made it unlikely that any one chemical had a chance to accumulate in the body. (For example, about four hundred carrots would have to be eaten, one after another, before signs of poisoning were observed.) And when earlier humans noted adverse reactions to foods, these must have been eliminated from the diet. Those who became the victims of foods whose deleterious effect was delayed or gradual, so that no identification of the cause of illness was possible, must have eventually died out. In the vast majority of cases, though, toxic foods can be assumed to have been eaten only sporadically and in small quantities—or else a technology was developed for detoxifying them.

Today, however, dangerous substances are eaten every day, year after year, throughout the life span, because the same chemicals appear in foods in many different guises. Almost all middle-aged people in North America alive today have consumed a dose of nitrites every day of their lives since infancy, and most of them have consumed a quantity of Yellow Dye No. 5 several times each week. The long-term effects of almost none of the 20,000 chemicals that are today used in food production have been studied. Evidence from such studies as have been made indicates that humans are now confronted with the problem of adapting to steady quantities of dangerous substances.

The number and kinds of additives that we ultimately continue to eat will depend upon the kind of society to which we belong and the values it holds dear. Certain of these values will determine the extent to which we continue to tamper chemically with the foods we eat. Paramount among these values is freedom from hunger. Here the choice is between letting events take their course—resulting in periodic famines, endemic malnutrition, and disease—and allowing the intervention of food technologists to promote the growth of food plants and animals, to enrich foods deficient in protein or vitamins, and to increase the seasonal availability of food by preservation. In placing a high value upon freedom from hunger and disease, North American and European societies are no different from others around the world—except that they are equipped with the technology to do something about it. The first question to be decided is whether in the face of hunger and disease we are willing to accept a technology that entails some degree of risk. Most people are probably willing to accept that risk.

A further question is economic. In capitalistic and socialistic countries alike, the providers of food must be rewarded for their efforts, with either a profit or some other incentive. So to entice the consumer, food is colored to make it more marketable and otherwise treated artificially to reduce cost and guarantee a profit. The questions to be asked are whether consumers will cease to buy raw potatoes if the tubers are not waxed and colored, or whether it is worth saving 3½¢ on a pound of beef by dosing everyone in the United States with low-level amounts of a carcinogenic hormone. For most people, the answer will surely be No. Yet another value is the humans' strong desire for variety in foods. Modern technology has now made it possible for large numbers of people in northern climates to obtain fresh vegetables throughout the year, and to make tropical fruits available in Canada and Finland. To do so, the processes of freezing, packing, and chemical preservation must be employed to protect against spoilage. Are these worth the risk?

In short, such questions can hardly be answered until we have first dealt with other, no less fundamental questions. Which of the values espoused by our society come first? In North America and Europe, freedom from hunger and disease undoubtedly rank at the top, and probably the desire for variety comes last. Similarly, the risks of tampering with a diet that has resulted from several million years of evolution must be assigned a place. Like so many other aspects of eating described in this book, the way we resolve the problem of technological tampering with food comes down in the end to a cultural statement: We will eat the way we are as a society.

Acknowledgments
Reference Notes
Bibliography
Index

Acknowledgments

Many people assisted in the preparation of this book from its original conception to publication. Some read sections and indeed the entire manuscript; others offered guidance and gave freely of their own work; still others contributed to research or to the preparation of the manuscript. Since the contributions of all were pervasive, it would be invidious to attempt to list them by categories. They are instead listed alphabetically; to all, our deepest appreciation:

Adina Armelagos; Carl Brandt, Brandt & Brandt Literary Agency; Virginia A. Beal, Department of Food Science and Nutrition, University of Massachusetts—Amherst; C. Loring Brace, Department of Anthropology, University of Michigan—Ann Arbor; George F. Cahill, Harvard University School of Medicine; Amy Clampitt; Robert Dirks, Department of Anthropology, Illinois State University; Mark Farb; Oriole Farb; Katherine V. Fite, Department of Psychology, University of Massachusetts—Amherst; Sheila Flynn; Sylvia H. Forman, Department of Anthropology, University of Massachusetts—Amherst; Sharon Fretwell; Stanley M. Garn, Department of Anthropology, University of Michigan—Ann Arbor; Kenneth E. Glander, Department of Anthropology, University of Michigan—Ann Arbor; Alan Goodman; Rebecca Huss–Ashmore; Kenneth H. Jacobs; Phillip S. Katz, School of Public Health, Yale University; Nancy Munn, Department of Anthropology, University of Chicago; Austin Olney, Houghton Mifflin Company; Gretel H. Pelto, Department of Anthropology, University of Connecticut; Oriol Pi–Sunyer, Department of Anthropology, University of Massachusetts—Amherst; Paul Rozin, Department of Psychology, University of Pennsylvania; Kenneth W. Samonds, Department of Food Science and Nutrition, University of Massachusetts—Amherst; Steve Sampson; William Stini, Department of Anthropology, University of Arizona; R. Brooke Thomas, Department of Anthropology, University of Massachusetts—Amherst; University of Massachusetts Libraries, Reference Department and Inter-Library Loan Office; Dennis P. Van Gerven, Department of Anthropology, University of Colorado; Marjorie Weinstein.

Reference Notes

PROLOGUE:
UNDERSTANDING SOCIETY AND
CULTURE THROUGH EATING

1–2   The intensity with which humans regard food, the
        ways they have made eating behavior an inseparable
        part of social customs and relations, the central place
        that eating has occupied along the trail of human
        evolution—these have made eating a hallmark of hu-
        manity. James Boswell was one of the first to seize
        upon this as a major distinguishing trait of humans.
        During a tour of the Scottish Hebrides Islands with
        Samuel Johnson in 1773, he wrote in his *Journal:*

> . . . I had found out a perfect definition of human
> nature as distinguished from the animal. An an-
> cient philosopher [Plato] said, Man was "a two-
> legged animal without feathers," upon which his
> rival sage [Diogenes Laertes] had a cock plucked
> bare, and set him down in the school before all his
> disciples, as a "Philosophick Man." Dr. [Ben-
> jamin] Franklin said, Man was "a tool-making
> animal," which is very well; for no animal but

271

man makes a thing, by means of which he can make another thing. But this applies to very few of the species. My definition of *Man* is, a "Cooking Animal." The beasts have memory, judgement, and all the faculties and passions of our mind, in a certain degree; but no beast is a cook.

This quotation is taken from *Journal of a Tour to the Hebrides with Samuel Johnson, L.L.D.*, edited by R. W. Chapman (London: Oxford University Press, 1930, pg. 179).

2   The item about Edmund Kean appeared in *Science*, vol. 199 (1978), pg. 26. The sources for the quotations are Brillat-Savarin (1926), pg. xxxiii (who possibly obtained it from a punning German proverb: *Mann ist was Mann isst*, "Man is what Man eats"); *Julius Caesar* by Shakespeare, Act 1, Scene 2. For the *Bhagavad Gita*, see XVII, 8–9. Many people in simple societies regard food and the individual as inseparable. To the Gimi of New Guinea even bodily wastes related to food—such as feces, urine, vomit, and the crumbs of saliva—are truly part of the individual. Should certain spirits get hold of these, it is the same as though they had gotten hold of the individuals themselves. For more about the Gimi, see Glick (1977).

3   Richards (1932) is the source for the Bantu and Anderson and Anderson (1977, 1968) for the Chinese. A general summary of the meaning of food as communication is Knutson (1965). For the acquisition of culture by children, see among others Shack (1971) and *Sex and Temperament in Three Primitive Societies* by Margaret Mead (New York: Morrow, 1935).

6   The information on the Malays comes from C. Wilson (1971), on the Bemba from Richards (1939). The quotation by Dorothy Lee is from her "Food and Human Existence," *Nutrition News*, vol. 25 (1962), pg. 10.

7   The place of food in the total Trobriand culture is
         discussed by Malinowski (1961, 1935, 1929).

10   For more on adaptation, see Alland (1973, 1970). A
         particular aspect of adaptation cannot always be de-
         termined to be simply beneficial or injurious. For
         example, twenty-two percent of the total amount of
         electricity generated in the United States in one re-
         cent year was devoted to the production and prepara-
         tion of food—producing a varied diet for most people
         in the United States, but at the same time proving
         maladaptive because of the degradation of the envi-
         ronment by strip-mining for coal and because of air
         pollution. Statistics on food-related energy require-
         ments can be found in Hirst (1974).

11   The point about the relation of cuisine to local re-
         sources is made by Miller (1978). See the more exten-
         sive treatment of cuisine in Chapter 10 of this book.

12   These, and other examples of seemingly irrational
         eating behavior can be found in Harrison *et al.* (1977),
         pg. 421, de Garine (1972), Dubos (1965), pp. 64–65,
         and Gillin (1944). For the processing of maize by
         Mexicans to improve nutrition, see Katz *et al.* (1974).
         A note on the beneficial effects of adding milk to tea
         appears in *Science,* vol. 204 (June 1, 1979), pg. 909.

13   It is often difficult to derive a cohesive and sustained
         theory from Lévi–Strauss' writings, but his basic
         views on eating can be found in his 1969 volume. A
         fuller discussion appears on pp. 124–28 of this book.

14   Regarding self-selection, the original paper that
         seemed to support a natural wisdom in the choice of a
         nutritious diet by children is Davis (1928). Dr. Spock's
         endorsement of her view can be found in *Baby and
         Child Care* (New York: Hawthorn, 1968, pp.
         278–281). A discussion of the controversy about self-

selection, together with excellent bibliographic references, is in Lytle (1977), pp. 23–27. A critique based on the methodology of Davis' experiments is by Arlin (1977).

Experiments with animals that raise doubts about self-selection are discussed by Young (1948); on the other hand, self-selection by rats has been supported by Epstein and Teitelbaum (1962) and by several other researchers. A summary of experiments that show self-selection by laboratory rats to be a combination of innate and learned behaviors can be found in Balagura (1973), pp. 134–148. That experiments with rats to determine self-selection are so often ambiguous is a result of laboratory variables: among them, the number of food items offered the rats, the ratio of liquid to solid foods, the palatability of the foods, the age and sex and general health of the rats, and even the placement of the food.

The notion of innate wisdom about the best diet fails to explain why neighboring groups of people do not agree about food preferences. After all, if every human were born with a wisdom about eating, then peoples inhabiting similar environments would be expected to select the same foods. An example of the way selections vary may be seen in two nearby tribes in Kenya, the Masai and the Akikuyu. The Masai consume large amounts of milk and blood from their cattle, and they sometimes eat meat as well. The Akikuyu, in contrast, live chiefly on cereals and potatoes, even though they maintain herds of goats (which they use for exchange and for prestige rather than for food). The Masai are generally healthy and vigorous and their children do not suffer from the bone deformities, anemia, and other nutritional diseases that plague the Akikuyu. What happened to the innate wisdom of self-selection among the Akikuyu? (The source of this example is Jensen, 1953.)

14   The three-sectored approach to explaining eating behavior is indebted to Harris (1975), pp. 156–158.

1. THE BIOLOGICAL BASELINE

20   The problems of the omnivore are discussed by
P. Rozin (1978).

21–22   The statistics on the calories of energy produced in
the United States by the reduction to ideal weight are
from "The Energy Cost of Overweight in the United
States" by Bruce G. Hannon and Timothy G.
Lohman, *American Journal of Public Health*, vol. 68
(1978), pp. 765–767.

22   The nutritional analysis of a North American dinner
used the University of Massachusetts—Amherst Nutritional Data Bank, compiled by Kenneth W. Samonds. The more than 1200 grams of edible substances in such a meal contain, among other
nutrients, the following:

838.4	grams of water
97	grams of protein
165.9	grams of carbohydrates
96.6	grams of total fat (of which 41.7 grams are saturated and 12 are unsaturated)
307.8	milligrams of calcium
998	milligrams of phosphorus
15	milligrams of iron
2600	milligrams of sodium
2600	milligrams of potassium
4042	International Units of vitamin A
.8	milligrams of thiamine
1.1	milligrams of riboflavin
22.7	milligrams of niacin

53.5   milligrams of vitamin C
          2.5   grams of crude fiber

All of this is in addition to vitamins B_6, B_{12}, folic acid, D, and E as well as magnesium, zinc, and other minerals—as well as just under 2000 calories.

One point should be made about these nutrients. Strictly speaking, when humans eat they do not feed the person but rather the cells that make up that person. Life began with single-celled organisms in the sea, and all through succeeding evolution the chemical composition of sea water has continued to set the preconditions for life. These have remained basically the same for all mammals, including humans, even though mammals evolved into very complex, multi-celled organisms. Our living cells are still really inhabitants of the seas—and that is why the human body might be looked upon as a vehicle for carrying around a tank of sea water and as a mechanism for getting food to each of the cells inhabiting the tank.

22   The discussion of what happens when humans eat is indebted to Olefsky (1978), Lytle (1977), and Arlin (1977). Davenport (1972) explains why the stomach does not digest itself. Balagura (1973) summarizes experimental evidence for many of the topics discussed in this section.

23–24   The sensory properties of food are discussed by Lepkovsky (1977). The flavors recollected by the Israelites are given in Numbers 11:5–7. A report on the beneficial effects of hot chicken soup appeared in *The Sciences,* vol. 18 (1978), no. 8, pp. 4–5.

24–25   See Dethier (1978), Bartoshuk (1976), and Gorman (1975) for the four primary tastes and Garcia and Hankins (1975) for the evolution of sensitivity to a *page* bitter taste. The sweetening effect of artichoke is reported on by Bartoshuk *et al.* (1972).

29 Excellent summaries concerning human motivations for eating can be found in Lytle (1977), Wooley *et al.* (1976), Teyler (1975), C. Hamilton (1973), and in chapter 2 of *Psychology* by Roger Brown and Richard J. Herrnstein (Boston: Little, Brown, 1975). Balagura (1973) summarizes pertinent animal experiments.

32 The information about basic nutritional needs is indebted largely to Olefsky (1978), Clydesdale and Francis (1977), and Young and Scrimshaw (1971). The item about Columbus' sailors is from P. Rozin (1976 A). The quotation from *Romeo and Juliet* is in Act 3, Scene 5.

36–37 The most recent revision of the Recommended Dietary Allowances is the eighth edition, published in 1974 by the Food and Nutrition Board of the National Academy of Sciences, Washington, D.C. An interpretation of these data is presented in Guthrie (1975), which is an excellent source for more detailed nutritional information than is given in this section, as is Arlin (1977).

37 Williams (1978) explains nutritional individuality. A. Ferro-Luzzi *et al.* (1975) and Oomen (1970) offer the example of New Guinea. The "walking legume" hypothesis has been questioned by Norgan *et al.* (1974).

38 Scrimshaw and Young (1976) raise the major problems of defining basic nutritional needs.

39–40 Draper (1977) and Nickerson *et al.* (1973) suggest ways in which some Eskimo groups achieve a bal-

page anced nutrition on a diet almost completely devoid of meat. The change in Eskimo diet in recent times is described by Kemp (1971). Saffirio (1975) compares the Eskimos' diet to that of the Cro-Magnons in prehistoric Europe.

42–43 Register and Sonnenberg (1973) discuss vegetarian diets. The vegetarian diet of fast days is given in greater detail by Knutsson and Selinus (1970). They point out that poor people are likely to suffer nutritional deficiencies when abstaining from animal products because they cannot always afford adequate plant substitutes. The largely vegetarian diet of Gambian peasants is summarized by G. Harrison *et al.* (1977), pp. 413–417.

43 The study of vegetarianism by choice in Israel is reported in Guggenheim *et al.* (1962).

44 Growth in stature by Harvard males over several generations is documented in *New Types of Old Americans at Harvard* by G. T. Bowles (Cambridge, Mass.: Harvard University Press, 1932) and in "Secular Trends in Height and Weight within Old American Families at Harvard, 1870–1965" by Albert Damon, *American Journal of Physical Anthropology,* vol. 29 (1968), pp. 45–50. Statistics for the increase in stature of the general United States population are from *The New York Times,* June 10, 1976.

44 Froehlich (1970) reported on the growth of Japanese in Hawaii, and Wenkam and Wolff (1970) on the changed food habits there.

2. THE EMERGING HUMAN PATTERN

47 Sources for the food habits of nonhuman primates are, among others, Gaulin and Konner (1977),

page   P. Wilson (1977), Teleki (1975, 1973), Jolly (1972), chapter 3, and Thorington (1970).

48   The implications for humans of the arboreal adaptation are presented in much greater detail in Tuttle (1975).

49   Food preferences of nonhuman primates are discussed by P. Wilson (1977).

50   See Teleki (1975, 1973) for hunting by chimpanzees.

50   The tendency of both nonhuman and human primates to switch to a meat diet whenever possible is discussed by Hamilton and Busse (1978).

50–51   The definitive work on insects as human food is Bodenheimer (1951).

52   General statements about steps toward the evolution of the human diet are from P. Rozin (1976 B).

53   Harrison *et al.* (1977), pg. 402, is the source for the estimates of energy expended in the quest for food by apes and humans.

53–54   The widely accepted view of hunting–gathering as the original human adaptation stems from an influential paper by Washburn and Avis (1958). The view has occasionally been challenged, among others by Perper and Schrire (1977).

54   Much of the speculation based on East African excavations is from G. Isaac (1978).

56   On sharing by the San, see Lee and DeVore (1976) and on that by the Cooper Eskimo, see Damas (1972). Because the San are the surviving hunter–gatherers

about whom most is known, they are given particular prominence in this book. The item about "hunter's appetite" is from *The Natural History of Man* by J. S. Weiner (New York: Doubleday Anchor, 1973, pg. 146).

57   Male power, stemming from the control of animal foods, is discussed by Friedl (1978, 1975).

59   Archeologists have been able to piece together the diets of early humans from various kinds of evidence. The patterns of tooth wear, fossilized food remains at butchering and living sites, and coprolites (dried feces) provide direct evidence. Inferences have also been drawn from tools, from what is known of ancient climates, from fossils of plants and animals inhabiting the same environment as humans, and from comparisons with the present-day eating habits of nonhuman primates and hunter–gatherers. Much more recent diets, dating from only some tens of thousands of years ago, are inferred from cave paintings that show various kinds of animals with spears and arrows imbedded in them. For still more recent humans, diets can be determined from food offerings in graves, from refuse heaps, from the stomach contents of mummies, and from coprolites; most recent of all is the considerable evidence in written documents. For a general discussion of the foods of early humans, see Brothwell and Brothwell (1969) and for a more technical one see G. Isaac (1971). An excellent summary of the foods of nonhuman primates and hunter–gatherers is Gaulin and Konner (1977).

59   All textbooks of physical anthropology and human evolution at least touch upon dentition, and many go into the subject in great detail. A study by Davies (1972) is wide-ranging, but is often anecdotal rather than scientific; a thorough but highly technical volume is Butler and Joysey (1978).

page

59   Information on the bite and the incisors is from Brace (1977). For more on chopsticks, see the index references in Chang (1977).

62   The prevalence of dental caries previous to modern diets is documented in Wells (1975). The shopping list is in Act 4, Scene 3 of *The Winter's Tale*.

63   Information about cooking is summarized in *Man's Place in Nature* by Charles F. Hockett (New York: McGraw–Hill, 1973.) Ways to boil without fireproof containers are from Tannahill (1973). For more about cooking methods on Tikopia, see Firth (1973, 1936). Lamb's essay was first published in *The London Magazine* and later collected in *Essays of Elia* (1833); it is often reprinted in anthologies, more to illustrate techniques about writing an essay than for its scientific validity.

65   The diet and health of the San are described by Truswell (1977). Lee and DeVore (1976) give a more extensive discussion.

66   Haviland (1967) analyzes the skeletons at Tikal.

3. EATING AS CULTURAL ADAPTATION

67   For material on Tikopia, see Firth (1973).

68   An excellent summary of the adaptive features of horticulture is Friedl (1975), to whom this discussion is indebted. For the adaptation of horticulture, and for others as well, see Lenski and Lenski (1974).

The adaptation that replaced hunting–gathering is sometimes called "agriculture," but is more accurately referred to as "horticulture." It continues to the present day, primarily in the tropics and subtropics. In agriculture, extensive fields are plowed *page* and harvested with the aid of animal power and machines, whereas in horticulture all of the tasks, from clearing the small garden to picking the crop, are accomplished by human muscle. Fields are cultivated almost continuously, generation after generation, but garden plots are cultivated for only a few years in succession, and then the wild growth of the forests is allowed to reclaim them. Among horticulturists, tracts of forest or brush are cleared by burning; the ashes fertilize the soil and the garden is then planted amid the stumps and debris. Because the soil becomes exhausted in a few years, it is necessary to leave it fallow and for new lands to be cleared. The growth of wild plants on the fallow land replenishes the soil to the extent that the land can be cleared again in perhaps ten years.

70   Much of the material on the East African cattle complex was derived from Netting (1977) and from Dyson–Hudson and Dyson–Hudson (1969). Two classic studies are Evans–Pritchard (1940) and Richards (1932).

74   Lenski and Lenski (1974) present characteristics of the modern adaptation in much greater detail. Clements (1970) discusses changes in the diet due to industrialization.

77   A controversial explanation for the modern rise in population, to which this book subscribes in general, has been offered by McKeown (1976). A carefully documented case for the influence of New World crops on Europe's food supply can be found in Langer (1975). The definitive source on the potato is Salaman (1940). The information on China is from Chang (1977).

78   The discussion of energy flow in various adaptations is indebted to Harris (1975), pp. 233–255 in particular.

The energy costs of food production can be found in Little and Morren (1976).

79 The data on the San are primarily from Lee and DeVore (1968), pp. 30–43, and from Lee and DeVore (1976).

79 The summary of energy input and yields in a Gambian village is from *Economics of Agriculture in a Savannah Village* by M. R. Haswell (London: Colonial Research Studies, Her Majesty's Stationery Office, 1953).

80 Information on the efficiency of the pastoral adaptation is from R. Brooke Thomas (personal communication).

81 Data on Chinese energy inputs and yields are from *Earthbound China* by Fei Hsiao-T'ung and Chang Chih-i (Chicago: University of Chicago Press, 1947).

83 The example of the Miskito Indians is based primarily upon the anthropological film "The Turtle People," produced by James Ward and distributed by B & G Films 1973, and upon the guide to the film written by Brian Weiss. Several works by Nietschmann, primarily his 1973 volume, were also helpful.

4. THE LIFE PASSAGE

87 Portions of this chapter are in particular indebted to McElroy and Townsend (1979) and Guthrie (1975). The classic work on rites of passage is van Gennep (1960); he frequently mentions eating and drinking with others as a social communion.

87 Why the Mbum Kpau women eat neither chicken nor many other animals is discussed by O'Laughlin (1974).

88   Pregnancy cravings and aversions in Albany, New York, are reported by Hook (1978).

88–89 The culture–nutrition interpretation of clay eating is from Hunter (1973). On the Ewe, see Vermeer (1971). The consumption of such nonfood items as clay and starch—as well as ashes, chalk, lead paint, and a variety of other substances—is technically known as "pica," from the Latin word for magpie, a bird noted for the diversity of things it eats or carries off. Cooper (1957) presents a history of observations about pica.

89–90 Much of the information in these pages is from McElroy and Townsend (1979).

90   Menzies (1970) discusses the influence of eating on the infant.

91   On the Gurage of Ethiopia, see D. Shack (1969).

93   Breast-feeding is discussed by McElroy and Townsend (1979) and by Guthrie (1975), among others. Various statistics on breast- and bottle-feeding are from Latham (1977) and Wade (1974); some have been recalculated to bring them up to date. One of many cases against bottle-feeding is given in brief by Jelliffe and Jelliffe (1977).

94   For the connection between lactation and ovulation, see Frisch (1978) and Van Ginneken (1974), among others. The possibility that the stimulus of sucking by the infant retards ovulation is suggested in "Lactation, Ovulation, Infanticide and Women's Work" by Richard B. Lee, in *Ecology and Society of the Kun San* (New York: Cambridge University Press, 1979).
       The relation between food supplies and fertility was noted by Darwin in his *The Variation of Animals and Plants Under Domestication* (1868). He stated that

domesticated animals, which expend much less energy in obtaining plentiful food supplies than do wild members of the same species, are more fertile; that an individual animal's fertility is affected by variations in the amount of food and by "hard living"; and he noted the difficulty of fattening a cow that is lactating. The effect of food supplies and of the expenditure of energy on fertility is much the same in human beings. A detailed analysis of the fertility of lower-class English and Scottish families in the early part of the last century showed that about half of the women who labored in the mills had "problems of the uterus," including the failure to menstruate, and that the diet of the laboring class in general was "inadequate for health and strength." These poorly nourished women nevertheless had anywhere from five to seven children—a rate of fertility that might seem high but is actually quite low compared to well-nourished contemporary populations who do not use contraception—among them the Hutterites, a group of religious communities in the northern plains of North America, who have an average of eleven or twelve children per family. (Information about fertility in nineteenth-century British families is from Frisch, 1978).

98   Much of the material in these pages is from McElroy and Townsend (1979), Guthrie (1975), and Niehoff and Meister (1972). The point about children absorbing the flavor of food is from P. Rozin (1976 B).

98   Richards (1939, 1932) discusses the Bantu.

99–100 Considerable information about the folklore of menstruation and food can be found in *The Curse* by Janice Delaney *et al.*, (New York: Dutton, 1976). The statement of Pliny is quoted from his *Natural History* (Cambridge, Mass.: Harvard University Press, 1961, pg. 549).

100   Malinowski (1961, 1935, 1929) discusses the place of
        food in Trobriand marriage and Firth (1973), pg. 259,
        gives information about the Tikopian marriage cere-
        mony.

102   The use of food terms by Australian Aborigines to
        describe sex is noted in *Children of the Desert* by
        Géza Róheim (New York: Basic Books, 1974, pg.
        245). The Sinhalese example is from Yalman (1969).

102–03 The sexual symbolism of food among the Tukano In-
        dians is discussed by Reichel–Dolmatoff (1976, 1971).

103   Willis (1977) describes in greater detail the sexual rites
        by the Fipa to encourage growth, particularly the
        relation of these rites to the people's cosmic view.

104   The similar operations of the nervous system in re-
        gard to sex and food are noted by Pullar (1970).

106   It is not true that the oyster is poisonous during the
        months whose names in English do not contain the
        letter *r*. The belief may once have had validity be-
        cause during the warm months of May, June, July,
        and August, oysters shipped unrefrigerated were
        likely to spoil. The summer is also the spawning sea-
        son for oysters; at this time they may taste somewhat
        flat, even though they are not dangerous to eat. Al-
        though it has no beneficial effect on humans, the folk-
        lore prohibition against eating oysters during those
        months does have the beneficial effect of protecting
        oysters during their spawning season.

107–08 Material for the section on aphrodisiacs was drawn
        from numerous sources, among them Cosman (1976),
        Benedek (1972), Pullar (1970), Trager (1970), and Bel-
        ham (1965). Falstaff's exclamation occurs in *The
        Merry Wives of Windsor,* Act 5, Scene 4. The story of

Leah and the mandrake root is told in the book of Genesis, 30:14–17. The quotations from Maimonides and Ogden Nash appear in Benedek (1972).

110 Guthrie (1975), chapter 19, discusses the eating habits of the elderly and also gives an excellent bibliography. Exton–Smith (1972) is the source for the California study. See Exton–Smith (1972) and Ross and Bras (1975) for material on animal experiments that relate nutrition to longevity. Longevity in the Caucasus is reported on by Benet (1976).

111–12 For more about Pacific Island funerals, see Firth (1973, 1936).

5. MEAL AS METAPHOR

115 General discussions of the metaphorical and symbolic importance given to eating can be found in Barthes (1975), Firth (1973), chapter 7, and Richards (1932), chapter 7, in addition to other works mentioned later in references for this chapter.

115 The example of Chad is given by de Garine (1971).

116 The quotation from the Beatitudes occurs in Matthew 5:6. The origin of the word "toast" is of interest in connection with the metaphorical uses of food and drink. Originally it referred to a woman whose beauty or charms are celebrated when quaffing a drink. The word itself comes from the practice during the Middle Ages of floating a piece of spiced and toasted bread in the glass—whence the metaphorical notion that the name of the woman toasted would add flavor to the drink.

116–17 Simoons (1976) dicusses the milk tie. The description of the Promised Land is from Exodus 3:8.

118 Numerous studies have been made of hot–cold categories, particularly among peasants in Latin America, including those by Molony (1975), Currier (1966), and Madsen (1955). Foster (1979) discusses the persistence of the categories in North American folk beliefs. *Yin* and *yang* concepts about food are discussed in Chang (1977), particularly pp. 10, 47–48, 228, and 369; see also Anderson and Anderson (1975, 1969).

121 Recent research indicates that starving a fever might actually be beneficial. A fever decreases the level of iron in the blood—and disease organisms cannot survive without adequate iron. People who eat less, and who consequently decrease the amount of iron in the blood, may so reduce its level that microorganisms cannot grow, thereby increasing resistance to infection. See "Fever" by Charles A. Dinarello and Sheldon M. Wolff, *Human Nature,* vol. 2 (1979), no. 2, pp. 66–72. For folk beliefs about this, see Foster (1979).

122 A study of English working-class meals is reported in Douglas (1974, 1972) and in Douglas and Nicod (1974).

123 Metaphors of a Japanese dinner are discussed by Befu (1974).

125 Lévi–Strauss' exposition of his culinary triangle appeared in English first in his 1966 paper and in somewhat different form in his 1978 book (original French edition 1968), pp. 478–495. For further elaboration of his views, see also his 1973 and 1969 volumes (French editions 1966 and 1964). Lévi–Strauss' theories are given a sympathetic though brief discussion in *Lévi–Strauss,* by Edmund Leach (London: Collins, 1970); the quotation here is from pg. 32. Critiques of Lévi–Strauss, both in regard to his facts and to his methodology, are numerous. Harris (1979), particu-

larly pp. 202–215, discusses in detail his distortion of fact. Lehrer (1972, 1969) has made a careful linguistic analysis of food words in different languages; she does not find support for most of Lévi–Strauss' hypotheses concerning the culinary triangle. See also a devastating analysis by Shankman (1969) of Lévi–Strauss' generalizations about ways in which cannibals cook human meat.

127–28 Lehrer (1972, 1969) presents a taxonomy of cooking words in English. For a general discussion of conceptual categories in language, see Farb (1974), in particular chapter 9.

129 The Basuto words for the evening star are from Richards (1932), pg. 197.

129 Information for the section on bread came from many sources: Bailey (1975), Darby *et al*. (1977) on Egypt; *Feast-Day Cakes* by Dorothy G. Spicer (New York: Holt, Rinehart and Winston, 1960), on hot-cross buns; and Arnott (1975) on Greek breads.

132 For the meal as a symbolic event, see the works of Douglas, particularly her 1972 paper which is also the source for the Chicken Marengo anecdote. Details about this dish can be found in *Larousse Gastronomique* by Prosper Montagné (New York: Crown, 1961, pg. 608). Napoleon's master chef, Dunand, feeling that the crayfish were out of place in Chicken Marengo, later eliminated them and substituted mushrooms. But Napoleon complained about the alteration of the recipe; the crayfish were restored and they are used as garnish for the dish to this day.

6. EAT NOT OF THEIR FLESH

133 Perper and Schrire (1977) point out the importance of the two biblical myths for understanding the relationship between humans and forbidden foods.

134   Simoons (1961) discusses taboos placed upon animal foods.

134–35 Basic sources of information on the causes of pork avoidance are Darby *et al.* (1977), vol. 1, pp. 171–209, Grivetti and Pangborn (1974), and Douglas (1970), pp. 40–44. An ecological explanation is offered by Harris in his 1977 volume, pp. 129–138, and in his 1974 one, pp. 35–80; Harris' views are opposed by Diener and Robkin (1978). Simoons (1961), chapter 3, gives a general discussion of pork avoidance in the Old World.

135   For a brief summary of the literature about trichinosis, see Darby *et al.* (1977), vol. 1, pp. 171–172 and 199–200.

136   Much of the material on the dietary rules in Leviticus is indebted both to Soler (1979) and to Douglas (1970), pp. 54–72, who in her 1972 paper revised her position somewhat.

139   The prominence given by the Maccabees to pork avoidance is discussed by Douglas (1973), pp. 60–64.

139–40 See Darby *et al.* (1977), vol. 1, among others, on pork avoidance by Moslems.

140   The item about permission given by the Koran to eat pork in cases of necessity is from Darby *et al.* (1977), vol. 1, pg. 203 and the item about swine in modern Israel is from Simoons (1961), pg. 40.

146   Taboos on beef are discussed by Simoons (1961). The discussion of the sacredness of the Indian cow owes a great debt to Harris' work, beginning with his "The Myth of the Sacred Cow" in *Man, Culture, and Animals* edited by A. Leeds and A. P. Vayda (Washington, D.C.: American Association for the Advance-

ment of Science, 1965, pp. 217–228). For his more recent statements, see his 1978 paper and his 1977 and 1974 volumes. Harris' position has been attacked by Heston (1971), who is answered by Harris in the same issue. Simoons' study (1973) of the provisions of Indian law for sacred cattle also leads him to disagree with Harris. Al–Biruni is quoted by Anderson (1977), pg. 552. The West Bengal study referred to, as well as several additional facts used in the discussion, are from Odend'hal (1972).

147   The quotation is from *Antony and Cleopatra,* Act 1, Scene 4, lines 66–68.

147   Gerlach (1964) is the source for the example about the Bantu, Malinowski (1929) for that about the Melanesians, and Welsh (1971) for that about the Omaha Indians.

148   Fischer *et al*. (1959) report on allergic reactions to the violation of food taboos.

149   The physiological explanation for death after eating a forbidden food is given by William Howells in *The Heathens* (Garden City, N.Y.: Natural History Press, 1962, pp. 98–99).

149   See Garb and Stunkard (1974) for bait shyness.

7. FOODS FOR THE GODS

152   Firth (1963) defines and discusses sacrifice and fasting.

153   Much information about sacrifice in the Old Testament can be found in the *Pictorial Biblical Encyclopedia* edited by G. Cornfeld (New York: Macmillan, 1964, pp. 638–648).

153 On Bantu sacrifices, see Richards (1932), chapter 7, and the primary sources she cites.

154–55 Evans–Pritchard (1956), chapter 8 in particular, describes the economic calculation in Nuer sacrifice.

155 The *Euthyphro* quotation is from the translation by B. Jowett in *The Dialogues of Plato* (New York: Random House, 1937, vol. 1, pg. 397).

156 The statement by Tylor is from *Primitive Culture* (New York: Harper & Row, 1958, vol. 2, pg. 485; originally published 1871).

157 Fasting in India is discussed by Katona–Apte (1975).

158 The spread of the grapevine by Jews and Christians is mentioned by Sopher (1967), pg. 33. For the spread of other plants for ritual purposes, see Fickeler (1962).

159 E. Isaac (1959) is the source material on the spread of citrus. "The fruit of the goodly tree," traditionally regarded as the citron, is mentioned in Leviticus 23:40. For Pliny's reference to the citron in his *Natural History,* see book 12, chapter 7.

161 Much of the material about the Eucharist and the Mass is from Tannahill (1975). See I Corinthians 11:24–26 for Paul's statement about making Jesus' words into a rite of the Church. That transubstantiation is literally true, and not just symbolic, was reaffirmed by Pope Paul VI in his encyclical letter *Mysterium Fidei* (1965):

> Nor is it right to treat of the mystery of transubstantiation without mentioning the marvelous change of the whole of the bread's substance into Christ's body and the whole of the wine's substance into his blood. . . . Nor, finally, is it right

to put forward and to give expression in practice to the view which maintains that Christ the Lord is no longer present in the consecrated hosts which are left over when the sacrifice of the Mass is over.

162 The literature on cannibalism is huge. Tannahill (1975) has presented an anecdotal survey, with a wide-ranging bibliography, mostly from historic sources. See also Sagan (1974), which relies heavily on a psychoanalytical approach, and Shankman (1969). Arens (1979) believes anthropophagy has never existed in any society except for exceptional cases of survival necessity; his view is very much a minority one. References are given below for cannibalism in several societies. The story of the cannibalism practiced by the Uruguayan rugby team after their plane crashed in the Andes is told in *Alive* by Piers Paul Read (Philadelphia: Lippincott, 1974). The hunger of the survivors overcame their revulsion against eating human flesh. Yet, so much were they prisoners of their culture that they debated the morality of the act and whether it was permissible to eat meat from relatives.

163–64 See Dole (1962) on endocannibalism among the Panoans.

164 Information about cannibalism in New Guinea is derived almost completely from Berndt (1962), with additional information from Glasse (1967).

166 *Kuru* is discussed by Glasse (1967) and by others who have written on New Guinea cannibalism. For the discovery of its cause, D. Carleton Gajdusek, of the United States National Institutes of Health, received the 1976 Nobel Prize in Physiology and Medicine. Gajdusek's Nobel Lecture (1977) on the subject is extremely technical.

169   The hypothesis of Aztec cannibalism was proposed by Harner (1977) and expanded upon by Harris (1979, 1977). Major attempts at rebuttal have been made by Ortiz de Montellano (1978) and by Price (1978), both of whom put forward other hypotheses. See also a critical review by Marshall Sahlins in *The New York Review of Books,* vol. 25, no. 18 (November 23, 1978), pp. 45–53, and the reply by Harris in the issue of June 28, 1979. The reports of Bernal Díaz are from *The Discovery and Conquest of Mexico, 1519–1521* (New York: Farrar, Straus, 1956, pg. 119). For a brief summary of Aztec culture and history, see Farb (1978 B), pp. 155–175.

169–70   Protein deficiency in New Guinea is pointed out by Berndt (1962), pg. 271. The analysis of the nutritional value of human meat in New Guinea is by Dornstreich and Morren (1974). The statement of Garn and Block (1970) that human meat is of limited nutritional value is answered in *American Anthropologist,* vol. 72 (1970), pp. 1462–1463, and vol. 73, pp. 269–270.

171   Furst (1978) reports on *Spirulina* as an Aztec food source. For the nutritional value of amaranth, see *Underexploited Tropical Plants with Promising Economic Value* by the Advisory Committee on Technology Innovation (Washington, D.C.: National Academy of Sciences, 1975, pp. 14–19).

172   The statement by Lévi-Strauss is quoted from his *A World on the Wane [Tristes Tropiques]* (New York: Criterion Books, 1961, pg. 388).

174–75   The health-food movement is discussed as a fad by Schafer and Yetley (1975). A recent summary of the various groups, examined as if they were religious cults, is Keen (1978). An entertaining book on the subject is Deutsch (1977). The attitudes of organic-food faddists in particular are discussed by Hufford (1971). On vegetarianism as a fad diet, see Majumder (1972). An excellent analysis of the health-food movement was presented by Gretel H. Pelto of the University of Connecticut at the 1976 Meetings of the American Dietetic Association in Boston.

8. THE FEAST AND THE GIFT

176   The information about mince pie and pretzels is from Lowenberg *et al.* (1974), pg. 157.

177   Geertz (1960) is the source for material on the *slametan*.

180   The potlatch, because of its seeming irrationality, has been the subject of a tremendous literature. For ecological explanations, see Adams (1973), Suttles (1968), and chapter 3 of Netting (1977). Farb (1978 B), chapter 8, presents a brief summary of Northwest Coast culture.

181   The literature on the "big man" of Melanesia is also extensive. Major studies are by Strathern (1971), Hogbin (1964), and Oliver (1955), with an important paper by Sahlins (1963). Harris discusses big men in both his 1977 and 1974 volumes. The quotation about the advantages of polygyny to the big man is from Sahlins (1963). M. Young (1971) offers an extended treatment of competitive feasting in Melanesia.

185   The description of eating in medieval England is from Cosman (1976).

185–86 Tannahill (1970) is the primary source on sumptuary laws.

186   For Bemba hospitality, see Richards (1939).

187 Food as a factor in caste hierarchy in tribal India is discussed by G. Ferro–Luzzi (1975). The summary of caste distinctions based on food transactions in Hindu villages is based on Marriott (1968); a definitive study of much the same subject, from a somewhat different point of view, is Dumont (1972).

189–90 The quotation about food gifts is from *Book of the Eskimo* by Peter Freuchen (Cleveland, Ohio: World, 1961, pg. 154).

190–91 General statements about sharing are indebted to Sahlins (1972) and to the sources he cites.

192 Mauss (1967, originally published 1925) was perhaps the first scholar to demonstrate that gifts are almost never given out of pure generosity. More recent discussions of gifts of food are Firth (1973), chapter 11, and Sahlins (1972). Richards (1939) describes attempts by the Bemba to avoid sharing. On the Maori, see "Proverbs in Native Life, with Special Reference to Those of the Maori" by Raymond Firth, *Folklore*, vol. 37 (1926), pp. 245–270. On the Gurage, see W. Shack (1971).

9. TASTE AND DISTASTE

198 Material on the unusual preferences and avoidances mentioned in these pages can be found in Simoons (1978), Jacobs (1975), Pyke (1968), and Cussler and De Give (1952), among others. The Emperor Vitellius' eating habits are described by Suetonius in *The Twelve Caesars* (Baltimore, Md.: Penguin, 1957, pg. 269). The statement by Lucretius, better known in the form "one man's meat is another man's poison," is from *De Rerum Natura,* IV, 637. The quotation from *Macbeth* appears in Act 4, Scene 1.

page

198–99 Food avoidances of the tribes of India are listed in G. Ferro–Luzzi (1975).

199   The foods that would be approved by many of the world's peoples are suggested by Moore (1970).

200   The relative ranking of domesticated plants in the United States is from Rick (1978).

200   On food preferences of the San, see Tanaka (1976).

201–03 The discussion of the sacred dog and also much about the avoidance of horsemeat is indebted to Sahlins (1976), chapter 4; see also Harris (1979). On attitudes toward dogs and horses, see Simoons (1961). Gade (1976) presents the history of the consumption of horsemeat in France and in western Europe.

204–05 Most of the information about beef is derived from Harris and Ross (1978).

206   A source on facial expressions connected with disgust is *The Face of Emotion* by C. E. Izard (New York: Appleton, 1971). Information about the cultural reaction of disgust is from P. Rozin (personal communication).

207   The anomaly of chili peppers and other spices is from P. Rozin (1978, 1977, 1976 B, and personal communication). See also Pangborn (1975). Pickersgill (1969) gives the early history of chili peppers.

210   The material on coffee is from P. Rozin (personal communication) and from Timson (1978). For the place of coffee in United States culture, see Taylor (1977).

210–12 Marshall (1979) and Mandelbaum (1965) provide general discussions of alcohol and culture. Information

page   on the Jívaro is from Harner (1973); on the Bemba,
from Richards (1939). Mentions of liquor in antiquity
are from Brothwell and Brothwell (1969). An excellent analysis of the place of beer in another African
society, the Kofyar of northern Nigeria, is by Netting
(1964).

213   Studies of the effects of alcohol on different populations are Reed *et al.* (1976), Bennion and Li (1976),
and Wolff (1972).

214   Heath (1962) reported the extraordinary consumption
of alcohol by the Camba; more recent information is
included in a comment by Heath at the conclusion of
Mandelbaum (1965).

216–17 The basic source on drinking in Ireland is Bales
(1962). Of interest also is *Family and Community in
Ireland* by C. M. Arensberg and S. T. Kimball (Cambridge, Mass.: Harvard University Press, 1940).

217   On drinking by Jews, see Snyder (1962); on drinking
by Italians, see Lolli (1958).

218   Individual taste profiles are discussed in *Heredity,
Evolution, and Society* by I. Michael Lerner and William J. Libby (San Francisco: Freeman, 1976 [second
edition], pp. 319, 338–340). For PTC, see *Human
Races* by Stanley Garn (Springfield, Ill.: Thomas,
1971 [third edition], pp. 44–46).

219   Yudkin (1969) proposes an evolutionary hypothesis of
palatability and food choice.

219–20 Chang (1977), pp. 87–140, is the source on T'ang
Dynasty China.

221   Beauchamp and Maller (1977) summarize the
influence of tastes and aromas on children. The quota-

page — tion from the Gadsup ceremony is given by Leininger (1970).

221–22 The flavor principle in cuisines has been put forth by E. Rozin (1973); the summary of distinctive flavors is derived from hers.

225–26 The discussion of the inability to digest milk is taken largely from Simoons (1973), Kretchmer (1972), and McCracken (1971). G. G. Harrison (1975) suggests a genetic approach.

10. THE WISDOM OF CUISINE

227   Food traditions of Japanese macaques are discussed in "Newly Acquired Precultural Behavior of the Natural Troops of Japanese Monkeys on Koshima Inlet" by M. Kawai, *Primates,* vol. 6 (1965), pp. 1–30.

228   Many of the statements made in defining a cuisine are indebted to P. Rozin (1976 A, 1976 B).

233   Material on the cuisine of China is largely from Chang (1977, 1973), Freeman (1977), Anderson and Anderson (1975), and Tannahill (1973). The source for material concerning food-and-sex in the restaurants of China is Chang (1977), particularly pp. 136–137 and 158–159.
         The restaurant originated in China, but its flowering in the modern world was directly influenced by France. The first such establishment was opened in Paris in the middle of the eighteenth century, and offered mostly soups with fowl and fresh eggs. The derivation of the word "restaurant" is either from the descriptive French term for a fortifying soup or from the sign above the doors of the first one: *Venite ad me omnes qui stomacho laboratis et ego restaurabo vos* ("Come to me all ye whose stomachs suffer and I will

page   restore you"). The number of restaurants increased rapidly when, following the French Revolution, numerous chefs who had once served the aristocracy opened eating places for the common people, thereby spreading the cuisine throughout the population. Information about restaurants in Europe can be found in Norman (1972).

239   Especially helpful on North American cuisine were Root and de Rochemont (1976), M. Bennion (1976), Gifft *et al.* (1972), Trager (1970), Hilliard (1969), Braudel (1967), and Weigley (1964). The item on convenience foods is from Tannahill (1970), pg. 99.

241   Reasons why maize, beans, and squash became superfoods are given by Farb (1978 A), pp. 125–126, by Cohen (1977), pp. 211–218, and by Flannery (1973).

242   On the mongongo nut, see Lee (1973).

243   Pyke (1968), chapter 8, discusses potatoes, spinach, onions, strawberries, and other toxic plants.

243   The preference for manioc, despite its toxicity, is summarized by Moore (1970). A considerable amount of effort is involved in making manioc beer. The Jívaro, as reported by Harner (1973), make it this way: The tubers are first peeled and washed in a stream near the garden; carried to the house, they are cut up and placed in a pot to boil. Once they have become soft, they are mashed and stirred for a long time with a special wooden paddle until a soft consistency is achieved. While the woman stirs the mash, she chews handfuls and spits them back into the pot, a process which may take more than a half an hour. The Jívaro believe that chewing the mash is essential for proper fermentation. In this they are correct; enzymes in the saliva, as well as bacteria in the mouth,

do indeed hasten the fermentation process. After the mash has been prepared, it is allowed to ferment in jars. Four or five days are needed to reach the maximum alcoholic content, though usually the beer is too much in demand to be allowed to sit for that long. The Jívaro consider beer far superior to plain water, which they drink only in emergencies.

243 Scudder (1971) describes the toxic plants of the Tonga.

244 Most of the information on the change in European table manners is from Elias (1978). Material on meals depicted in art is from Braudel (1967), pp. 140–141. An interesting study of United States table manners, as distinguished from the European ones presented here, is Schlesinger (1947).

EPILOGUE:
HUNGER IN THE SOCIAL AND HUMAN BODY

250 The literature on famine is immense. For the biological effects, see among others Cox (1978), Cahill (1978, 1970), Stini (1975, 1972), Stein and Susser (1975), and Young and Scrimshaw (1971).

On the relation between famine and sociocultural behavior, a classic study is Keys *et al.* (1950); more anecdotal is Sorokin (1942). A general discussion is Jelliffe and Jelliffe (1971). A recent and major synthesis of the subject is Dirks (In Press), and it is to him that the analysis of the responses to famine along the lines of stress theory is indebted. See also the collection of papers that touch on various aspects of hunger in Laughlin and Brady (1978).

Two widely publicized examples of the effects of famine on social relations—the Siriono of Bolivia (*Nomads of the Long Bow* by Allan R. Holmberg, *page* Garden City, N.Y.: Natural History Press, 1969) and the Ik of Uganda *(The Mountain People* by Colin Turnbull, New York: Simon and Schuster, 1972)— have not been discussed in this book because recent evaluation shows that the effects of famine were due more to population fluctuations and enforced migrations into new ecological niches than to indigenous factors within these two societies. For a major critique of the former, see *Human Ecology,* vol. 5, no. 2 (1977), pp. 137–154; on the latter, see *Current Anthropology,* vol. 15 (1974), pp. 99–102 and vol. 16 (1975), pp. 343–358.

250   Statistics on the prevalence of famine are from Nicol (1971).

250–51 MacSwiney's hunger strike is mentioned in Grande (1964).

251   The effects of famine on the Tikopians are discussed in Firth (1959) and in Spillius (1957).

254   Changes in the United States diet are documented by Brewster and Jacobson (1978) and by Winikoff (1978), who provides the statistics on life expectancy.

254   This brief discussion of obesity relied primarily on the summaries in Rodin (1978), Beller (1977), and Kolata (1977).

256   A nutritional analysis of fast-food meals appears in *Consumer Reports,* vol. 44 (September 1979), pp. 508–513.

256–57 Eating at McDonald's is discussed as a ritual by Kottak (1978).

258   The information on milling is from a variety of sources, among them Clydesdale and Francis (1977)

page and Haas and Harrison (1977). Statistics on the loss of nutrients through processing are from Mount (1975), who also gives this comparison of the nutritional values of wholemeal bread and enriched white bread:

	WHOLE-MEAL BREAD	ENRICHED WHITE BREAD
	(in milligrams per 100 grams)	
VITAMINS		
Thiamine (B₁)	0.2	0.18
Riboflavin	0.1	—
Nicotinic acid	3.5	1.7
Pyridoxine (B₆)	0.5	0.15
Pantothenic acid	0.8	0.34
Folic acid	0.026	0.014
Tocopherol (E)	2.2	0.85
MINERALS		
Sodium	466	515
Potassium	261	106
Calcium	26	92
Magnesium	89	22.6
Manganese	2.4	0.3
Iron	2.8	1.8
Copper	0.46	77
Phosphorus	240	0.13
Sulphur	81	81

260 A summary of information on salt in the North American diet, and its effects on health, written by Jane E. Brody, appears in *The New York Times,* July 11, 1979.

261 Nitrites, dyes, antibiotics, hormones, and other additives are discussed in detail by Hall (1976). The material on adulterated potatoes is from Bodley (1976).

263 The labeling for beefsteak is from *The New York Times,* July 12, 1978.

265   The menu analyzed for toxins is part of a larger one offered by Clydesdale and Francis (1977), pp. 104–111, who use it to document their position as food technologists that additives and adulterants are "natural" and harmless. For a different point of view, see Hall (1976) and Mount (1975), among others.

266   The societal values involved in food technology are discussed by Stumpf (1978).

Bibliography

ADAMS, JOHN W. 1973. *The Gitkson Potlatch*. New York: Holt, Rinehart and Winston.

ALLAND, ALEXANDER, JR. 1970. *Adaptation in Cultural Evolution*. New York: Columbia University Press.

———— and BONNIE MC CAY. 1973. "The Concept of Adaptation in Biological and Cultural Evolution." In *Handbook of Social and Cultural Anthropology* edited by John J. Honigmann (Chicago: Rand McNally, pp. 143–178).

ANDERSON, E. N., JR. 1977. "On an Early Interpretation of India's Sacred Cattle." *Current Anthropology,* vol. 18, no. 3, pg. 552.

———— and MARJA L. ANDERSON. 1977. "Modern China: South." In Chang (1977), pp. 317–382.

————. 1975. "Folk Dietetics in Two Chinese Communities and Its Implications for the Study of Chinese Medicine." In *Medicine and Chinese Culture* edited by A. Kleinman *et al*. (Washington, D.C.: U.S. Public Health Service, 1975, pp. 143–171).

————. 1969. "Cantonese Ethnohoptology." *Ethnos,* vol. 34, pp. 107–117.

ARENS, WILLIAM. 1979. *The Man-Eating Myth*. New York: Oxford University Press.

305

ARLIN, MARIAN. 1977 (2nd edition). *The Science of Nutrition*. New York: Macmillan.

ARNOTT, MARGARET L., editor. 1975 A. *Gastronomy: The Anthropology of Food and Food Habits*. The Hague: Mouton.

————. 1975 B. "The Breads of Mani." In Arnott (1975 A), pp. 297–303.

BAILEY, ADRIAN. 1975. *The Blessings of Bread*. New York: Paddington Press.

BALAGURA, SAUL. 1973. *Hunger: A Biopsychological Analysis*. New York: Basic Books.

BALES, ROBERT F. 1962. "Attitudes Toward Drinking in the Irish Culture." In *Society, Culture, and Drinking Patterns* edited by David J. Pittman and Charles R. Snyder (New York: Wiley, pp. 157–187).

BARNESS, LEWIS A. 1977. "Breast Milk for All." *New England Journal of Medicine*, vol. 297, pp. 939–940.

BARTHES, ROLAND. 1975. "Toward a Psychosociology of Contemporary Food Consumption." In Forster and Forster (1975), pp. 47–59.

BARTOSHUK, LINDA M. 1976. "Taste Quality." In *Appetite and Food Intake* edited by Trevor Silverstone (Berlin, W. Germany: Dahlem Konferenzen, 1976, pp. 229–253).

BARTOSHUK, LINDA M. *et al*. 1972. "Sweet Taste of Water Induced by Artichoke *(Cynara scolymus)*." *Science*, vol. 178, pp. 988–989.

BATES, MARSTON. 1968. *Gluttons and Libertines*. New York: Random House.

BEAUCHAMP, GARY K. and OWEN MALLER. 1977. "The Development of Flavor Preferences in Humans: A Review." In *The Chemical Senses and Nutrition* edited by Morley R. Kare and Owen Maller (New York: Academic Press, 1977, pp. 291–311).

BEFU, HARUMI. 1974. "An Ethnography of Dinner Entertainment in Japan." *Arctic Anthropology*, vol. 11, Supplement, pp. 196–203.

BELHAM, GEORGE. 1965. *The Virility Diet*. London: Wolfe.

BELLER, ANNE S. 1977. *Fat and Thin: A Natural History of Obesity*. New York: Farrar, Straus.

BENEDEK, THOMAS G. 1972. "Food and Drink as Aphrodisiacs." *Sexual Behavior*, vol. 2, no. 7, pp. 5–10.

BENET, SULA. 1976. *How to Live to Be 100*. New York: Dial.

BENNION, LYNN J. and TING-KAI LI. 1976. "Alcohol Metabolism in American Indians and Whites." *New England Journal of Medicine*, vol. 294, pp. 9–13.

BENNION, MARION, 1976. "Food Preparation in Colonial America." *Journal of The American Dietetic Association*, vol. 69, pp. 16–23.

BERNDT, RONALD M. 1962. *Excess and Restraint: Social Control Among a New Guinea Mountain People*. Chicago, Ill.: University of Chicago Press.

BEY, PILAFF (pseud. for Norman Douglas). 1952. *Venus in the Kitchen: or Love's Cookery Book*. London: Heinemann.

BLIX, GUNNAR *et al.*, editors. 1971. *Famine: A Symposium*. Uppsala: Almqvist & Wiksells.

BODENHEIMER, FRIEDRICH S. 1951. *Insects as Human Food*. The Hague: W. Junk.

BODLEY, JOHN M. 1976. *Anthropology and Contemporary Human Problems*. Menlo Park: Cummings.

BRACE, C. LORING. 1977. "Occlusion to the Anthropological Eye." In *The Biology of Occlusal Development* edited by James A. McNamara, Jr. (Ann Arbor: University of Michigan Press, 1977, pp. 179–209).

BRAUDEL, F. 1967. *Capitalism and Material Life, 1400–1800*. New York: Harper & Row.

BREWSTER, LETITIA and MICHAEL F. JACOBSON. 1978. *The Changing American Diet*. Washington, D.C.: Center for Science in the Public Interest.

BRILLAT–SAVARIN, JEAN A. 1926. *The Physiology of Taste*. New York: Liveright (originally published 1825).

BRINGÉUS, NILS–ARVID. 1970. "Man, Food, and Milieu." *Folk Life*, vol. 8, pp. 45–55.

BROTHWELL, DON and PATRICIA BROTHWELL. 1969. *Food in Antiquity: A Survey of the Diet of Early Peoples*. London: Thames and Hudson.

BUTLER, P. M. and K. A. JOYSEY. 1978. *Development, Function and Evolution of Teeth*. New York: Academic Press.

CAHILL, GEORGE F., JR. 1978. "Physiology of Acute Starvation in Man." *Ecology of Food and Nutrition,* vol. 6, pp. 221–230.

―――. 1970. "Starvation in Man." *New England Journal of Medicine,* vol. 282, pp. 668–675.

CHANG, K. C. 1973. "Food and Food Vessels in Ancient China." *Transactions of The N.Y. Academy of Sciences,* vol. 35, pp. 495–520.

―――, editor. 1977. *Food in Chinese Culture*. New Haven, Conn.: Yale University Press.

CHAPELLE, MARY LOU. 1972. "The Language of Food." *American Journal of Nursing,* vol. 72, pp. 1294–1295.

CLARK, F. LE GROS. 1968. "Food Habits as a Practical Nutrition Problem." *World Review of Nutrition and Dietetics,* vol. 9, pp. 56–84.

CLASTRES, PIERRE. 1974. "Guayaki Cannibalism." In *Native South Americans* edited by Patricia J. Lyon (Boston: Little, Brown, 1974, pp. 309–321).

CLEMENTS, F. W. 1970. "Some Effects of Different Diets." In *The Impact of Civilisation on the Biology of Man* edited by S. V. Boyden (Toronto, Canada: University of Toronto Press, 1970, pp. 109–141).

CLYDESDALE, FERGUS M. and FREDERICK J. FRANCIS. 1977. *Food, Nutrition, and You*. Englewood Cliffs, N.J.: Prentice–Hall.

COHEN, MARK N. 1977. *The Food Crisis in Prehistory*. New Haven, Conn.: Yale University Press.

COOPER, MARCIA. 1957. *Pica*. Springfield, Ill.: Charles C. Thomas.

COSMAN, MADELEINE P. 1976. *Fabulous Feasts: Medieval Cookery and Ceremony*. New York: Braziller.

COX, GEORGE W. 1978. "The Ecology of Famine: An Overview." *Ecology of Food and Nutrition,* vol. 6, pp. 207–220.

CURRIER, RICHARD L. 1966. "The Hot-Cold Syndrome and Symbolic Balance in Mexican and Spanish–American Folk Medicine." *Ethnology,* vol. 5, pp. 251–263.

Bibliography

CUSSLER, MARGARET and MARY L. DE GIVE. 1952. *'Twixt the Cup and the Lip*. New York: Twayne.

DAMAS, DAVID. 1972. "Central Eskimo Systems of Food Sharing." *Ethnology*, vol. 11, pp. 220–240.

DARBY, WILLIAM J. *et al*. 1977. *Food: The Gift of Osiris*. New York: Academic Press.

DAVENPORT, HORACE W. 1972. "Why the Stomach Does Not Digest Itself." *Scientific American*, vol. 226, no. 1, pp. 86–92.

DAVIES, D. M. 1972. *The Influence of Teeth, Diet, and Habits on the Human Face*. London: Heinemann.

DAVIS, CLARA M. 1928. "Self Selection of Diet by Newly Weaned Infants." *American Journal of Diseases of Children*, vol. 36, pp. 651–679.

DEETZ, JAMES and JAY ANDERSON. 1972. "The Ethnogastronomy of Thanksgiving." *Saturday Review*, vol. 55 (Nov. 25), pp. 29–39.

DE GARINE, IGOR. 1972. "The Socio-Cultural Aspects of Nutrition." *Ecology of Food and Nutrition*, vol. 1, pp. 143–163.

———. 1971. "Food Is Not Just Something to Eat." *Ceres*, vol. 4, pp. 46–51.

DETHIER, VINCENT G. 1978. "Other Tastes, Other Worlds." *Science*, vol. 201, pp. 224–228.

DEUTSCH, RONALD M. 1977. *The New Nuts Among the Berries*. Palo Alto, Calif.: Bull Publishing.

DIENER, PAUL and EUGENE E. ROBKIN. 1978. "Ecology, Evolution, and the Search for Cultural Origins: The Question of Islamic Pig Prohibitions." *Current Anthropology*, vol. 19, pp. 493–540.

DIRKS, ROBERT. In Press. "Socio-Behavioral Responses to Famine." *Current Anthropology*.

DOLE, GERTRUDE E. 1962. "Endocannibalism Among the Amahuaca Indians." *Transactions of The N.Y. Academy of Sciences*, vol. 24, Series 2, pp. 567–573.

DORNSTREICH, MARK D. and GEORGE E. MORREN. 1974. "Does New Guinea Cannibalism Have Nutritional Value?" *Human Ecology*, vol. 2, pp. 1–12.

DOUGLAS, MARY. 1974. "Food as an Art Form." *Studio International,* vol. 188, pp. 83–88.

———. 1973. *Natural Symbols.* New York: Vintage.

———. 1972. "Deciphering a Meal." *Daedalus,* vol. 101 (Winter), pp. 61–81.

———. 1970. "The Abominations of Leviticus." In *Purity and Danger: An Analysis of Concepts of Pollution and Taboo* by Mary Douglas (Baltimore, Md.: Penguin, 1970, pp. 54–72).

——— and MICHAEL NICOD. 1974. "Taking the Biscuit: The Structure of British Meals." *New Society,* vol. 30, pp. 744–747.

DRAPER, H. H. 1977. "The Aboriginal Eskimo Diet in Modern Perspective." *American Anthropologist,* vol. 79, pp. 309–316.

DUBOS, RENÉ. 1965. *Man Adapting.* New Haven, Conn.: Yale University Press.

DUMONT, LOUIS. 1972. *Homo Hierarchicus: The Caste System and Its Implications.* London: Paladin.

DYSON–HUDSON, RADA and NEVILLE DYSON–HUDSON. 1969. "Subsistence Herding in Uganda." *Scientific American,* vol. 220, no. 2, pp. 76–89.

ELIAS, NORBERT. 1978. *The Civilizing Process: The History of Manners.* New York: Urizen Books.

EVANS–PRITCHARD, E. E. 1956. *Nuer Religion.* New York: Oxford University Press.

EXTON–SMITH, A. N. 1972. "Physiological Aspects of Aging: Relationship to Nutrition." In Watkin (1972), pp. 853–859.

FAITHORN, ELIZABETH. 1975. "The Concept of Pollution Among the Káfe of the Papua New Guinea Highlands." In *Toward an Anthropology of Women* edited by Rayna R. Reiter (New York: Monthly Review Press, 1975).

FARB, PETER. 1978 A. *Humankind.* Boston: Houghton Mifflin.

———. 1978 B (2nd edition). *Man's Rise to Civilization: The Cultural Ascent of the Indians of North America.* New York: Dutton.

———. 1974. *Word Play: What Happens When People Talk.* New York. Knopf.

FERRO–LUZZI, ANNA *et al.* 1975. "Food Intake, Its Relationship to Body Weight and Age, and Its Apparent Nutritional Adequacy in New Guinean Children." *American Journal of Clinical Nutrition,* vol. 28, pp. 1443–1453.

FERRO–LUZZI, GABRIELLA E. 1975. "Food Avoidances of Indian Tribes." *Anthropos,* vol. 70, pp. 385–428.

FICKELER, PAUL. 1962. "Fundamental Questions in the Geography of Religions." In *Readings in Cultural Geography* edited by Philip L. Wagner and Marvin W. Mikesell (Chicago, Ill.: University of Chicago Press).

FIRTH, RAYMOND. 1973. "Food Symbolism in a Pre-Industrial Society." In *Symbols: Public and Private* by Raymond Firth (Ithaca, N.Y.: Cornell University Press, pp. 243–261).

———. 1963. "Offering and Sacrifice." *Journal of Royal Anthropological Institute of Great Britain and Ireland,* vol. 93, part 1, pp. 12–24.

———. 1959. *Social Change in Tikopia.* New York: Macmillan.

———. 1936. *We, the Tikopia.* London: Allen & Unwin; Boston: Beacon Pr.

FISCHER, J. L. *et al.* 1959. "Totemism and Allergy." *International Journal of Social Psychiatry,* vol. 5, pp. 33–40.

FLANNERY, KENT V. 1973. "The Origins of Agriculture." *Annual Review of Anthropology,* vol. 2, pp. 271–310.

FORSTER, ELBORG and ROBERT FORSTER. 1975. *European Diet from Pre-Industrial to Modern Times.* New York: Harper & Row.

FOSTER, GEORGE M. 1979. "Humoral Traces in United States Folk Medicine." *Medical Anthropology Newsletter,* vol. 10, no. 2, pp. 17–20.

FREEMAN, MICHAEL. 1977. "Sung." In Chang (1977), pp. 141–176.

FRIEDL, ERNESTINE. 1978. "Society and Sex Roles." *Human Nature,* vol. 1, no. 4, pp. 68–75.

———. 1975. *Women and Men: An Anthropologist's View.* New York: Holt, Rinehart and Winston.

FRIEDMAN, MARK I. and EDWARD M. STRICKER. 1976. "The Physiological Psychology of Hunger." *Psychological Review,* vol. 83, pp. 409–431.

FRISCH, ROSE E. 1978. "Population, Food Intake, and Fertility." *Science,* vol. 199, pp. 22–30.

FROELICH, J. W. 1970. "Migration and the Plasticity of Physique in the Japanese–Americans of Hawaii." *American Journal of Physical Anthropology,* vol. 32 (1970), pp. 429–442.

FURST, PETER T. 1978. "Spirulina." *Human Nature,* vol. 1, no. 3, pp. 60–65.

GADE, DANIEL W. 1976. "Horsemeat as Human Food in France." *Ecology of Food and Nutrition,* vol. 5, pp. 1–11.

GADJUSEK, D. CARLTON. 1977. "Unconventional Viruses and the Origin and Disappearance of Kuru." *Science,* vol. 197, pp. 943–960.

GARB, JANE L. and ALBERT J. STUNKARD. 1974. "Taste Aversions in Man." *American Journal of Psychiatry,* vol. 131, pp. 1204–1207.

GARCIA, JOHN and WALTER G. HANKINS. 1975. "The Evolution of Bitter and the Acquisition of Toxiphobia." In *Olfaction and Taste V* edited by Derek A. Denton and John P. Coghlan (New York: Academic Press, 1975, pp. 39–45).

GARN, STANLEY M. and WALTER D. BLOCK. 1970. "The Limited Nutritional Value of Cannibalism." *American Anthropologist,* vol. 72, pp. 106–107.

GAULIN, STEVEN J. and MELVIN KONNER. 1977. "On the Natural Diet of Primates, Including Humans." In *Nutrition and the Brain* edited by Richard J. Wurtman and Judith J. Wurtman (New York: Raven Press, 1977, vol. 1, pp. 1–86).

GEERTZ, CLIFFORD. 1960. *The Religion of Java.* Glencoe, Ill.: The Free Press.

GELFAND, MICHAEL. 1971. *Diet and Tradition in an African Culture.* Edinburgh, Scotland: Livingstone.

GERLACH, LUTHER P. 1964. "Socio-Cultural Factors Affecting the Diet of the Northeast Coastal Bantu." *The American Dietetic Association,* vol. 45, pp

GIFFT, HELEN H. *et al.* 1972. *Nutrition, Beha͙ Change.* Englewood Cliffs, N.J.: Prentice–Hall.

GILLIN, JOHN. 1944. "Custom and Range of Human Response." *Journal of Personality,* vol. 13, pp. 101–134.

GLASSE, ROBERT. 1967. "Cannibalism in the Kuru Region of New Guinea." *Transactions of The N.Y. Academy of Sciences,* Series II, vol. 29, pp. 748–754.

GLICK, L. B. 1977. "Medicine as an Ethnographic Category: The Gimi of the New Guinea Highlands." In *Culture, Disease, and Healing* edited by David Landy (New York: Macmillan).

GORMAN, JAMES. 1975. "The Taster's Puzzling Perception." *The Sciences,* vol. 15, no. 6, pp. 6–10.

GOULD, RICHARD A. 1969. *Yiwara: Foragers of the Australian Desert.* New York: Scribners.

GRANDE, FRANCISCO. 1964. "Man Under Calóric Deficiency." In *Adaptation to the Environment, Handbook of Physiology* edited by D. B. Dill *et al.* (Washington, D.C.: American Physiological Society, Section 4, pp. 911–937).

GRIVETTI, LOUIS E. 1978. "Culture, Diet, and Nutrition." *BioScience,* vol. 28, no. 3, pp. 171–177.

GRIVETTI, LOUIS E. and ROSE M. PANGBORN. 1974. "Origin of Selected Old Testament Dietary Prohibitions." *Journal of The American Dietetic Association,* vol. 65, pp. 634–638.

GUGGENHEIM, K. *et al.* 1962. "Composition and Nutritive Value of Diets Consumed by Strict Vegetarians." *British Journal of Nutrition,* vol. 16, pp. 467–474.

GUTHRIE, HELEN A. 1975 (3rd edition). *Introductory Nutrition.* St. Louis, Mo.: Mosby.

HAAS, JERE D. and GAIL G. HARRISON. 1977. "Nutritional Anthropology and Biological Adaptation." *Annual Review of Anthropology,* vol. 6, pp. 69–101.

HALL, ROSS H. 1974. *Food for Nought: The Decline in Nutrition.* New York: Harper & Row.

Bibliography

HAMILTON, C. L. 1973. "Physiologic Control of Food Intake." *Journal of The American Dietetic Association*, vol. 62, pp. 35–40.

HAMILTON, W. J., III and C. D. BUSSE. 1978. "Primate Carnivory and Its Significance to Human Diets." *BioScience*, vol. 28, pp. 761–766.

HARNER, MICHAEL. 1977. "The Ecological Basis for Aztec Sacrifice." *American Ethnologist*, vol. 4, pp. 117–135.

———. 1973. *The Jívaro: People of the Sacred Waterfalls*. New York: Doubleday Anchor.

HARRIS, MARVIN. 1979. *Cultural Materialism*. New York: Random House.

———. 1978. "India's Sacred Cow." *Human Nature*, vol. 1, no. 2, pp. 28–36.

———. 1977. *Cannibals and Kings: The Origins of Cultures*. New York: Random House.

———. 1975 (2nd edition). *Culture, People, Nature*. New York: Crowell.

———. 1974. *Cows, Pigs, Wars, and Witches: The Riddles of Culture*. New York: Random House.

——— and ERIC B. ROSS. 1978. "How Beef Became King." *Psychology Today*, vol. 12, no. 5, pp. 88–94.

HARRISON, G. A. *et al.* 1977. *Human Biology*. New York: Oxford University Press.

HARRISON, GAIL G. 1975. "Primary Adult Lactase Deficiency: A Problem in Anthropological Genetics." *American Anthropologist*, vol. 77, pp. 812–835.

HATHCOCK, JOHN N. and JULIUS COON, editors. 1978. *Nutrition and Drug Interactions*. New York: Academic Press.

HAVILAND, WILLIAM A. 1967. "Stature at Tikal, Guatemala: Implications for Ancient Maya Demography and Social Organization." *American Antiquity*, vol. 32, pp. 316–325.

HEATH, DWIGHT B. 1962. "Drinking Patterns of the Bolivian Camba." In *Society, Culture, and Drinking Patterns* edited by David J. Pittman and Charles R. Snyder (New York: Wiley, pp. 22–36).

HENKIN, ROBERT I. 1977. "New Aspects in the Control of Food Intake and Appetite." In Moss and Mayer (1977), pp. 321–334.

HESTON, ALAN. 1971. "An Approach to the Sacred Cow of India." *Current Anthropology,* vol. 12, pp. 191–209.

HILLIARD, SAM. 1969. "Hog Meat and Cornpone: Food Habits in the Ante-Bellum South." *Proceedings of The American Philosophical Society,* vol. 113, pp. 1–13.

HIRST, ERIC. 1974. "Food-Related Energy Requirements." *Science,* vol. 184, pp. 134–138.

HOGBIN, IAN. 1964. *A Guadalcanal Society.* New York: Holt, Rinehart and Winston.

HOOK, ERNEST B. 1978. "Dietary Cravings and Aversions During Pregnancy."*American Journal of Clinical Nutrition,* vol. 31, pp. 1355–1362.

HUFFORD, DAVID. 1971. "Organic Food People: Nutrition, Health, and World View." *Keystone Folklore Quarterly,* vol. 16, pp. 179–184.

HUNTER, JOHN M. 1973. "Geophagy in Africa and in the United States: A Cultural-Nutrition Hypothesis." *Geographical Review,* vol. 63, pp. 170–195.

ISAAC, ERICH. 1959. "Influence of Religion on the Spread of Citrus."*Science,* vol. 129, pp. 179–186.

ISAAC, GLYNN. 1978. "The Food-Sharing Behavior of Proto-human Hominids." *Scientific American,* vol. 238, no. 4, pp. 90–108.

———. 1971. "The Diet of Early Man: Aspects of Archaeological Evidence from Lower and Middle Pleistocene Sites in Africa." *World Archeology,* vol. 2, pp. 278–299.

JACOBS, JAY. 1975. *Gastronomy.* New York: Newsweek Books.

JANICK, JULES *et al.* 1976. "The Cycles of Plant and Animal Nutrition." *Scientific American,* vol. 235, no. 3, pp. 74–86.

JELLIFFE, DERRICK B. 1975. "Human Milk Nutrition and the World Resource Crisis." *Science,* vol. 188, pp. 557–561.

——— and E. F. P. JELLIFFE. 1977. " 'Breast Is Best': Modern Meanings." *New England Journal of Medicine,* vol. 297, pp. 912–915.

———. 1971. "The Effects of Starvation on the Function of the Family and of Society." In Blix *et al.* (1971), pp. 54–61.

JENSEN, LLOYD B. 1953. *Man's Foods*. Champaign, Ill.: Garrard.

JONES, WILLIAM O. 1959. *Manioc in Africa*. Stanford, Calif.: Stanford University Press.

KANDEL, RANDY F. and GRETEL H. PELTO. In Press. "Vegetarianism and Health Food Use Among Young Adults in Southern New England." In *Nutritional Anthropology* edited by N. Jerome *et al*.

KATONA–APTE, JUDIT. 1975. "Dietary Aspects of Acculturation: Meals, Feasts, and Fasts in a Minority Community in South Asia." In Arnott (1975 A), pp. 297–303.

KATZ, S. H. *et al*. 1974. "Traditional Maize Processing Techniques in the New World." *Science*, vol. 184, pp. 765–773.

KEEN, SAM. 1978. "Eating Our Way to Enlightenment" and "The Pure, the Impure, and the Paranoid." *Psychology Today*, vol. 12, no. 5, pp. 62–87.

KEMP, WILLIAM B. 1971. "The Flow of Energy in a Hunting Society." *Scientific American*, vol. 224, no. 3, pp. 104–115.

KEYS, ANCEL *et al*. 1950. *The Biology of Human Starvation*. Minneapolis: University of Minnesota Press.

KNUTSON, A. L. 1965. "The Meaning of Food." In *The Individual, Society and Health Behavior* by A. L. Knutson (New York: Russell Sage Foundation, 1965, pp. 132–143).

KNUTSSON, KARL E. and RUTH SELINUS. 1970. "Fasting in Ethiopia: An Anthropological and Nutritional Study." *American Journal of Clinical Nutrition*, vol. 23, pp. 956–969.

KOLATA, GINA B. 1977. "Obesity, a Growing Problem." *Science*, vol. 198, pp. 905–906.

KOTTAK, CONRAD P. 1978. "Ritual at McDonald's." *Natural History Magazine*, vol. 87, no. 1, pp. 75–82.

KRETCHMER, NORMAN. 1972. "Lactose and Lactase." *Scientific American*, vol. 227, no. 4, pp. 71–78.

KUPPER, JESSICA, editor. 1977. *The Anthropologists' Cookbook*. New York: Universe Books.

LANGER, WILLIAM. 1975. "American Foods and Europe's Population Growth 1750–1850." *Journal of Social History,* Winter, pp. 51–66.

LATHAM, MICHAEL C. 1977. "Infant Feeding in National and International Perspective." In Moss and Mayer (1977), pp. 197–209.

LAUGHLIN, CHARLES D., JR. and IVAN A. BRADY, editors. 1978. *Extinction and Survival in Human Populations.* New York: Columbia University Press.

LEE, RICHARD B. 1973. "Mongongo: The Ethnography of a Major Wild Food Resource." *Ecology of Food and Nutrition,* vol. 2, pp. 307–321.

——— and IRVEN DE VORE, editors. 1976. *Kalahari Hunter–Gatherers.* Cambridge, Mass.: Harvard University Press.

———. 1968. *Man the Hunter.* Chicago: Aldine.

LEHRER, ADRIENNE. 1972. "Cooking Vocabularies and the Culinary Triangle of Lévi–Strauss." *Anthropological Linguistics,* vol. 14, pp. 155–171.

———. 1969. "Semantic Cuisine." *Journal of Linguistics,* vol. 5, pp. 39–55.

LEININGER, M. 1970. "Some Cross-Cultural and Non-Universal Functions, Beliefs, and Practices of Food." In *Dimensions of Nutrition* edited by Jacqueline Dupont (Ft. Collins, Colo.: Proceedings of the Colorado Dietetic Conference, pp. 153–179).

LENSKI, GERHARD and JEAN LENSKI. 1974. *Human Societies.* New York: McGraw–Hill.

LEPKOVSKY, SAMUEL. 1977. "The Role of the Chemical Senses in Nutrition." In *The Chemical Senses and Nutrition* edited by Morley R. Kare and Owen Maller (New York: Academic Press, pp. 413–428).

LÉVI–STRAUSS, CLAUDE. 1978. *The Origin of Table Manners.* New York: Harper & Row.

———. 1973. *From Honey to Ashes.* New York: Harper & Row.

———. 1969. *The Raw and the Cooked.* New York: Harper & Row.

———. 1966. "The Culinary Triangle." *Partisan Review,* vol. 33, pp. 586–595.

MICHAEL A. and GEORGE E. MORREN, JR. 1976. *Ecol-y, Energetics, and Human Variability.* Dubuque, Iowa: William C. Brown.

LOLLI, GEORGIO *et al.* 1958. *Alcohol in Italian Culture.* Glencoe, Ill.: The Free Press.

LOOMIS, ROBERT S. 1976. "Agricultural Systems." *Scientific American,* vol. 235, no. 3, pp. 98–105.

LOWENBERG, MIRIAM E. *et al.* 1974 (2nd edition). *Food and Man.* New York: Wiley.

LYTLE, LOYD. 1977. "Control of Eating Behavior." In *Nutrition and the Brain* edited by Richard J. Wurtman and Judith J. Wurtman (New York: Raven Press, 1977, pp. 1–145).

MCCRACKEN, ROBERT D. 1971. "Lactase Deficiency: An Example of Dietary Evolution." *Current Anthropology,* vol. 12, pp. 479–517.

MCELROY, ANN and PATRICIA K. TOWNSEND. 1979. *Medical Anthropology.* North Scituate, Mass.: Duxbury Press.

MCKEOWN, THOMAS. 1976. *The Modern Rise of Population.* New York: Academic Press.

MADSEN, WILLIAM. 1955. "Hot and Cold in the Universe of San Francisco Tecospa, Valley of Mexico." *Journal of American Folklore,* vol. 68, pp. 123–139.

MAJUMDER, SANAT K. 1972. "Vegetarianism: Fad, Faith, or Fact?" *American Scientist,* vol. 60, pp. 175–179.

MALINOWSKI, BRONISLAW. 1961. *Argonauts of the Western Pacific.* New York: Dutton (originally published 1922).

———. 1935. *Coral Gardens and Their Magic.* New York: American Book Co.

———. 1929. *The Sexual Life of Savages in North-Western Melanesia.* New York: Harcourt, Brace.

MANDELBAUM, DAVID G. 1965. "Alcohol and Culture." *Current Anthropology,* vol. 6, pp. 281–293.

MANGELSDORF, PAUL C. 1974. *Corn: Its Origin, Evolution, and Management.* Cambridge, Mass.: Harvard University Press.

MARRIOTT, MCKIM. 1968. "Caste Ranking and Food Transactions: A Matrix Analysis." In *Structure and Change in*

Indian Society edited by Milton Singer and Bernard S. Cohn (Chicago: Aldine–Atherton, 1968, pp. 133–171).

MARSHALL, MAC, editor. 1979. *Beliefs, Behaviors, and Alcoholic Beverages*. Ann Arbor: University of Michigan Press.

MAUSS, MARCEL. 1967. *The Gift: Forms and Functions of Exchange in Archaic Societies*. New York: Norton (originally published 1925).

MAYER, JEAN. 1976. "The Dimensions of Human Hunger." *Scientific American*, vol. 235, no. 3, pp. 40–49.

MELLOR, JOHN W. 1976. "The Agriculture of India." *Scientific American*, vol. 235, no. 3, pp 154–163.

MENZIES, ISABEL E. 1970. "Psychosocial Aspects of Eating." *Journal of Psychosomatic Research*, vol. 14, pp. 223–227.

MIRACLE, MARVIN P. 1966. *Maize in Tropical Africa*. Madison: University of Wisconsin Press.

MOLONY, CAROL H. 1975. "Systematic Valence Coding of Mexican Hot–Cold Food." *Ecology of Food and Nutrition*, vol. 4, pp. 67–74.

MOORE, FRANK W. 1970. "Food Habits in Non-Industrial Societies." In *Dimensions of Nutrition* edited by Jacqueline Dupont (Ft. Collins, Colo.: Proceedings of the Colorado Dietetic Conference, pp. 182–221).

MORAN, EMILIO F. 1975. "Food, Development, and Man in the Tropics." In Arnott (1975 A), pp. 169–186.

MORGANE, P. J. and H. L. JACOBS. 1969. "Hunger and Satiety." *World Review of Nutrition and Dietetics*, vol. 10, pp. 100–213.

MOSS, N. HENRY and JEAN MAYER, editors. 1977. *Food and Nutrition in Health and Disease*. New York: N.Y. Academy of Sciences.

MOUNT, JAMES L. 1975. *The Food and Health of Western Man*. New York: Wiley.

NETTING, ROBERT MC C. 1977. *Cultural Ecology*. Menlo Park, Calif.: Cummings.

———. 1964. "Beer as a Locus of Value among the West African Kofyar." *American Anthropologist*, vol. 66, pp. 375–384.

NEUMANN, THOMAS W. 1977. "A Biocultural Approach to Salt Taboos: The Case of the Southeastern United States." *Current Anthropology,* vol. 18, pp. 289–308.

NEWMAN, MARSHALL T. 1975. "Nutritional Adaptation in Man." In *Physiological Anthropology* edited by Albert Damon (New York: Oxford University Press, 1975, pp. 210–259).

NICKERSON, N. H. *et al.* 1973. "Native Plants in the Diets of North Alaskan Eskimos." In *Man and His Foods* edited by C. Earle Smith, Jr. (University, Ala.: University of Alabama Press).

NICOL, B. M. 1971. "Causes of Famine in the Past and in the Future." In Blix *et al.* (1971), pp. 10–15.

NIEHOFF, ARTHUR and NATALIE MEISTER. 1972. "The Cultural Characteristics of Breast-Feeding: A Survey." *Journal of Tropical Pediatrics,* vol. 18, pp. 16–20.

NIETSCHMANN, BERNARD. 1973. *Between Land and Water: The Subsistence Ecology of the Miskito Indians.* New York: Seminar Press.

NISBETT, R. E. 1972. "Eating Behavior and Obesity in Men and Animals." *Advances in Psychosomatic Medicine,* vol. 7, pp. 173–193.

NORGAN, N. G. *et al.* 1974. "The Energy and Nutrient Intake and the Energy Expenditure of 204 New Guinean Adults." *Philosophical Transactions, Royal Society of London,* vol. 208, pp. 309–348.

NORMAN, BARBARA. 1972. *Tales of the Table: A History of Western Cuisine.* Englewood Cliffs, N.J.: Prentice–Hall.

ODEND'HAL, STEWART. 1972. "Energetics of Indian Cattle in Their Environment." *Human Ecology,* vol. 1, pp. 3–22.

O'LAUGHLIN, BRIDGET. 1974. "Mediation of Contradiction: Why Mbum Women Do Not Eat Chicken." In *Woman, Culture, and Society* edited by Michelle Z. Rosaldo and Louise Lamphere (Stanford, Calif.: Stanford University Press, 1974, pp. 301–318).

OLEFSKY, JERROLD. 1978. "What Happens to Your Lunch." *Human Nature,* vol. 1, no. 4, pp. 38–47.

OLIVER, DOUGLAS. 1955. *A Solomon Island Society*. Cambridge, Mass.: Harvard University Press.

OMOLOLU, A. 1971. "Changing Food Habits in Africa." *Ecology of Food and Nutrition,* vol. 1, pp. 165–168.

OOMEN, H. A. 1970. "Interrelationship of the Human Intestinal Flora and Protein Utilization." *Proceedings of The Nutrition Society (Great Britain),* vol. 29, pp. 197–206.

ORTIZ DE MONTELLANO, BERNARD R. 1978. "Aztec Cannibalism: An Ecological Necessity?" *Science,* vol. 200, pp. 611–617.

PAGE, LOUISE and BERTA FRIEND. 1978. "The Changing United States Diet." *BioScience,* vol. 28, pp. 192–198.

PANGBORN, ROSE M. 1975. "Cross-Cultural Aspects of Flavor Preferences." *Food Technology,* vol. 29, no. 6, pp. 34–36.

PELTO, GRETEL H. 1976. "Culture and the Health Food Movement." Paper presented at the Annual Meeting of the American Dietetic Association, Boston, 1976.

PERPER, TIMOTHY and CARMEL SCHRIRE. 1977. "The Nimrod Connection: Myth and Science in the Hunting Model." In *The Chemical Senses and Nutrition* edited by Morley R. Kare and Owen Maller (New York: Academic Press, 1977, pp. 447–459).

PICKERSGILL, BARBARA. 1969. "The Domestication of Chili Peppers." In Ucko and Dimbleby (1974), pp. 443–450.

PITTMAN, DAVID J. and CHARLES R. SNYDER, editors. 1962. *Society, Culture and Drinking Patterns*. New York: Wiley.

PRICE, BARBARA J. 1978. "Demystification, Enriddlement, and Aztec Cannibalism: A Materialist Rejoinder to Harner." *American Ethnologist,* vol. 5, pp. 98–115.

PULLAR, PHILIPPA. 1970. *Consuming Passions: A History of English Food and Appetite*. London: Hamish Hamilton.

PYKE, MAGNUS. 1968. *Food and Society*. London: John Murray.

RADCLIFFE–BROWN, A. R. 1922. *The Andaman Islanders: A Study in Social Anthropology*. Cambridge, England: Cambridge University Press.

REED, T. EDWARD *et al.* 1976. "Alcohol and Acetaldehyde Metabolism in Caucasians, Chinese and Amerinds." *Canadian Medical Association Journal,* vol. 115, pp. 851–855.

REGISTER, U. D. and L. M. SONNENBERG. 1973. "The Vegetarian Diet." *Journal of The American Dietetic Association,* vol. 62, pp. 253–261.

REICHEL–DOLMATOFF, GERARDO. 1976. "Cosmology as Ecological Analysis: A View from the Rain Forest." *Man,* vol. 11, pp. 307–318.

———. 1971. *Amazonian Cosmos: The Sexual and Religious Symbolism of the Tukano Indians.* Chicago, Ill.: University of Chicago Press.

RENNER, H. D. 1944. *The Origin of Food Habits.* London: Faber and Faber.

RICHARDS, AUDREY I. 1939. *Land, Labour and Diet in Northern Rhodesia.* London: Oxford University Press.

———. 1932. *Hunger and Work in a Savage Tribe.* London: Routledge.

RICK, CHARLES M. 1978. "The Tomato." *Scientific American,* vol. 239, no. 2, pp. 76–88.

RODIN, JUDITH. 1978. "The Puzzle of Obesity." *Human Nature,* vol. 1, no. 2, pp. 38–47.

ROOT, WAVERLY and RICHARD DE ROCHEMONT. 1976. *Eating in America: A History.* New York: Morrow.

ROSS, M. H. and G. BRAS. 1975. "Food Preference and Length of Life." *Science,* vol. 190, pp. 165–167.

ROZIN, ELISABETH. 1973. *The Flavor-Principle Cookbook.* New York: Hawthorn.

ROZIN, PAUL. 1978. "The Use of Characteristic Flavorings in Human Culinary Practice." In *Flavor: Its Chemical, Behavioral, and Commercial Aspects* edited by Charles M. Apt (Boulder, Colo.: Westview Press, 1978, pp. 101–127).

———. 1976 A. "Selection of Foods by Rats, Humans, and Other Animals." In *Advances in the Study of Behavior 6* edited by Jay S. Rosenblatt *et al.* (New York: Academic Press, 1976, pp. 21–76).

———. 1976 B. "Psychological and Cultural Determinants of

Food Choice." In *Appetite and Food Intake* edited Trevor Silverstone (Berlin, W. Germany: Dahlem Konferenzen, 1976, pp. 286–312).

SAFFIRIO, LUIGI. 1975. "Monophagy in the European Upper Paleolithic." In Arnott (1975 A), pp. 79–88.

SAGAN, ELI. 1974. *Cannibalism: Human Aggression and Cultural Form*. New York: Harper & Row.

SAHLINS, MARSHALL. 1976. *Culture and Practical Reason*. Chicago, Ill.: University of Chicago Press.

———. 1972. *Stone Age Economics*. Chicago, Ill.: Aldine–Atherton.

———. 1963. "Poor Man, Rich Man, Big-Man, Chief: Political Types in Melanesia and Polynesia." *Comparative Studies in Society and History*, vol. 5, pp. 285–303.

SALAMAN, REDCLIFFE N. 1949. *The History and Social Influence of the Potato*. New York: Cambridge University Press.

SCHAFER, ROBERT and ELIZABETH A. YETLEY. 1975. "Social Psychology of Food Faddism." *Journal of The American Dietetic Association*, vol. 66, pp. 129–133.

SCHLESINGER, ARTHUR M., SR. 1947. *Learning How to Behave: A Historical Study of American Etiquette Books*. New York: Macmillan.

SCRIMSHAW, NEVIN S. and VERNON R. YOUNG. 1976. "The Requirements of Human Nutrition." *Scientific American*, vol. 235, no. 3, pp. 55–70.

SCUDDER, THAYER. 1971. *Gathering Among Woodland Savannah Cultivators: The Gwembe Tonga*. Lusaka: University of Zambia, Zambian Papers No. 5.

SHACK, DOROTHY N. 1969. "Nutritional Processes and Personality Development Among the Gurage of Ethiopia." *Ethnology*, vol. 8, no. 3, pp. 292–300.

SHACK, WILLIAM A. 1971. "Hunger, Anxiety, and Ritual: Deprivation and Spirit Possession among the Gurage of Ethiopia." *Man*, vol. 6, pp. 30–43.

SHANKMAN, PAUL. 1969. "Le Rôti et le Bouilli: Lévi–Strauss' Theory of Cannibalism." *American Anthropologist*, vol. 71, pp. 54–69.

SIMOONS, FREDERICK J. 1978. "Traditional Use and Avoidance of Foods of Animal Origin: A Cultural Historical View." *BioScience,* vol. 28, pp. 178–184.

———. 1976. "Food Habits as Influenced by Human Culture: Approaches in Anthropology and Geography." In *Appetite and Food Intake* edited by Trevor Silverstone (Berlin, W. Germany: Dahlem Konferenzen, 1976, pp. 313–329).

———. 1973 A. "The Sacred Cow and the Constitution of India." *Ecology of Food and Nutrition,* vol. 2, pp. 281–295.

———. 1973 B. "The Determination of Dairying and Milk Use in the Old World: Ecological, Physiological and Cultural." *Ecology of Food and Nutrition,* vol. 2, pp. 83–90.

———. 1961. *Eat Not This Flesh: Food Avoidances in the Old World.* Madison: University of Wisconsin Press.

SNYDER, CHARLES R. 1962. "Culture and Jewish Sobriety: The Ingroup–Outgroup Factor." In *Society, Culture, and Drinking Patterns* edited by David J. Pittman and Charles R. Snyder (New York: Wiley, 1962, pp. 188–225).

SOLER, JEAN. 1979. "The Semiotics of Food in the Bible." In *Food and Drink in History* edited by Robert Forster and Orest Ranum (Baltimore, Md.: Johns Hopkins University Press, pp. 126–138).

SOPHER, DAVID E. 1967. *Geography of Religions.* Englewood Cliffs, N.J.: Prentice–Hall.

SOROKIN, PITIRIM A. 1942. *Man and Society in Calamity.* New York: Dutton.

SORRE, MAX. 1962. "The Geography of Diet." In *Readings in Cultural Geography* edited by Philip L. Wagner and Marvin W. Mikesell (Chicago, Ill.: University of Chicago Press, 1962, pp. 445–456).

SPILLIUS, JAMES. 1957. "Natural Disaster and Political Crisis in a Polynesian Society." *Human Relations,* vol. 10, nos. 1–2, pp. 3–27 and 113–125.

STINI, WILLIAM A. 1975. "Adaptive Strategies of Human

Populations Under Nutritional Stress." In Watts *et al.*
(1975), pp. 19–41.

———. 1972. "Malnutrition, Body Size and Proportion."
Ecology of Food and Nutrition, vol. 1, pp. 121–126.

———. 1971. "Evolutionary Implications of Changing Nutritional Patterns on Human Populations." *American Anthropologist*, vol. 73, pp. 1019–1030.

STRATHERN, ANDREW. 1971. *The Rope of Moka: Big Men and Ceremonial Exchange*. New York: Cambridge University Press.

STUMPF, SAMUEL E. 1978. "Culture, Values, and Food Safety." *BioScience*, vol. 28, pp. 186–190.

SUTTLES, WAYNE. 1968. "Coping with Abundance: Subsistence on the Northwest Coast." In Lee and DeVore (1968), pp. 56–68.

TAMBIAH, S. J. 1969. "Animals Are Good to Think and Good to Prohibit." *Ethnology*, vol. 8, pp. 423–459.

TANAKA, JIRO. 1976. "Subsistence Ecology of the Central Kalahari San." In Lee and DeVore (1976), pp. 98–119.

TANNAHILL, REAY. 1975. *Flesh and Blood: A History of the Cannibal Complex*. London: Hamish Hamilton.

———. 1973. *Food in History*. New York: Stein and Day.

———. 1970. *The Fine Art of Food*. Cranbury, N.J.: Barnes.

TAYLOR, LAWRENCE. 1977. "Coffee: The Bottomless Cup." In *The American Dimension: Cultural Myths and Social Realities* edited by W. Arews and S. P. Montague (Port Washington, N.Y.: Alfred Publishing, 1977, pp. 141–148).

TELEKI, GEZA. 1975. "Primate Subsistence Patterns: Collector–Predators and Gatherer–Hunters." *Journal of Human Evolution*, vol. 4, pp. 125–184.

———. 1973. "The Omnivorous Chimpanzee." *Scientific American*, vol. 228, no. 1, pp. 32–42.

TEUTEBERG, H. J. 1975. "The General Relationship between Diet and Industrialization." In Forster and Forster (1975), pp. 61–109.

TEYLER, TIMOTHY J. 1975. *A Primer of Psychobiology.* San Francisco, Calif.: Freeman.

THORINGTON, R. W., JR. 1970. "Feeding Behavior of Nonhuman Primates in the Wild." In *Feeding and Nutrition of Nonhuman Primates* edited by Robert S. Harris (New York: Academic Press, 1970, pp. 15–27).

TIMSON, JOHN. 1978. "Is Coffee Safe to Drink?" *Human Nature,* vol. 1, no. 12, pp. 56–59.

TODHUNTER, E. NEIGE. 1973. "Food Habits, Food Faddism, and Nutrition." *Food, Nutrition and Health,* vol. 16, pp. 286–317.

TOLLEFSON, KENNETH D. 1975. "Potlatch and Stratification among the Tlingit." Paper presented at the Annual Meeting of the American Anthropological Association, San Francisco, 1975.

TRAGER, JAMES. 1972. *The Bellybook.* New York: Grossman.
———. 1970. *The Foodbook.* New York: Grossman.

TRUSWELL, A. S. 1977. "Diet and Nutrition of Hunter–Gatherers." In *Health and Disease in Tribal Societies* (Ciba Foundation Symposium; New York: Elsevier Excerpta Medica, 1977).

TUTTLE, RUSSEL H., editor. 1975. *Socioecology and Psychology of Primates.* Chicago: Aldine.

UCKO, PETER J. and G. W. DIMBLEBY, editors. 1969. *The Domestication and Exploitation of Plants and Animals.* Chicago, Ill.: Aldine.

VAN GENNEP, ARNOLD. 1960. *The Rites of Passage.* Chicago, Ill.: University of Chicago Press.

VAN GINNEKAN, JEROEN K. 1974. "Prolonged Breastfeeding as a Birth Spacing Method." *Studies in Family Planning,* vol. 5, pp. 201–206.

VERMEER, DONALD E. 1971. "Geophagy Among the Ewe of Ghana." *Ethnology,* vol. 10, pp. 56–72.

WADE, NICHOLAS. 1974. "Bottle-Feeding: Adverse Effects of a Western Technology." *Science,* vol. 184, pp. 45–48.

WASHBURN, SHERWOOD L. and VIRGINIA AVIS. 1958. "Evolution of Human Behavior." In *Behavior and Evolution*

edited by Anne Roe and George G. Simpson (New Haven, Conn.: Yale University Press, 1958, pp. 421–436).

WATKIN, DONALD M., editor. 1972. "Symposium: Nutrition and Aging." *American Journal of Clinical Nutrition,* vol. 25, pp. 809–859.

WATSON, LYALL. 1971. *The Omnivorous Ape.* New York: Coward, McCann.

WATTS, ELIZABETH S. *et al.* 1975. *Biosocial Interrelations in Population Adaptation.* The Hague: Mouton.

WEIGLEY, EMMA S. 1964. "Food in the Days of the Declaration of Independence." *Journal of The American Dietetic Association,* vol. 45, pp. 35–40.

WELLS, CALVIN. 1975. "Prehistoric and Historical Changes in Nutritional Diseases and Associated Conditions." *Progress in Food and Nutrition Science,* vol. 1, pp. 729–779.

WELSH, ROGER L. 1971. " 'We Are What We Eat': Omaha Food as Symbol." *Keystone Folklore Quarterly,* vol. 16, pp. 165–170.

WENKAM, NAO S. and ROBERT J. WOLFF. 1970. "A Half Century of Changing Food Habits Among Japanese in Hawaii." *Journal of The American Dietetic Association,* vol. 57, pp. 29–32.

WHITEMAN, JOSEPHINE. 1966. "The Function of Food in Society." *Nutrition,* vol. 20, pp. 4–8.

WILLIAMS, ROGER J. 1978. "Nutritional Individuality." *Human Nature,* vol. 1, no. 6, pp. 46–53.

WILLIS, R. G. 1977. "Pollution and Paradigms." In *Culture, Disease, and Healing* edited by David Landy (New York: Macmillan, 1977, pp. 278–285).

WILSON, CHRISTINE S. 1971. "Food Beliefs Affect Nutritional Status of Malay Fisherfolk." *Journal of Nutrition Education,* vol. 2, no. 3, pp. 96–98.

WILSON, PETER J. 1977. "La Pensée Alimentaire: The Evolutionary Context of Rational Objective Thought." *Man,* vol. 12, pp. 320–335.

WINIKOFF, BEVERLY. 1978. "Changing Public Diet." *Human Nature,* vol. 1, no. 1, pp. 60–65.

WOLFF, PETER H. 1972. "Ethnic Differences in Alcohol Sensitivity." *Science,* vol. 175, pp. 449–450.

LEY, S. C. *et al.* 1976. "Psychological Aspects of Feeding Group Report." In *Appetite and Food Intake* edited by Trevor Silverstone (Berlin, W. Germany: Dahlem Konferenzen, pp. 331–354).

WURTMAN, RICHARD J. 1978. "Food for Thought." *The Sciences,* vol. 18, no. 4, pp. 6–9.

YALMAN, NUR. 1969. "On the Meaning of Food Offerings in Ceylon." In *Forms of Symbolic Action* edited by Robert F. Spencer (Seattle: University of Washington Press, 1969, pp. 81–96).

YOUNG, M. W. 1971. *Fighting with Food: Leadership, Values, and Social Control in a Massim Society.* New York: Cambridge University Press.

YOUNG, VERNON R. and NEVIN S. SCRIMSHAW. 1971. "The Physiology of Starvation." *Scientific American,* vol. 225, no. 4, pp. 14–21.

YUDKIN, JOHN. 1969. "Archeology and the Nutritionist." In Ucko and Dimbleby (1969), pp. 547–552.

Index

Abomination, Judaic determination of, 138. *See also* Food taboos

Abundance, of food in North America, 236

Activity, calories for, 21

Adaptation: maladaptation, 83; nature of, 273*n;* strategies, 10, 95

Addiction, caffeine, 209. *See also* Alcoholism

Additivies, 257, 303; common, 260; consumption of, 265; nitrites, 261; sodium, 260. *See also* Carcinogens; Salt

Adolescence, and food and sex, 87, 101

Adrenal glands, 26

Adulterants, 257, 259–60, 303*n*

Africans, cuisine of, 237. *See also specific nationalities and tribes*

Agave plant, 212

Agribusiness, 239

Agricultural Revolution, 74

Agriculture: Indian, 143; invention of, 53–54; irrigation, 80; irrigation *vs.* modern, 81–82; mechanized, 82; of Middle America, 168; spread of, 200. *See also* Horticulture

Akikuyu (Kenya), 274

Al-Biruni, 144, 291*n*

Alcohol: as aphrodisiac, 107; and cultural attitudes, 218; effects of, 210, 298*n;* and fat absorption, 28; and hunger pangs, 28–29; and stomach lining, 27, 210–12; wine, 107, 158, 212, 217. *See also* Beer

Alcoholism: cultural expectations and, 216; food supply and, 216–17; and genetic potential, 213–14

Allergic reactions, and food taboos, 147–48

Alpaca, 168, 223

Amaranth plant, 171

American Indians: alcoholic consumption of, 213; cuisine of, 236, 240; nutritional balance in diet of, 40; putrefied food eaten by, 12; subsistence patterns of, 233. *See also specific tribes*

Amhara (Ethiopia): linguistic categories associated with food, 128; vegetarianism of, 41

Amino acids: in digestive process, 28; maize deficiency of, 241; utilization of, 39. *See also* Protein

Andean pastoralists, food efficiency of, 80

Anemia, iron-deficiency, 36

Animal foods: European preferences for, 186; female, 199; overconsumption of, 52; pastoralist consumption of, 72; and sexual division of labor, 58. *See also* Meat

Animals, unclean, 137–38

Animal sacrifice, 136–37; and Buddhism, 142; economic aspects of, 153; among Israelites, 153

Anthropophagy, 162, 173. *See also* Cannibalism

Antibiotics: fed to livestock, 262; in processed foods, 303*n*

Antiochus IV, 139

Anxiety, food, 92, 192

Ape(s): diet of, 47–48, 49; food-related behavior of, 52. *See also* Primates

Aphrodisiacs: alcohol as, 107; claims for, 104–05. *See also* Sexuality

Arabs: citrus introduced by, 160; milk intolerance of, 226; milk tie among, 116–17. *See also* Moslems

Arboreal environment, nutritional adaptation to, 48

Arizona Indians, alcoholic tolerance of, 214

Aroma(s): and food preferences, 24; infant socialization to, 220. *See also* Odor

Artichokes, as sugar substitutes, 25

Ascorbic acid. *See* Vitamin C

Asiatic peoples, response to alcohol of, 214. *See also* Chinese; Japanese

Aspirin, and stomach lining, 27

Astronauts, food preferences of, 228

Athletes, glucose storage for, 33

Atkins, Robert, 174

Australian Aborigines, 285*n;* cooking practices of, 64

Avoidances, food, 30, 193, 296*n;* "bait shyness," 149–50; of Indians, 198–99; insects, 50–51; milk, 225. *See also* Food preferences; Food taboos

Aztecs, cannibalism of, 167–73, 293*n*

Baboon(s): diet of, 51; hunting by, 50–51. *See also* Primates

Bacon, "bringing home," 205

"Bait shyness," 149–50

Baking, 127. *See also* Cooking practices

Bantu (Zimbabwe), 291*n;* eating customs of, 98; food taboos of, 147; initiation ceremonies of, 99; sacrifice of, 153

Barbecue, 122–23, 248; origins of, 236

Bassano, Jacopo, 246

Bean porridge, 234

Beans: amino acids from, 39; domestication of, 241–42; in North American cuisine, 233; as staple, 241, 300*n*

Bean sprouts, 11

Beef, prohibition against eating, 141, 290*n*. *See also* Meat

Beefsteak, contents of, 263, 303*n*

Beer: as aphrodisiac, 107; in Bemba society, 211; in Jívaro Indian culture, 211; from manioc, 212, 300*n*

Belief systems, testing of, 147

Bemba (Zambia): beer drinking of, 211; definition of witch of, 192; eating patterns of, 6; hospitality of, 186, 295; putrefied food eaten by, 12; reciprocity among, 191–92; weaning practices of, 95

Beverages, intoxicating, 210–18. *See also* Alcohol

Bhagavad Gita, 2

Biafra, and diet disparities between sexes, 96

Bible. *See* New Testament; Old Testament

"Big men," 181, 295*n*

Birth, food celebration associated with, 87

Biscuit, as metaphor, 122

Bison, 206

Bite, of modern humans, 61, 280*n*

Bitterness, detection of, 26

Black Americans, eating habits of, 88–90

Black Death, 186

Blanching, 256

Blood, pastoralist consumption of, 72, 73

Bohemians, cuisine of, 236

Boiling, 64; linguistic categories associated with, 127; *vs.* steaming, 126. *See also* Cooking practices

Bone, and vitamin D, 35

Boston baked beans, 236

Boswell, James, 271*n*

Bottle-feeding, 92–93, 284*n*

Bouillon cube, 234

Brain: eating regulated by, 30–31; glucose supply to, 32–33; in human evolution, 49

Braising, 127

Bran, in balanced diet, 43

Bread, color of, 130; liquid, 212; metaphorical associations with, 129–30; modern white, 258; symbolism of, 130, 210; whole-meal *vs.* enriched white, 302*n*–303*n*

Breakfast, American, 237

Breast-feeding, 92, 284*n.* *See also* Milk

Breasts, human, as sexual signaling device, 98–99

Breeding practices, among pastoralists, 71

Brillat-Savarin, Jean Anthelme, 2

British: beer drinking of, 212; cuisine of, 236; tea drinking of, 13. *See also* English

Broccoli, popularity of, 199

"Brushwood eels," 230

"Brushwood shrimps," 230

Buddhism: and hippophagy, 202; and meat eating, 142; vegetarianism in, 41

Buffet, 122

Bushmen. *See* San

Butchering, of humans, 164–65. *See also* Cannibalism

Butler, 185

B vitamins, 39

Caffeine: in coffee, 208, 264; and hunger pangs, 28–29; and stomach lining, 27; in tea, 209

Calcium, 36; for pregnant women, 88–89; in tortillas, 12

Calipee (defined), 84

Calorie(s), 20; calculating amount needed, 21; detecting, 29; and longevity, 110; and overeating, 254

Camba Indians (Bolivia), alcohol consumption of, 214–15, 298*n*

Camel meat, tabooed, 134

Canadian Ojibways, alcoholic tolerance of, 213

Canadians. *See* North Americans

Cancer: of colon, 258; esophageal, 13. *See also* Carcinogens

Canines (teeth), 59–60

Cannibalism, 293*n;* of Aztecs, 168–72; and colonial powers, 162; cooking practices in, 126–27; in Europe, 162; kinds of, 163

Canning, 258

Cantharides, 107. *See also* "Spanish fly"

Cantonese cuisine, 221, 231–32

Capsicin, 207, 208

Carbohydrates: in beer, 212; calories provided by, 21; consumed in U.S., 254; nutritional function of, 32

Carcinogens: dyes, 261; polynuclear aromatic hydrocarbons, 264; nitrites, 261. *See also* Additives

Carnivores, teeth of, 19. *See also* Teeth

Carob seed, 159

Carotoxin, 264

Carrots: as aphrodisiac, 107; in balanced diet, 43; carotoxin in, 264

Carving, of meat, poultry, fish: prestige associated with, 184–85; social changes associated with, 246. *See also* Roasting

Cassava, 243

Caste system: food as reinforcement of, 187, 295*n;* and food exchange, 188. *See also* Hindus

Cattle: East African, 73; selective breeding of, 74;

Cattle (*cont.*)
  value associated with, 72.
    See also Cow
Cattle complex, East African, 70–71, 73, 282*n*
Caucasus Mountain peoples, diet of, 110–11
Central Americans, flavor principles of, 222
Chaga (East Africa), postpartum sex taboos of, 94
Chaucer, Geoffrey, 108
Chicken, in North American cuisine, 234–35. *See also* Poultry
Chicken Marengo, 132, 289*n*
Chicken soup, 24
Children: and aromas, 220; and eating patterns, 4–5; and flavors, 221; food selection of, 14–15, 96–97, 272*n;* and food sharing, 98; malnutrition in, 96. *See also* Weaning
Chileans, breast-feeding among, 92–93
Chili peppers, widespread use of, 207–08, 297*n*
Chimpanzees: food-related behavior of, 53; hunting by, 50. *See also* Primates
Chinese: alcohol consumption of, 213; cannibalism of, 163; cooking styles of, 230–32; cuisine of, 229–33; dog eating of, 201; eating habits during pregnancy, 88; eating patterns of, 3; eating utensils of, 247, 280*n;* during famine, 253; food preferences of, 198, 220, 229; meals of, 34; soybeans in diet of, 11;

sweet potato consumption in, 77; village production of, 81–82; yin and yang duality of, 119–20
Chitterlings, 239
Cholesterol, 65
Chopsticks, 247, 280*n*
Chou Dynasty, cuisine of, 230–31
Chow, Ethiopian food, 208
Christians: communion ritual of, 161; food taboos of, 9; and hippophagy, 202–03; and wine, 158
Christmas, food associated with, 176
Cigarette smoke, and stomach lining, 27
Cinchona bark, 105
Circulatory disorders, 45–46
Citron, 159–60
Citrus trees: in Mediterranean area, 158; spread of, 292*n*
"Clanship of porridge," 3
Class structure: and food, 67; 184–85; and table manners, 245. *See also* Society
Clay: craving of pregnant women for, 88; nutritional value of, 88–89
Clay eating, interpretation of, 283*n*
Cloven hoofs, category of, 137
Coddling, 127
Codfish, in North American cuisine, 233
Coffee, 263–64, 297*n;* popularity of, 208; preference for, 219; symbolism of, 209; variations in tolerance of, 209

Cola beverages, 209
Coldness of food, 118
Colitis, 254
Colobus monkeys, specialized digestive tracts of, 47–48. *See also* Primates
Colon, cancer of, 258
Colonialism, consequences of, 200
Color, in food preferences, 23
Coloring agents, 259, 261
Commanche Indians, 162
Communication, food as, 242*n*. *See also* Language
Communion, Christian, 161
Companion, definition of, 3
Company stores, 84
Conception, during lactation, 93–94
Confucius, 229
Convenience foods, North American reliance on, 234
Cooking practices: of cannibals, 126–27; Chinese, 231–32; Eskimo, 41; flavor principles, 221–22; French, 11; Italians, 11–12; Japanese, 10–11; kinds of, 63–65; language for, 127–28; origin of, 63–65. *See also* Cuisine; Food preparation
Cookout, 122–23
Copper, 36
Coprolites, 280*n*
Corn. *See* Maize
Corn belt, 205
Corn dodgers, 239
Corn muffins, 239
Coronary heart disease, 65, 254

Cortés, Hernán, 167
Cosmopolitanism, of North American cuisine, 237
Coumarin (in strawberries), 264
Cow, India's sacred, 141–46. *See also* Cattle
Cow dung, as fuel, 145
Critical-weight hypothesis, 94
Crops: cash, 83–84; New World, 77; rotation of, 74. *See also* Agriculture
Cuisine(s), 11, 226; Chinese, 228–33, 299*n;* defined, 228; European, 246; and local resources, 273*n;* North American, 300*n;* origin of, 229; staples in, 240; and table manners, 244–49; of United States, 233
"Culinary triangle," 125–26, 127, 288*n*
Cultural systems, 15
Culture, human metabolism and, 45–46. *See also* Language; Society; Symbolism
Curaçao, 34
Cyanide, in manioc, 243

Dairying, 225. *See also* Milk
Danes, horsemeat consumed by, 203
Darwin, Charles, 284–85
Davis, Adelle, 174
Death: food celebration associated with, 87, 111; and violation of food taboos, 149, 291*n*
Deep-frying, 127

Dehydration, 258
del Castillo, Bernal Díaz, 167
Dental caries (decay), 65, 281*n;* in human evolution, 62
Dentition, 280*n. See also* Teeth
DES. *See* Diethylstilbestrol
Developing countries: bottle-feeding in, 92–93; breast-feeding in, 92
Diabetes, 254
Diarrhea, 250
Diet: Aztec, 170–71; and class structure, 65; cosmopolitan, 237; and dental decay, 62; of early humans, 280*n;* for elderly, 108–09; Eskimo, 277*n;* fad, 175; insects in, 50–51; of lactating women, 95; and longevity, 111; modern adaptations, 279; New Guinean, 37; and physical characteristics, 43–44; origins of, 47–48; reducing, 32–33; universality of, 219; vegetarian, 279*n (see also* Vegetarianism); and yin-yang system, 120
Dietary laws, 140
Diethylstilbestrol (DES), 262
Digestive process, 19, 21–23; and cultural appetite, 21–22; enzymes in, 27–28; large intestine in, 28; mouth, 22–23, 48, 101; salivary glands, 26; small intestine, 27–28; stomach, 27–28; tongue, 24
Dining, cultural differences in, 122–23
Dinner, North American, 275*n*–77*n*
Disease: among Eskimo, 40; *kuru,* 166; and population increase, 75; rickets, 9; scurvy, 34; and technological advances, 266; and weaning process, 95
Disgust reaction, 207
Dishes, combinations of, 222
Diverticulitis, 258
Doctrine of Signatures, 107, 174
Dog: domestication of, 168; human consumption of, 198; North American attitudes toward, 200–02
Drinking, social, 215, 216. *See also* Alcohol
Drinking bouts, social motivation of, 214–15
Drugs, and hunger pangs, 28–29
Duck, tabooed, 134
Dutch: cuisine of, 236; tea drinking of, 13
Dyes, 303*n*

Eating: and evolution of human head, 49; human pattern of, 227, 254; internal controls over, 29; linguistic categories connected with, 127–28; metaphorical/symbolic importance of, 287*n;* motivation to begin, 29; North American, 239–40;

Eating (*cont.*)
overeating, 235, 254; patterns among elderly, 110; regulation of, 30–31; and sex, 101–07; special room for, 245; symbolic character of, 124; utensils for, 246–47; values attached to, 122–23; vocabulary of, 117–18

Ecology: of Aztec cannibalism, 168–73; of East African herding, 72–74; and food customs, 14; of Indian population increase, 143; and magic, 8; of raising beef, 205–06

Edward III, 186

Egg bread, 239

Egyptians, ancient: animal sacrifice of, 135; bread symbolism of, 129–30; cannibalism of, 163

Elderly, eating practices of, 108, 287*n*

Elite, and food, 184

Emotions: and eating, 3–4; and hunger pangs, 28–29; and infant feeding, 90–91; and stomach lining, 27

Enculturation: and food customs, 14–15; of food preferences, 97–98

Endocannibalism, 163, 167

English: eating patterns of, 2; meals of, 121–22. *See also* British

Enrichment, 258. *See also* Additives

Entertaining, cultural differences in, 123. *See also* Restaurants

Environment: adaptation to, 9–10; arboreal, 48. *See also* Ecology

Enzymes, in digestive process, 27–28

Erasmus, 245

Eskimos: balanced diet of, 40–41; changing subsistence patterns of, 201; diet of, 277*n;* food distribution among, 190; food sharing among, 56–57; food symbolism of, 124; food taboos of, 134; meat-eating of, 115; putrefied food eaten by, 12

Esophageal cancer, and tea drinking, 12

Esophagus, in digestive system, 27

Esthetics, of food preparation, 10–11

Ethiopia, coffee from, 208, 209

Ethiopians, fast days of, 157

Etiquette: of hunter-gatherers, 190; of intoxicating beverages, 210–11; of North American meals, 131–32, 192; of saki service, 123; table manners, 244–46

Eucharist, 161, 292*n*

Europeans: cannibalism among, 162; during famine, 253; flavor principles of, 221–22; folk beliefs of, 120; food production efficiency of, 82; horsemeat consumed by, 204; overeating of, 254; response to alcohol of, 214; table manners of, 301*n*

Evolution: cooperative hunting in, 54; dentition in, 58–60; and food habits, 26; human eating adaptations in, 43–44; meat-eating in, 52; nutritional adaptations in, 48; and taste sensation, 25–26

Ewe (Ghana), clay consumed by, 89

Exocannibalism, 164, 167

Experiments: with vegetarianism, 42–43; with taste, 218–19; on weight maintenance, 30

Eyes, in human evolution, 48

Facial expressions, associated with revulsion, 206–07; 297n

Faddists, 173

Family: as consumption unit, 246; during famine, 253; origin of, 55. *See also* Kinship groups

Famine: and Aztec civilization, 168; Irish potato, 76; occurrence of, 250; studies of, 301n. *See also* Hunger

Fast-food restaurants, 256; growth of, 256; nutritional analysis of meals in, 256, 302n; rapid expansion of, 228

Fat-cell theory, 255

Fats: calories provided by, 21; in digestive process, 28; in human milk, 93; nutritional function of, 33–34

Fatty acids, 33–34

Fear, shock associated with, 149

Feast of Tabernacles, 159

Feast of Tents, 159

Feasts, 93; competitive, 180–81, 183; during famine, 251; Melanesian, 181; potlatch, 178–80, 296n; *slametan,* 177–78, 295n; Thanksgiving, 116, 176, 185

Fellahin, folk beliefs of, 93

Females, reluctance to eat, 199

Femininity: boiled food symbolizing, 124; and food, 121. *See also* Masculinity

Fermentation, of soybeans, 11. *See also* Alcohol

Fertility: bread as symbol of, 131; cannibalistic rites associated with, 165; food supplies and, 284–85; ritual, 103–04

Festivals, 176. *See also* Feasts

Fiber, 257

Filet mignon, 205

Fipa (Tanzania), 286n; fertility rites of, 103

Fish: cooking with, 12; tabooed, 134

Flambé, 128

"Flavor principle," 221–22, 227

Flavors: awareness of, 97; children's familiarity with, 221; combining, 222; and food preferences, 23; synthetic, 258

Flesh pies, 185

Flour, white, 259

Fluids, in digestive process, 28

Fluorine, 36

Folk beliefs: about breast-feeding, 93; about carrots, 35–36

Folk taxonomies, 120

Food(s): categories for, 124; "cult of," 7; fear of new, 228–29; femininity of, 121; feelings of revulsion about, 150; folk taxonomies for, 118–20; hot and cold classifications for, 118; masculinity of, 121; medical applications of: chicken soup, 24, and kaolin, 12, (*see also* Health); metaphoric associations with, 175; processing of, 261; raw *vs.* cooked *vs.* rotted, 125; raw *vs.* prepared, 111–12; self-selection of, 274*n;* sensory properties of, 276*n;* social importance of, 7–9, 190; symbolic status given to, 116; technological tampering with, 266

Food customs: as adaptive strategies, 11; explanations for, 13–15

Food distribution: and male dominance, 96; in Melanesia, 181; reciprocity, 69, 192; and redistributive system, 183; at *slametan,* 177–78. *See also* Sharing relationships

Food energy, calculating efficiency of, 79–82. *See also* Calorie

Food fads, 173

Food habits, in evolution, 26–27. *See also* Cuisine; Eating

Food and Nutrition Board, U.S., 36–37, 89

Food preferences, 30, 297*n;* acquisition of, 63; attitudes about, 226; of children, 97, 272*n;* and cultural prejudices, 200; enculturation, 97–98; European, 186; meat, 52 (*see also* Meat-eating); for milk, 225 (*see also* Milk); of nonhuman primates, 50, 278*n;* and sensory perceptions, 23; variations in, 197

Food preparation, 227; cutting into small pieces, 61; as language, 126; linguistic categories for, 127. *See also* Cooking practices

Food taboos: and allergic reactions, 149; and "bait shyness," 149–50; during famine, 251; India's sacred cows, 141–46; pork prohibition, 134–41; of pregnant women, 87–90; prevalence of, 150; structuralist view of, 13; violations of, 148; and weaning, 147

Food use, variations in, 38–39

Fore tribes (New Guinea), *kuru* among, 166

Fork: adoption of, 247; introduction of, 247–48; use of, 61. *See also* Utensils

Four Humors, doctrine of, 119

Fourth of July, food associated with, 176

Fox, human consumption of, 198

Franklin, Benjamin, 235

Fredericks, Carlton, 174

Freezing, 258

French: cooking styles of, 11; cuisine of, 236; eating habits describing, 115; eating patterns of, 2; flavor principles of, 222; height and diet of, 44; horsemeat consumed by, 203–04; linguistic categories associated with food preparation of, 128

French-frying, 127

Freuchen, Peter, 190

Frogs, human consumption of, 115, 198

Fruit: dyeing of, 261; universal appeal of, 219

Fruit of Knowledge, 101

Fuel: and cooking styles, 11; cow dung as, 145; and food preparation, 10. *See also* Cooking practices

Funerals, and famine, 253. *See also* Death

Gambians: diet of, 42; food efficiency of, 79

Game, in North American cuisine, 234

Gandhi, 9, 142, 174

Genesis, book of, 133. *See also* Old Testament

Genetic potential: and increase in height, 44; and milk intolerance, 225; for obesity, 255; and taste ability, 218–19; and tolerance of intoxicating beverages, 213–14

Germans: cuisine of, 236–37; eating habits describing, 115; eating patterns of, 2

Germination, of soybeans, 11

Ghee, 188

Gifts: ambivalence about, 191; during famine, 252; food as, 152, 189–90, 296n

Gimi (New Guinea), 272n

Glucose, 33. *See also* Sugar

Gluten, inherited sensitivity to, 226. *See also* Wheat

Glycosides, 264

God-eating, 162

Goldsmith, Oliver, 74

Gorillas: diet of, 50; specialized digestive tract of, 48. *See also* Primates

Graduation ceremonies, food celebration associated with, 87

Grapevine, spread of, 292n. *See also* Wine

Grasshoppers, 51

Greeks: bread symbolism of, 130; flavor principles of, 222; milk intolerance of, 226

Greeks, ancient fertility symbolism of, 131; human sacrifice, 152–53

Green peppers, in balanced diet, 43

"Greensickness," 36

Green vegetables, amino acids from, 39. *See also* Vegetables

Grilling, 126; French concept of, 128

Grits, 239

Grubs, human consumption of, 198

Guava, in balanced diet, 43

Gurage (Ethiopia): and diet disparities between sexes, 96; food anxiety of, 192; infant feeding of, 91–92

Haggis, Scottish, 197

Ham, popularity of, 205

Hand, in human evolution, 48–49

Hanukkah, 139

Harrison, William Henry, 235

Harvard student study, 44, 278*n*

Harvey, William, 119

Hauser, Gayelord, 174

Hawaiians: cuisine of, 229; food taboos of, 147; height and diet of, 45–46

Head, in human evolution, 49

Headcheese, 239

Health, and Chinese cuisine, 233

Health-food movement, 173, 294*n*

Health problems, associated with modern diets, 65–66. *See also* Disease; Food, medical applications of

Height, and diet, 44–45

Herbivores, teeth of, 19

Herds: East African, 73; kinship investment in, 72. *See also* Cattle; Pastoralists

Herodotus, 130

Hindus: eating as status among, 187; fasting of, 157–58; food customs of, 11; food taboos of, 9. *See also* Indians

Hippocrates, 119, 173

Hippophagy, and religion, 202–03. *See also* Meat-eating

Hoe-cakes, 239

Hog belt, 205

Hominy, introduced by American Indians, 236

Homo erectus: anthropophagy of, 163; cooking done by, 63; dental decay of, 62. *See also* Evolution

Honey: cancer-causing substances of, 260; in cave paintings, 212–13; "organic," 173; symbolic status of, 117

Hormones, in processed foods, 303*n*

Horses: as food, 202–04; as luxury, 204

Horsemeat, cultural prejudice toward, 202–04

Horticulture, 66; nature of, 281*n*

Horticulturists: association of food and sex among, 103; limitations placed on, 69–70; warfare of, 68–69. *See also specific groups*

Host, of Christian mass, 161

Hot-cold categories, 287*n*

Hot-cross buns, 129

Hotness, of food, 118

"Household deer," 230

Housman, A. E., 211

Howler monkeys, specialized digestive tracts of, 47–48. *See also* Primates

Human behavior, 13–14; control over eating, 30; omnivorous, 20. *See also* Evolution; Society

Human sacrifice, 152–53; of Aztecs, 168–72

Hunger, 29; and sexual intercourse, 102, 104; and technological advance, 266

Hunter-gatherers: associations between food and sex among, 103; changes in diet of, 52; conflict among, 68–69; cooking practices of, 64; dentition of, 61; diet of, 65; diet disparities between sexes among, 96–97; etiquette of, 190; food distribution among, 55–56; food-related behavior of, 54; food sharing of, 65–66; *vs.* horticulturists, 67–68, 80; insects consumed by, 51; milk intolerance of, 224; modern vestiges of, 54; sharing relationships among, 58; staples of, 242

"Hunter's appetite," 56

Hunting: early anthropological view of, 55–56; in human evolution, 54; as sport, 249

Hutterites, 285

Hutu (Ruanda), diet of, 43–44

Hydrocarbons, polynuclear aromatic, 264

Hydrochloric acid, 27, 37

Hypertension, 65, 250, 254

Hypothalamus, regulation of eating by, 30

Ideology, 14–15; and pork prohibition, 139. *See also* Food taboos

Ik (Uganda), 301*n*

Incisors, 59, 280*n*; in human evolution, 61

Indians: cuisine of, 228; flavor principles of, 221; food avoidances of, 198–99; food categories of, 188; food customs of, 11; milk tie among, 116; sacred cows of, 141–46; soybean consumption of, 11. *See also* American Indians; Hindus

Indonesians, flavor principles of, 221

Industrialization: consequences of, 200; and diet, 282*n*

Industrial Revolution, 74

Inedibility, determining, 31. *See also* Food preferences

Infants, bottle *vs.* breast feeding of, 92–93. *See also* Children; Weaning

Infection: and breast milk, 92; and nutrition, 75; viral, 75, 166. *See also* Disease

Initiation ceremonies: dietary changes associated with, 99; food celebration associated with, 87

Innate behavior, and food customs, 14–15. *See also* Human behavior

Insects: human consumption of, 279*n*; in primate diets, 48, 50–51

Intelligence, and omnivorous behavior, 20

Intestinal bacteria, 38
Invertebrates, in human diet, 51
Iodine, 36, 259
Iranians: cuisine of, 228; flavor principles of, 221; weaning practices of, 95
Irish: alcohol consumption of, 216–17; cuisine of, 236; dependence on potato, 76; during famine, 253; horsemeat consumed by, 203; social drinking of, 217
Iron, 36; in red meat, 38
Iroquois Indians, cannibalism of, 163
Irrigation, food efficiency associated with, 80
Islamic tradition, myths about eating in, 133
Israelites, ancient: animal sacrifice of, 135–36, 153; concept of perfection of, 136–37
Italians: alcohol consumption of, 216; cooking styles of, 11; cuisine of, 237; drinking habits of, 217–18, 298n; eating habits describing, 115; flavor principles of, 222

Jamaicans, nutritional balance in diet of, 39
Japanese: alcoholic consumption of, 212; cuisine of, 10–11, 237; entertaining by, 123; flavor principles of, 221; food esthetics of, 10–11; height and diet of, 44; horsemeat consumption of, 202;

overeating of, 254; tea drinking of, 13
Japanese-Hawaiians, height and diet of, 44
Java Man, dental decay in, 62
Javanese, *slametan* of, 176–78
Jefferson, Thomas, 237
Jerky, 54
"Jewish penicillin," 24
Jews: alcohol consumption of, 216, 298n; and citriculture, 160; cuisine of, 236; fasting by, 157; flavor principles of, 222; food avoidances of, 51; food taboos of, 9, 134; and hippophagy, 202; milk intolerance of, 226; and prohibition of pork, 134–41; ritual consumption of alcohol by, 216–17; and wine, 152. See also Israelites
Jívaro Indians: beer drinking of, 211; food symbolism of, 124; manioc beer of, 297n
Johnnycake, 234
Johnson, Samuel, 271n
Judeo-Christian tradition: adolescence in, 101; myths about eating in, 133
Julius Caesar, 2

Kamehameha II, 147
Kaolin, in clay, 12
Karimojong (Uganda), cattle raising of, 70–71
Kean, Edmund, 2
Kenyans, breast-feeding among, 93. See also *specific groups*

Kilocalorie, 20

King, Martin Luther, Jr., 9

Kinship groups: and food sharing, 85; and land apportioning, 68. *See also* Family; Tribe

Knife, use of, 247. *See also* Carving; Utensils

Kola nuts, 209

Koran: taboo against pork of, 139–40, 290n. *See also* Moslems

Koreans, flavor principles of, 221

Kosher procedures, 134

"Krause's end bulbs," 104

Kumiss, 202

Kuru, 166, 293n

Kwakiutl (Northwest coast), 179

Labor: and food production, 82; sexual division of, 54, 55, 58

Lactase, and milk intolerance, 226

Lactating women: and conception, 93–94; increased demand for calcium of, 88; nursing patterns of, 94–95. *See also* Weaning

Lamb, Charles, 63, 64

Land: apportioning, 68; defense of, 68–69. *See also* Agriculture; Horticulture

Language: categories of, 117–18; of cooking, 127; food preparation as, 126, 205; in human evolution, 49

Latin Americans, hot and cold categories of, 118

Laundry starch, craving of pregnant women for, 90

Law of the minimum, 179

Leach, Edmund, 126

Lee, Dorothy, 6

Lemon, 160

Lepchas (Sikkim), putrified food eaten by, 12

Lévi-Strauss, Claude, 13, 124, 125, 126, 171, 273n, 288n

Leviticus, dietary rules in, 270n. *See also* Old Testament

"Limeys," 34

Lind, James, 34

Lineage, 68. *See also* Pastoralists

Linguistics, of beef eating, 205. *See also* Language

Livestock, antibiotics fed to, 262. *See also* Cattle

Llama, 168, 223

Lobster, in North American cuisine, 235

Locusts, 51–52

Longevity, and nutritional habits, 109–10, 111

"Love apples," 106

Lysine, 242

Macaque, Japanese, 227. *See also* Primates

Macbeth, 198

Maccabeus, Judas, 139

McDonald's, 256, 257, 302n. *See also* Fast-food restaurants

Macrobiotics, 174

MacSwiney, Terence, 250–51

Magic, among Trobrianders, 8. *See also* Religion; Ritual

Maimonides, 134

Maize, 6; amino acids from,

Maize (*cont.*)
39; Chinese dependence on, 77; crop of, 234; domestication of, 241; fossil remains of, 240; in North American cuisine, 233; and population increase, 76; processing of, 273n; as staple, 240, 300n; varied uses of, 238

Maladaptation, 83. *See also* Adaptation

Malaria, 105

Malays(ians), eating patterns of, 5–6; meals of, 121

Male dominance, and food distribution, 97. *See also* Masculinity

Malnutrition: and infection, 75–76; and weaning, 96. *See also* Hunger; Starvation

Mammals, diet of, 19

Mandrake, 107

Manioc, 212, 243; preference for, 300n. *See also* Cassava

Manna, 23

Maori (New Zealand): food symbolism of, 124; reciprocity among, 192

Maple syrup, 212, 233

Market economy, and peasant maladaptation, 85

Marriage: animal sacrifice for, 153–54; food celebration associated with, 87, 100–01. *See also* Family; Sex roles

Martineau, Harriet, 238

Martyrs, killing of, 160

Masai (Kenya), 274n

Masculinity: and food, 121; North American meat-eating associated with, 238; roast symbolizing, 124

Massasoit, 185

Masturbation, ritual, 103

Maté, of South American Indians, 209

Mbum Kpau (Chaud), food taboos of, 87–88

Mead, 213. *See also* Alcohol

Meal(s): definition of, 122; North American formula for, 132, 275–76n; rules for, 227; serving of, 128–29; social events organized around, 122; space for, 128–29; as symbolic event, 289n; timing of, 128; universal 199–200. *See also* Cuisine; Eating

Meat: beef, 204–05; dog as, 201–02; horsemeat, 202–04; in hunter-gatherer societies, 56–57; iron in, 38–39; in North American cuisine, 237–38; preference for, 53; universal appeal of, 219. *See also* Roast

Meat-eating: attitudes toward, 115; of Buddhists, 41–42; in human evolution, 52; Judeo-Christian myth about, 133; limitations placed on, 42–43; of North Americans, 204; of pastoralists, 73; prohibition against, 141; ritual, 72. *See also* Vegetarianism

Medicine, humoral, 119
Medieval England: competitive feasting in, 184; table manners of, 244–45
Megavitamin diets, 174
Melanesians, 291*n;* "big men," 295; food reciprocity among, 192; food taboos of, 148
Memory, and omnivorous behavior, 20
Menstruation: folklore of, 285; taboos associated with, 99–100
Metabolism: and human adaptation, 45–46; human differences in, 37–38
Metaphor, food as, 129, 175. *See also* Symbolism
Mexican peasants, tortilla making of, 12
Mexicans: cuisine of, 228; flavor principles of, 222; nutritional balance in diet of, 39
Mice, 19
Microorganisms, effect of hot spices on, 207–08. *See also* Infection
"Middle-age spread," 65
Middle Americans, agriculture of, 168. *See also* North Americans
Middle Easterners, flavor principles of, 222
Milk: cultural attitudes toward, 223–26; evaporating, 258; human *vs.* cow, 93; intolerance of, 224–26; as North American staple, 240; vitamin fortification of, 35
Milk, human, and infant's

immunologic system, 92
"Milk tie," 116–17, 287*n*
Milling, 302*n*
Mince pie, 176, 295*n*
Mind-altering substances, 210–11. *See also* Alcohol
Minerals: in beer, 211; in digestive process, 27–28; in Eskimo diet, 40; nutritional function of, 36–37; and salt consumption, 260
Minimum, law of, 179–80
Miskito Indians, maladaptation of, 83–85, 285*n*
Modernization, 75; and obesity, 255; and population increase, 75
Modern societies, and food efficiency, 81–82
Molars, 60
Mongongo nuts, 242, 300*n*
Monkeys, diet of, 47–48, 50. *See also* Primates
Moses, books of, and prohibition on pork, 136. *See also* Old Testament
Moslems: coffee consumption of, 209–10; fasting of, 157; and hippophagy, 202–03; and prohibition on pork, 134–35, 139–41. *See also* Islamic tradition
Mouth: in digestive process, 22–23; in human evolution, 48; as major erogenous zone, 101. *See also* Teeth
"Mouth-watering," 23
Mud, eating of, 171. *See also* Clay
Myristicin, 264

Mythology, and food
taboos, 13; about meat-
eating, 133. *See also*
Food taboos; Religion;
Ritual

Napkins, 245
Nash, Ogden, 108
National Committee on Nu-
tritional Sciences, British,
37
Neophobia, 228
New Guineans: cannibalism
of, 164, 169; food customs
of, 11; *kuru* among, 166;
nutritional adaptation of,
37; protein deficiency in,
294*n*
New Testament, on gifts,
191. *See also* Old Testament
Nicaragua, peasant
maladaptation in, 83–85
Nigerians, and diet dis-
parities between sexes, 96
"Nipples of the Virgin," 197
Nitrites, 261, 264, 303*n*
North Americans: cuisine
of, 233–39, 300*n;* cultural
prejudices of, 201–02; diet
of, 40; eating habits of,
21–22, 38; eating habits
during pregnancy, 87–89;
excess calories of, 20–21;
folk beliefs of, 120–21;
food preferences of, 25;
food production efficiency
of, 81–82; food standards
of, 37; and food taboos,
150; hunting by, 249; im-
portance of food among,
192–93; meals of, 131–32;
meat consumption of,
204, 237–38; obesity

among, 254; overeating
by, 235, 254; proteins in
diet of, 32; salt consumption of, 260; toxins con-
sumed by, 265
Northwest Coast Indian
tribes, 66; potlatch of,
179–80
Nuer (Sudan), animal
sacrifice among, 154–55;
meat distribution among,
155
"Nun's thighs," 197
Nursing, and milk tie, 116–
17. *See also* Lactating
women
Nutrients, RDA for, 36
Nutrition: and infection, 75;
and magic, 8; of North
Americans, 239–40. *See
also* Adaptation; Food;
specific nutrients
Nutritional blueprint, 37

Obesity, 45–46, 302*n;* attitudes toward, 111;
causes of, 255; among
North Americans, 254
Obligation, and animal
sacrifice, 154. *See also*
Food distribution
Odors: detection of, 25–26;
and food preferences, 23.
See also Aromas
Offerings, 155; and ancestor
worship, 232; of food,
152. *See also* Sacrifice
Old Testament, 33, 291*n;*
eating scenes in, 160;
taboo against pork in,
139. *See also* New Testament
Olla podrida, 125

Omaha Indians, Wind Clan of, 148, 291*n*

Omnivores, 20, 275*n;* primates, 48; teeth of, 59

On Civility in Children (Erasmus), 245

Onions: introduced by American Indians, 236; toxins associated with, 243

Orange, 160

Organic-food movement, 175

Oven-baking, 127

Overeating, 253–54; of North Americans, 235

Oxen, role in India of, 143–44. *See also* Cattle

Oyster: in North American cuisine, 235; prohibition against, 286*n*

Pakot (Kenya), ritual meat-eating of, 72

Pan-frying, 127. *See also* Cooking practices

Panhandlers, 189

Panoans, cannibalism of, 163–64

Panter, 185

Par-boiling, 127. *See also* Boiling

Parching, 128

Paris, siege of, 252

Passenger pigeon, in North American cuisine, 234

Pastoralism, 66

Pastoralists: cattle complex, 70–71; diet disparities between sexes among, 96–97; East African, 71; food efficiency of, 79–80. *See also specific groups*

Peanuts, introduced by American Indians, 236

Peas, amino acids from, 39

Peasant leagues, 215

Peasants: Chinese, 81–82; Greek, 130; maladaptation of, 83–86; Mexican, 12; potato consumption of, 76

Peking cuisine, 231

Peking Man, cooking done by, 63

Peppers, in North American cuisine, 233. *See also* Chili peppers

Pepsin, human secretion of, 37

Phoenicians, hot-cross buns of, 129

Phosphorus, 36

"Pica," 284*n*

Pig: as abomination, 146; ecology of, 139; efficiency of, 238–39; preeminence of, 205; taboo on, 134–35. *See also* Pork; Swine

Pilgrims: food of, 185; Thanksgiving feasts of, 116

Pithecanthropus erectus, dental decay in, 62

Pituitary gland, 30

Plant foods: human emphasis on, 54; metaphorical qualities for, 116; and sexual division of labor, 51–52; toxins associated with, 243. *See also* Animal foods; Vegetarianism

Plato, 155

Plenty, tradition of, 235

Pliny the Elder, 100

Plums, introduced by American Indians, 236

Poaching, 128

"Pocket soup," 234
Political organization: and feasts, 68; and food use, 9–10; and starvation, 251–52. *See also* Famine; Society
Polo, Marco, 231
Polynesians: competitive feasting of, 184; food taboos of, 134
Ponapeans (Caroline Islands), food taboos of, 148
Ponce de León, Juan, 236
"Pone," 239
Popcorn, forerunner of, 65
"Pope's nose," 197
Population increase: and cannibalism, 168; China's, 230; explanation for, 282*n;* and famine, 77; and food production, 77; among horticulturists, 69–70; in India, 143; and law of minimum, 179; modernization and, 75
Pork: in North American cuisine, 238–39; preeminence of, 206; prohibition on, 134–41. *See also* Pig; Swine
Pork barrel, 205
Potassium, availability of, 260. *See also* Minerals
Potato: introduced by American Indians, 235; modern processing of, 262; and population increase, 76; sweet, 38, 77; toxins associated with, 242
Potato chips, 263
Potlatches, 178–80, 295*n*
"Pot likker," 35

Potpourri, 125
Poultry, antibiotics fed to, 262
Pregnant women: food taboos for, 87–90; increased demand for calcium of, 88; and special foods, 88
Premolars, 60
Preservatives, 259
Prestige: associated with carving, 184–85; and eating practices, 99; of meat, 204; of Melanesian "big men," 182. *See also* Status
Pretzel, symbolic connection of, 176, 295*n*
Primates, nonhuman: animal foods in diet of, 50–51; diet of, 19, 47–48, 50; food habits of, 26; food preferences of, 278*n;* teeth of, 59. *See also specific primates*
Pritikin, Nathan, 174
Processing, of foods, 261. *See also* Additives
Prosimians, diet of, 50
Prostitution, meals associated with, 232
Protein(s): calories provided by, 20–21; excessive intake of, 31–33; nutritional function of, 32. *See also* Meat
Proust, Marcel, 220
PTC (phenylthiocarbamide), 218
Pueblo Indians, and maize, 6
Pulque, 212
Pumpkin, symbolic status of, 116

Putrefied food, consumption of, 12

Quechua Indians, potato consumption of, 12
Quinine, 105

Rainfall, and pastoralism, 71
Rats, 19; omnivorous behavior of, 20; and weight maintenance, 30–31
RDA. *See* Recommended Dietary Allowances
Reciprocity: and eating practices, 69; and social obligations, 192–93. *See also* Food distribution; Sharing relationships
Recommended Dietary Allowances (RDA), 36–37, 277*n;* and fast-food restaurants, 256
"Red deer," 203
Redistributive system, 183–84. *See also* Food distribution
Refining process, 257–58
Religion: Aztec, 167; cooking associated with, 65; and cultural adaptation, 142–43; and eating patterns, 5; fasting and, 157; and food faddism, 175; and food use, 9; and hippophagy, 203. *See also* Ritual; Sacrifice
Requirements, nutritional, standardization of, 36–37, 38
Restaurants: fast-food, 228; origins of, 299*n;* during Sung Dynasty, 232; Western-style, 123

Revulsion, human expression of, 206
Rhubarb, toxins associated with, 243
Rice, 53; in North American cuisine, 233; symbolism of, 5; white, 259; wine from, 212
Rickets, 9
Rissoles, 128
Rites of passage, and food use, 9, 87, 283*n. See also specific rites*
Ritual: Christian, 160–61; cooking associated with, 65; and eating, 116; of fast-food restaurants, 257; sacrifice, 154–55 (*see also* Sacrifice); *slametan,* 177–78; wine for, 158. *See also* Religion
Roasting, 63–64, 128; *vs.* grilling, 127; linguistic categories associated with, 127–28; symbolic meaning of, 124
Rockwell, Norman, 249
Rodents, teeth of, 19
Roman Catholics, fasting of, 157
Romans, ancient: hot-cross buns of, 129; human sacrifice of, 152–53
Ruminants, 137
Russians: during famine, 253; flavor principles of, 222

Saccharin, tendency to taste, 218
Sacrifice: animal, 136, 137, 142, 152, 153; human, 152–53, 168–72; modern

Sacrifice (*cont.*)
view of, 156. *See also* Religion; Ritual

Saki, 123; effects of, 213

Salinity, of body fluids, 26

Salish Indians, status of food among, 190–91

Saliva, 23

Salivary glands, 26–27; of children, 97; of elderly, 108–09

Salt: craving for, 26; danger of, 260; in North American diet, 303*n*

Saltiness, detection of, 26

San (Bushmen of southern Africa): birth intervals among, 94; changing subsistence patterns of, 199–200; diet of, 65; food efficiency of, 79; food preferences of, 200, 296*n;* sharing of food among, 56; 279*n;* staples of, 242

Sanio-Hiowe (New Guinea), food taboos of, 90

Sautéing, 127

Saxons, hot-cross buns of, 129–30

Scandinavians: alcohol consumption of, 216; flavor principles of, 222

Scotch: cuisine of, 236; haggis of, 197

Scrapple, of Pennsylvania "Dutch," 236

Scurvy, 34

Scythians, cannibalism of, 163

Sea slug, 106

Serving, of meals, 128–29. *See also* Etiquette; Meal

Sesame seeds, in balanced diet, 43

Sex roles, and eating, 4–5. *See also* Femininity; Masculinity

Sexual differences: in diet and height, 45; in food distribution, 96

Sexual division of labor: and food-related behavior, 54–55; in hunter-gatherer societies, 58

Sexual intercourse: bread as metaphor for, 129; and hunger, 102, 104

Sexuality, and food, 100–08

Shanghai cuisine, 231

Shakespeare, William, 36, 62, 106, 147

Sharing relationships, 54–58, 183; children's learning of, 98. *See also* Food distribution

Shaw, George Bernard, 174

Shelley, Percy Bysshe, 174

Shirring, 127

Shoshonean Indians, changing subsistence patterns of, 200

Sinhalese (Sri Lanka), sex and food among, 102

Siriono (Bolivia), 301*n*

Size, body, and diet, 44–45

Slametan, 177–78, 295*n*

Small intestine, in digestive system, 27–28

Smoked foods, 264

Snack, *vs.* meal, 121. *See also* Meal

Social class, and diet, 66

Social groupings, and eating practices, 98

Society: and fast-food restaurants, 257; social structure, 15 (*see also* Caste system); and starvation, 250. *See also* Horticulturists; Hunter–gatherers; Pastoralists

Socrates, 155

Sodium, dangers of, 260. *See also* Salt

Soft drinks, 254

Sound, in food preferences, 23

Sourness, detection of, 26

Soybeans: in balanced diet, 43; uses of, 11, 231

Spanish, cuisine of, 236; horsemeat consumed by, 203

"Spanish fly," 107

Spinach, 38; toxins associated with, 242

Spock, Benjamin, 14

Spoilage, problem of, 259

Spoon, 248. *See also* Utensils

Sport, hunting for, 249

Squash: in North American cuisine, 233; as staple, 240, 300*n*

Staples: as basis of cuisine, 240 (*see also* Cuisine); metaphorical associations with, 129. *See also* Maize; Potato; Rice

Starch: craving of pregnant women for, 90; in digestive systems, 27

Starvation: effects of, 250; and food avoidance, 31. *See also* Famine

Status: and breast-feeding, 93–94; and food-related behavior, 8–9, 187, 190–91. *See also* Prestige; Sex roles

Steaks, prestige associated with, 205

Steaming, 126; of soybeans, 11. *See also* Boiling

Stereotypes, and eating patterns, 2–3

Stewing, 127. *See also* Boiling

Stir-frying, 230

Stomach, in digestive system, 27–28

Stomach lining, and acid, 27–28

Strategies, adaptive, 10; temporary suspension of ovulation, 94. *See also* Adaptation; Food taboos

Stress, and neophobia, 228–29

Stroke, 254

Structuralism, and food customs, 13–14

Subsistence bond, 58

Subsistence groups. *See* Hunter-gatherers; Horticulturalists; Pastoralists; Peasants

Succotash, introduced by American Indians, 236

Succoth, 159

Sugar: artichoke as substitute for, 25; craving for, 25–26; and dental decay, 62; in digestive process, 27–28; harmful effects of, 259–60

Sugar cane, in North American cuisine, 233

Sumptuary laws, 186, 295*n*

Sunflowers, introduced by American Indians, 236
Sung Dynasty, 232
Supernatural, devotion to, 157. *See also* Magic; Religion; Ritual
Superstitions, about food, 9
Sweeteners, artificial, 259
Sweetness, detection of, 25
Sweet potato: Chinese dependence on, 77; dietary dependence on, 38
"Sweet tooth," 26
Swine: as abomination, 146; ecological adaptation of, 136; in North American cuisine, 234. *See also* Pig; Pork
Symbolism: of alcohol, 211; of food, 124–25, 176; of roast carving, 54. *See also* Language; Ritual
Szechwan cuisine, 231–32; flavor principles of, 221

Table manners, 244; carving, 246–47; U.S. *vs.* European, 301*n*. *See also* Etiquette
Taboos, 134–35; maintenance of, 146–47. *See also* Food taboos
Tamerlane, 202
T'ang Dynasty, 232
Tannin, and tea, 13
Tapioca, 243
Tarnower, Herman, 174
Tasmanians, cooking practices of, 64
Taste: detection of, 25–26; experiments with, 218–19; and genetic potential, 218; primary, 276*n*; sensations of, 24–25. *See also* Food preferences
Tea: and esophageal cancer, 13; milk in, 273*n*; popularity of, 209; symbolism of, 210
Techno-environmental system, 15; of San, 79. *See also* Environment; *specific subsistence patterns*
Teeth: canines, 59–60; of elderly, 110; human, 19; incisors, 59; molars, 60; of omnivores, 59; premolars, 60. *See also* Mouth
Temperature, body, and eating habits, 30
Termites, fried, 51
Terror, shock associated with, 149
Texture, and food preferences, 23
Thanksgiving feast, 116, 176, 185
Thickeners, 259
Thinners, 259
Thiocyanate, 264
Thonga (southern Africa), weaning practices of, 95
Tierra del Fuegians, cooking practices of, 64
Tikopians: cooking practices of, 64; famine among, 253, 302*n*; funeral ritual of, 111; marriage celebration of, 100–01; meal preparation of, 67
Toasting, 128, 287*n*
Tobacco, and hunger pangs, 29
Tomato: as aphrodisiac, 106; popularity of, 199

Tonga (Zimbabwe), food testing of, 243–44
Tongue, in digestive process, 301. *See also* Mouth
Tool-making, in human evolution, 48
Toxins: and cooking, 63; effect of hot spices on, 208; in human evolution, 264–65; human overcoming of, 242. *See also* Plant foods
Transaction, and animal sacrifice, 155
Transportation, and population increase, 77. *See also* Population increase
Transubstantiation, 161, 292n
Trencherman, 185
Tribe, 68; and food preferences, 187; lineages, 68
Trichinosis, 135
Trobrianders: eating patterns of, 7; food-related behavior of, 7–9; marriage celebrations of, 100
Trumai Indians, food symbolism of, 124
Tuberculosis, 9
Tukano Indians (Colombia), food taboos of, 102–03, 286n
Tumeric plant, 158
Tunisian pastoralists, food efficiency of, 80
Turkey: domestication of, 168; in North American cuisine, 234
Tylor, Edward B., 156

Ulcers, stomach, 27
Upright posture, in human evolution, 49

Utensils, eating, 246; chopsticks, 247, 280n; fork, 247; knife, 247; spoon, 248

Values, and famine, 253. *See also* Famine; Food taboos; Ideology
Van Buren, Martin, 235
Vedas, Indian, 141
Vedda (Sri Lanka), putrefied food eaten by, 12
Vegetables: in balanced diet, 43; vitamins in, 35. *See also* Staples; *specific vegetables*
Vegetarianism, 41, 174, 278n; cultural aspects of, 174; limitations of, 42–43
Venison, status associated with, 185
Villagers, and food surplus, 81. *See also* Peasants
Viral infection, and nutrition, 75–76
Viruses, slow, 166
Vitamin(s): in beer, 212; chili peppers as source of, 207–08; deficiences, 34–35, 109; in digestive process, 27–28; in Eskimo diet, 40; fat-soluble, 35; and food processing, 260–61; nutritional function of, 34–37; water-soluble, 35
Vitamin A, 35; deficiency, 36; in seal oil, 40
Vitamin B complex, 39
Vitamin C (ascorbic acid): in Eskimo diet, 40; human synthesis of, 37; nutritional function of, 34

Vitamin D, 35
Vitamin E, 35
Vitamin K, 39
Vocabulary, of beef cuts, 205. *See also* Language

Walbiri (Australia), 162
"Walking legumes," 38
Water buffalo, stomach contents of, 220
Warfare, 68–69; in Aztec society, 172; and cannibalism, 164
Water, taste of, 25
Watt, James, 74
Weaning: criticalness of, 95; and food preferences, 220; and food taboos, 147; among Gurage, 91
Weight, body, maintenance of, 29, 30–31
Weight loss, physiology of, 251
Western societies, allergic reactions in, 147–48. *See also* Europeans; North Americans
Wheat, 53; intolerance of, 226; in Middle America, 171
Wheat germ, 258; in balanced diet, 43
Wilson, Alexander, 234

Wine: as aphrodisiac, 107; consumption of, 217–18; from rice, 212; sacramental value of, 158
"Wisdom teeth," 60
Wok, food preparation in, 10
Women: balanced diet for, 42–43; and food taboos, 87–90; menstrual behavior of, 100; role as plant gatherers, 55. *See also* Lactating women; Pregnant women; Sex roles
Wood, rotted, eating of, 12
Work, and food production, 81–82. *See also* Sexual division of labor
World view, 14–15

Yagua Indians, food symbolism of, 124
Yale University Center of Alcohol Studies, 218
Yams, among Trobrianders, 8, 9
Yellow Dye No. 5, 265
Yin-yang system, 120, 288*n*
Yohimbene, 107

Zebu cattle, 144–45. *See also* Cow

Look for these popular titles from Washington Square Press at your bookseller now

Graham Greene
THE END OF THE AFFAIR
"One of the best, most true and moving novels of my time, in anybody's language"—William Faulkner.
44535-9/$2.95/240 pp.

THE HONORARY CONSUL
A compelling tale of political intrigue and heartfelt passion by "the finest living novelist, bar none, in our language"—Harper's.
42881-0/$3.95/320 pp.

ORIENT EXPRESS
A stunning novel of violence and psychological intrigue.
43514-0/$2.75/256 pp.

Joan Didion
PLAY IT AS IT LAYS
At the center of this powerful novel is Maria, a young actress caught off balance by Hollywood, her husband, her hopelessly retarded daughter—and most of all, herself.
43596-5/$2.75/266 pp.

RUN RIVER
An unforgettable novel from one of America's most elegant and brilliant writers.
44258-9/$2.95/256 pp.

WSP
WASHINGTON SQUARE PRESS
Published by Pocket Books